IMAGES of America

PORTLAND ROSE FESTIVAL

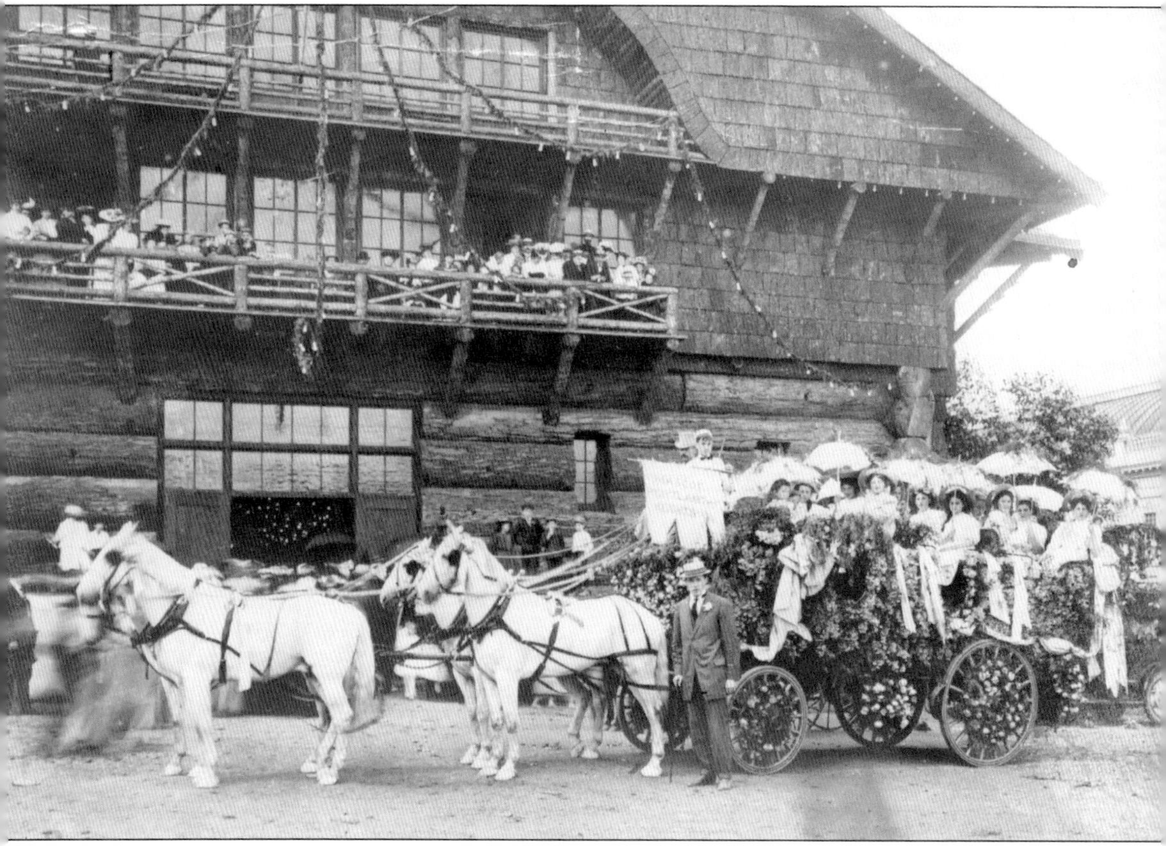

A horse-drawn float sits in front of the old Forestry Building in Northwest Portland, part of the 1905 Lewis & Clark Exposition and World's Fair. The Forestry Building, which burned down in 1964, was constructed of about 300 logs and dubbed "the world's largest log cabin." After the success of the exposition, Mayor Harry Lane decided the city should have an annual festival of roses, and the Rose Festival was born in 1907. (Courtesy the *Oregonian*.)

ON THE FRONT COVER: World War II halted all outdoor Rose Festival events, including the Grand Floral Parade. In 1946, after four years without a parade, eager spectators crowded the route so much that they hindered the forward motion of the entries. By 1947, an "honor line" was painted on the streets to hold people back, a system still used today. (Courtesy the Portland Rose Festival Foundation.)

IMAGES of America

PORTLAND ROSE FESTIVAL

George R. Miller and the
Portland Rose Festival Foundation

ARCADIA PUBLISHING

ISBN 978-0-7385-9614-3

Published by Arcadia Publishing
Charleston, South Carolina

Printed in the United States of America

Library of Congress Control Number: 2012940881
For all general information, please contact Arcadia Publishing:
Telephone 843-853-2070
Fax 843-853-0044
E-mail sales@arcadiapublishing.com
For customer service and orders:
Toll-Free 1-888-313-2665

Visit us on the Internet at www.arcadiapublishing.com

This book is dedicated to the thousands of volunteers, supporters, sponsors, participants, and especially to the millions of spectators who have kept the festival flourishing.

Contents

Acknowledgments

So many individuals have worked closely with me on this book that it would be difficult to list everyone here. The Portland Rose Festival Foundation has given me access to its catalog of Rose Festival–associated items—from written documentation to countless photographs—and without it this book would have been impossible. Chief operating officer Marilyn Clint, public relations manager Richard Jarvis, Rose Festival president Sue Bunday, and volunteer curator Nancy Benson Hopkins have been strong advisors to the author, and their knowledge of Rose Festival activities and community contacts were invaluable. Marilyn has lived, breathed, and worked for the Rose Festival more years than she can remember, and Nancy and Sue know more about Rose Festival history than this book could possibly contain. The Royal Rosarias, the official greeters to Portland, provided photographs. The Oregon Historical Society has also provided photographs and guidance; chief librarian Geoff Wexler, digital assets manager Scott Rook, and archivist Shawna Gandy have been invaluable. Several individuals have helped with proofreading the document, including my wife, Janice. As with every book I have written, Janice has proofread every word (several times) and has provided excellent suggestions. Finally, Arcadia Publishing associate editors Elizabeth Bray and Jared Nelson were there when I needed guidance. They have been excellent coaches. We have made every effort possible to identify people in the photographs.

Introduction

Several visionary leaders at the turn of the century are credited with the idea of starting the Rose Festival—men like John Carroll and E.W. Rowe. In 1905, a world's fair, the Lewis & Clark Exposition, which celebrated the centennial of the expedition of those famous explorers, was held in Portland with an estimated attendance of two million people. The fair was so successful (with revenue reported at $1.4 million) that the mayor of Portland, Dr. Harry Lane, made a speech at the close of the exposition calling for a "permanent rose carnival" to keep Portland on the map as the "summer capital of the world."

The rose was selected as the theme for the festival because of its history and popularity locally and because it was a positive symbol that would take the emphasis off another indigenous Portland feature—the rain.

During the early years, the Rose Festival was known as many things, including "Rose Carnival," "Rose Show," "Rose Fete," "Rose Fiesta," and "Feast of Roses." Following the first event in June 1907, a group of 10 businessmen formally organized the Portland Rose Festival Association as a nonprofit civic enterprise to plan and finance the annual event.

The Rose Festival took root, and the rest is history. Despite occasional financial woes and interruptions by a couple world wars, the festival marched on, literally and figuratively. Other organizations like the Royal Rosarians—founded in 1912—rose up in support of the Rose Festival. Business leaders continued to be invested in the festival's governance, which evolved over a century into what is now known as the Portland Rose Festival Foundation. Today, the Rose Festival is a 501(c)3 nonprofit association run by a board of directors of up to 75 dedicated volunteers and a professional staff of 12 to 15. The modern Rose Festival is a leader in the special events industry, recognized for its innovative programming and top-notch events. In both 2007 and 2011, the Rose Festival was named the "Best Festival in the World" by the International Festivals and Events Association—the trade organization for festivals and events worldwide.

The first Rose Festival lasted just three days. Today, the festival encompasses five weekends of celebration events, with a season that begins in March with the announcement of the Rose Festival Court. The court itself became a major feature of the festival in 1930, when princesses were first selected from local high schools. One of the earliest organizations in Oregon to offer scholarships to young women, the Rose Festival continues to emphasize the court, one of its most enduring programs. The court dominated the festival during World War II, when large outdoor events—like parades—were canceled by the US government.

The Rose Festival draws people to the Portland area from across the United States and around the world. Its most popular events are still its famous parades, including the iconic Grand Floral Parade, which annually draws more than 400,000 spectators to the streets of Portland. The more light-hearted Starlight Parade is the successor to the illuminated Electric Parade, or Merrykhana Parade, and attracts at least 250,000 people every year. The Junior Parade, which officially joined the festival lineup in 1936, is considered one of the largest children's parades in the world, delighting thousands of children of all ages.

Over the years, events and programs have come and gone. In the 1920s, the Rose Festival offered its first air races, an event that returned on a large scale in the late 1980s as the Rose Festival Airshow. In the 1950s, the festival featured an arts festival, which reappeared on the schedule in the late 1990s. Balloon races, ski races, milk carton boat races, and road races of all description have been included in the festival's events. For 22 years, an Indy-style auto race was a highlight of the annual calendar. And the Rose Cup Races celebrated its 50th in 2011. Throughout its history, the festival has included a maritime element, attracting an annual fleet of ships from the US military and other countries around the world.

Tom McCall Waterfront Park in downtown Portland became the home of the Rose Festival's "Fun Center" in the 1970s. One of the festival's most popular events, this urban fair was reformatted and rebranded many times throughout the next three decades, and today, it emphasizes music, food, and carnival rides as Rose Festival CityFair. In 2009, the span of this event was stretched to include Memorial Day weekend, and a patriotic theme was added to the weekend's activities.

In 2010, the Rose Festival was finally declared "Portland's Official Festival" by the city council after more than a century of celebrations. That same year, the festival's staff moved into a historic building at Waterfront Park, built in the late 1940s to serve as Portland's Visitor Information Center. Remodeled to serve as the festival's headquarters, the city charges the Rose Festival $1 a month on a 25-year lease.

With all the notoriety of the Portland Rose Festival and the multimillion-dollar annual economic impact the festival brings to the region, it may seem strange that one of the major topics discussed around town every year is the most obvious one: the weather. While the festival itself was originally started to help take people's minds off Portland's liquid sunshine, if anything, the Rose Festival adds emphasis to the Pacific Northwest's quixotic spring climate. The "Rose Festival Low" is often used to describe a stormy weather system sitting off the Northwest Coast.

For the most part, the weather has cooperated over the years, although there have been notable occasions when it did not, such as in 1948, when the Vanport Flood nearly shut down the festival after wiping away Oregon's second-largest city. Rain insurance has been purchased more than once, and the policy paid off in 2007, when incessant rain poured nonstop on the Rose Festival's Centennial Grand Floral Parade. In 1980, there was no insurance available to guard against Mother Nature's ultimate curve ball, the continued rumblings from Mount St. Helens that sent plumes of ash southward to Portland—including a major ashfall just 48 hours prior to the Grand Floral Parade. While the crowd was estimated at half its regular size, some hardy paradegoers shielded their faces behind painter's masks.

This book is for all those hardy festival folks—from planners to decorators to participants to viewers—anyone who has endured almost every element Mother Nature could generate. It has been their perseverance that has made the Portland Rose Festival known throughout the world, bringing spectators and participants from its far corners.

Included in the book are some amazing sights, many historical facts, a few curiosities, a little crazy weather, and even a bit of humor. The purpose is not to simply show photographs of beautiful parade floats, but to blend the above items into an entertaining story. Hopefully, those who have seen the festival up close and in person, or anyone who has marched, danced, sung, or waved through the countless Rose Festival events over more than 100 years, will find something to remember and enjoy.

One

1907–1918
The Budding Years

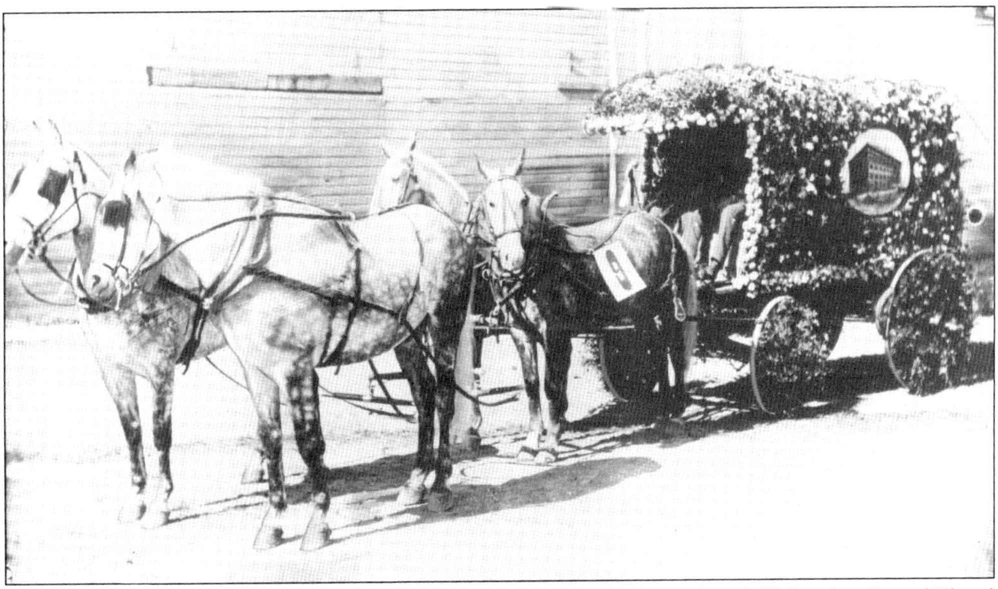

Portland mayor Harry Lane declared a half-holiday on Friday, June 21, 1907, for the Grand Floral Parade. Municipal offices were closed as well as almost every business house in the city, possibly due to a letter sent by a local citizen making this request. The Meier & Frank Company entered this horse-drawn float. It was a mostly sunny day. (Courtesy of Oregon Historical Society; OrHi75577.)

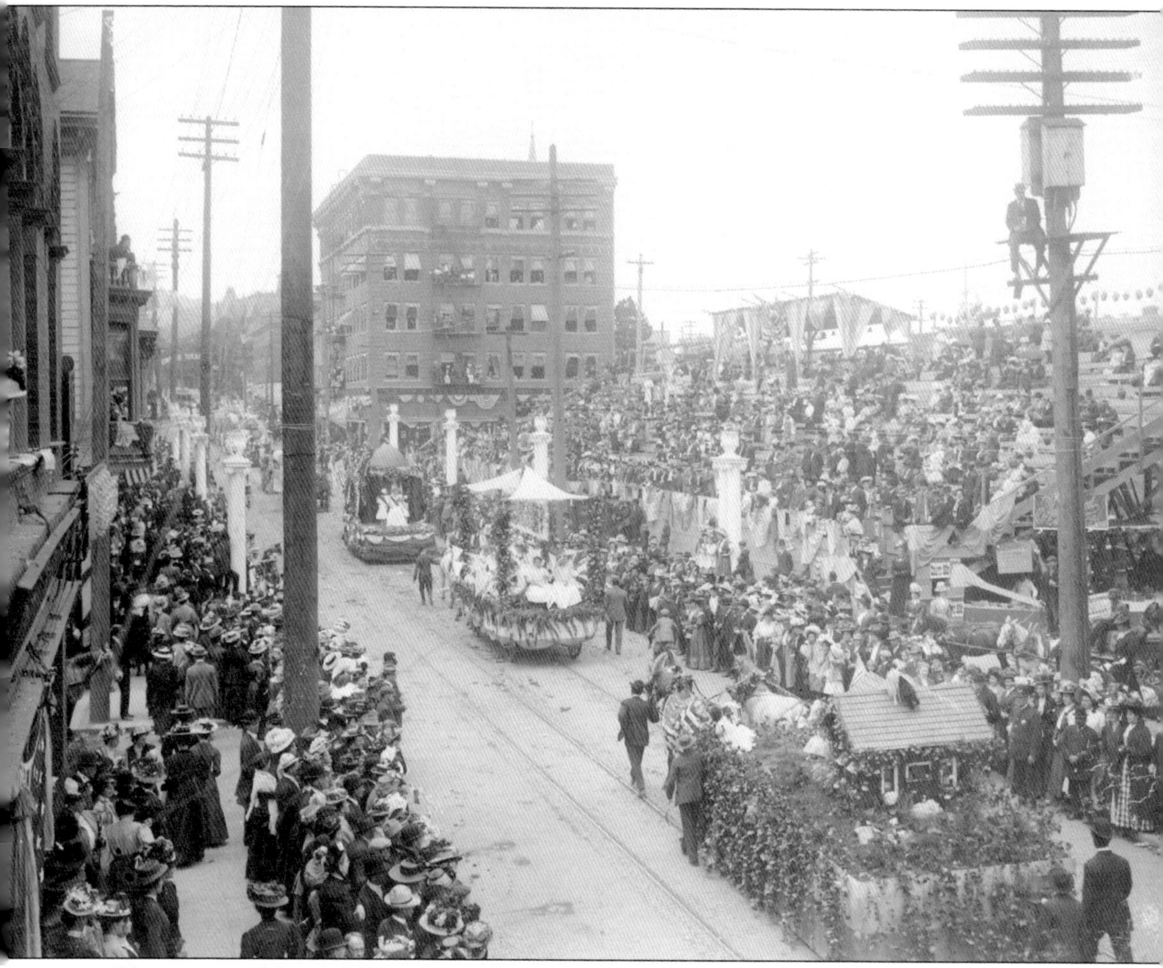

The success of the 1907 Rose Festival was manifest in the large crowd that gathered for the 1908 Grand Floral Parade; no doubt the article that appeared in *Sunset Magazine* in 1908 gave the fledgling festival even more stature. Several more parades were added, including the Feast of Lanterns and General Illumination parades, a Spirit of the Golden West Parade, and a Parade of Decorated Floral Vehicles. Festival attendees could enjoy a lobster salad with mayonnaise dressing for 20¢ or chicken potpie for 30¢ at the American Restaurant. Perhaps Lola Green Baldwin, Portland's first policewoman, helped with crowd control at one of the parades. (Courtesy Portland Rose Festival Foundation.)

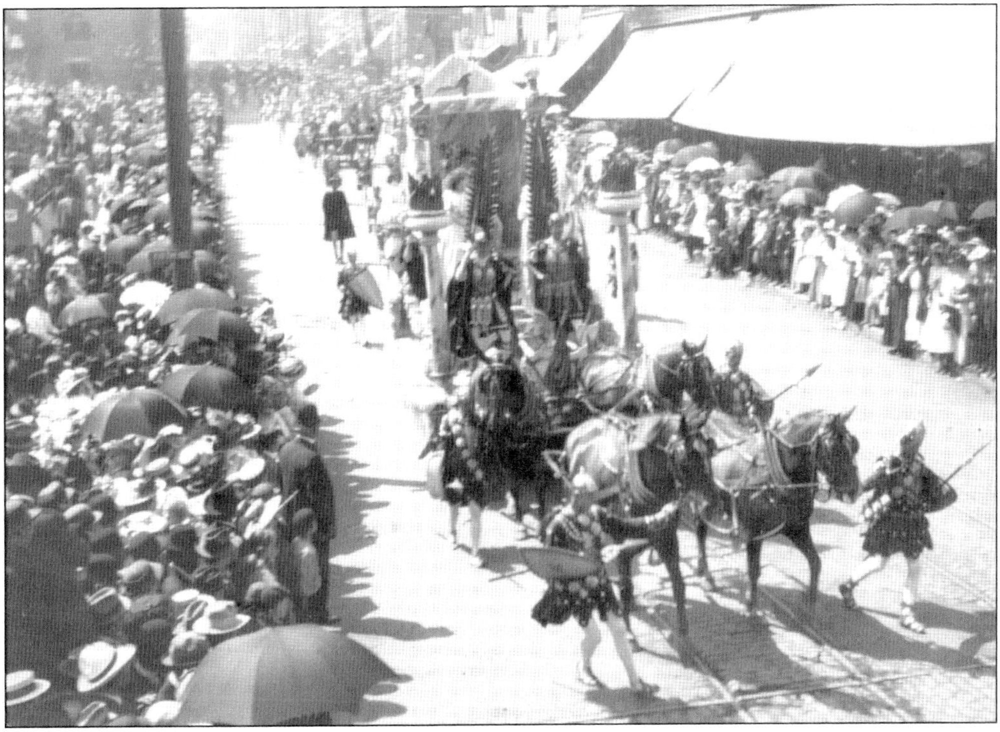

Sunny weather bathed the Horse and Vehicle Parade, when umbrellas were used for shade. By now, the Rose Festival had captured the attention of the United States, including its president. On Monday, June 7, 1909, Pres. William Taft, from his office in the nation's capital, precisely at the hour of noon—Portland time—pressed a button that remotely operated a fire gong at the headquarters of the Portland Fire Department. A telegram read: "R.W. Hoyt, president, Portland Rose Festival Association—I have pleasure in sending good wishes for the success of the Rose Festival, and a hearty greeting to all those participating in it." (Courtesy of Oregon Historical Society; OrHi72460.)

EXTRAORDINARY
ATTRACTION

JUNE 12

Three great Automobile Races on the Country Roads adjacent to Portland. Two Races of Fifty Miles each. One of One Hundred Miles for the Wemme Trophy. Forty of the Fastest Cars in America to Contest, driven by some of the most noted drivers in the world.

A Fifteen-Mile Motor Cycle Race in which Thirty Motor Cycles will Contest.

This natural Race Course is pronounced by experts to excel any other in America. Records will be broken.

These Races under the auspices of the Portland Automobile Club.

Indeed, it was a success, as the festival cost $34,000 and ran without a deficit, despite adding new features that included an automobile race. On Sunday, June 13, the *Oregon Journal* reported, "Driving the course of 102.8 miles, in only 18 seconds over 164 minutes and at a rate of averaging for the distance 58 miles an hour, Bert Dingley yesterday won the Wemme trophy offered by President Henry Wemme of the Portland Auto Club." (Courtesy Estate of Bob Dunsmore.)

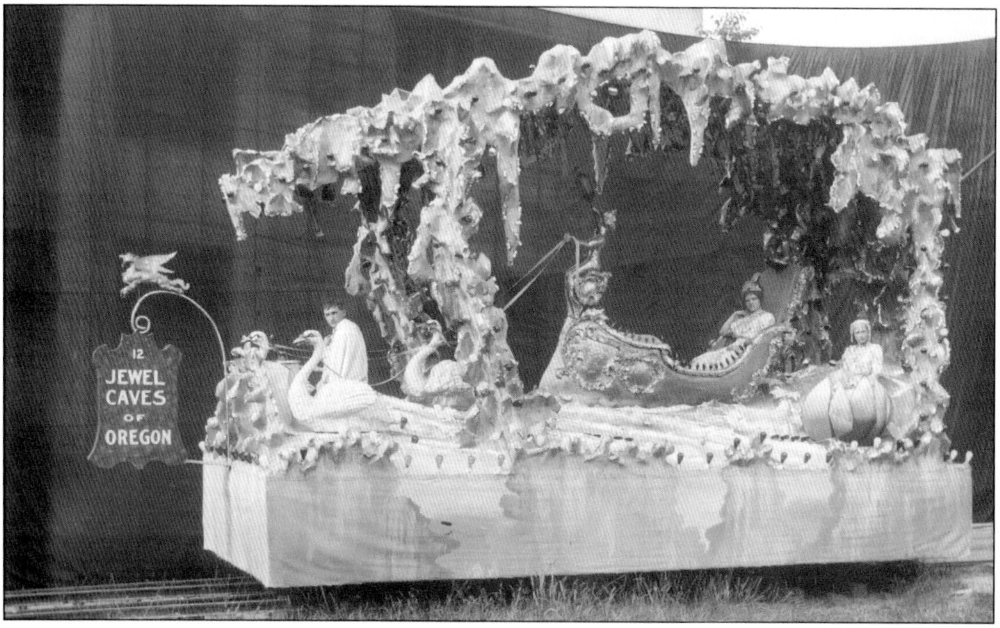

One of the mysterious figures from early festivals was Rex Oregonus. This Carnival King was selected from the business community by the Rose Festival president and general manager. His identity was kept secret behind a beard and a mask. He was revealed in different ways, including on a float in the Electric Parade, such as the one shown, or at a Grand Rex Ball. He sometimes arrived at the Rose Festival via a horse-drawn carriage or riding on a barge on the Willamette River. (Courtesy Portland Rose Festival Foundation.)

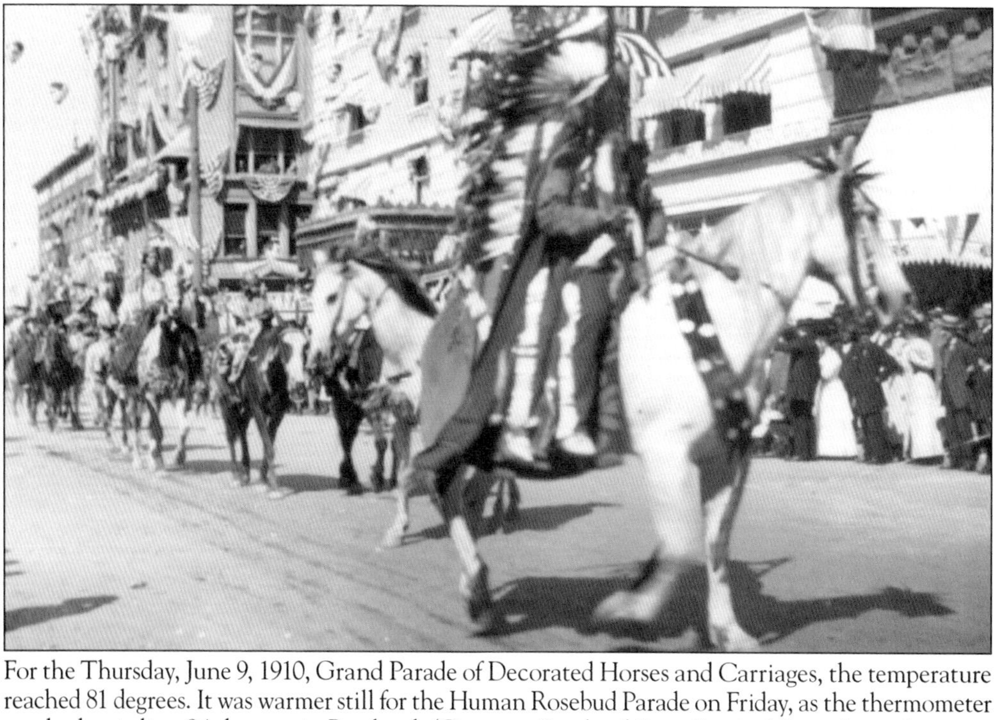

For the Thursday, June 9, 1910, Grand Parade of Decorated Horses and Carriages, the temperature reached 81 degrees. It was warmer still for the Human Rosebud Parade on Friday, as the thermometer reached a sizzling 94 degrees in Portland. (Courtesy Portland Rose Festival Foundation.)

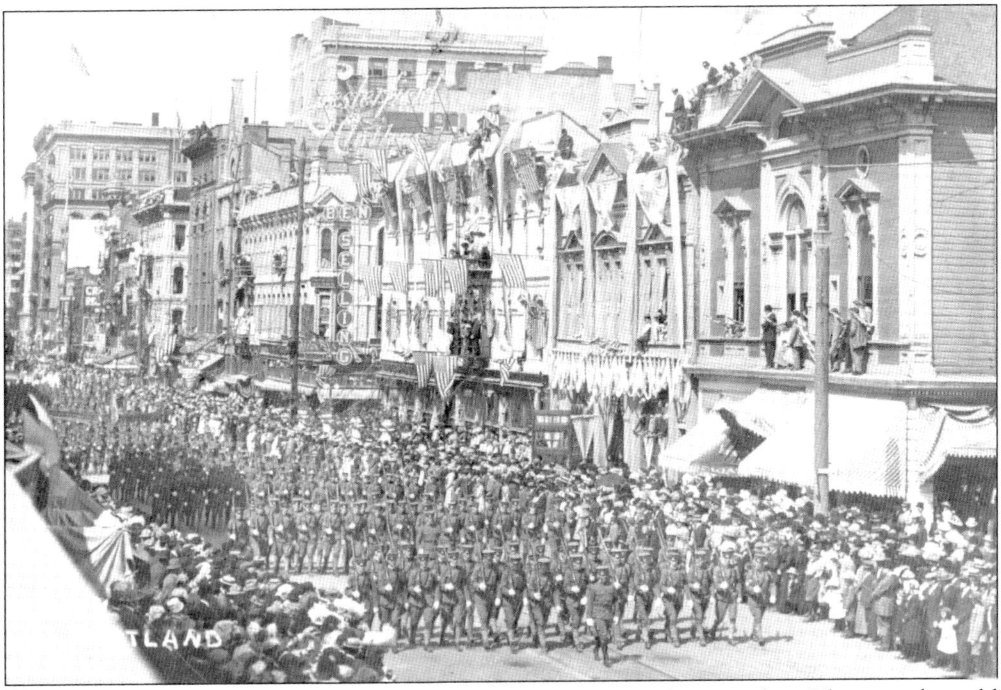

Since its beginning, the Rose Festival enjoyed generally rain-free weather. That trend would continue for 1911. Thursday's Decorated Horse and Vehicle Parade started with overcast skies that soon broke. Military units often marched in the parades, adding color and pageantry. (Courtesy Portland Rose Festival Foundation.)

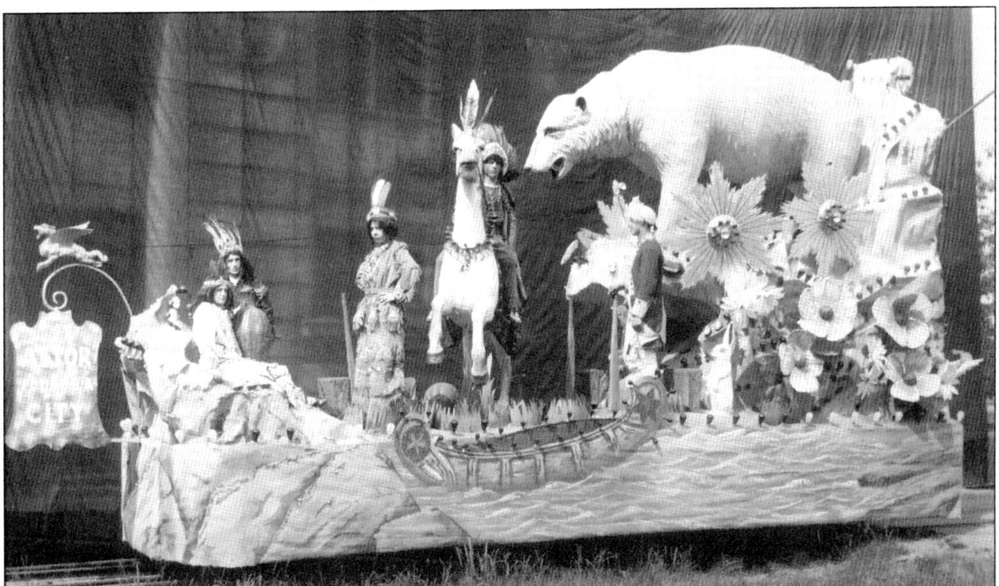

Electric parades were an integral part of early Rose Festivals. They usually occurred on Tuesday and Saturday evenings. Illumination was the key to these parades that ran on trolley tracks. The 1911 entry featured the 100th anniversary of the founding of the City of Astoria, the oldest American settlement west of the Mississippi. In 2011, Astoria celebrated its bicentennial with the first-ever electric-powered float in the Grand Floral Parade. (Courtesy Portland Rose Festival Foundation.)

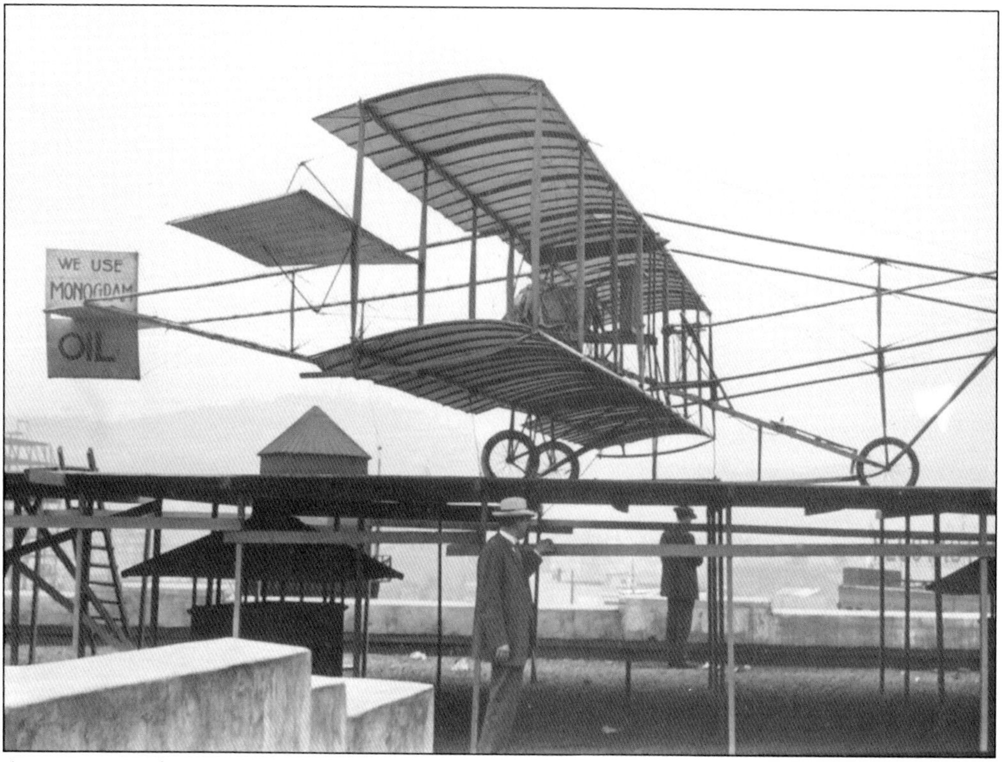

An interesting feature of the 1912 Rose Festival was a stunt by young daredevil Silas Christofferson. Silas was an inventor and pilot who proposed flying his Curtiss pusher biplane off the roof of the Multnomah Hotel in downtown Portland. As thousands of bystanders watched from below and from nearby roof tops, anticipating disaster, the plane took off, landing across the Columbia River 12 minutes later at Pearson Field in Vancouver. The *Oregonian* described the event on Wednesday, June 11. "The day was ideal for a perfect flight. The drizzly weather had apparently forced the cold strata of air to the streets and the cross currents of cold and warm ozone, so feared in the maze of streets and office structures, were absent." (Both, courtesy Oregon Historical Society.)

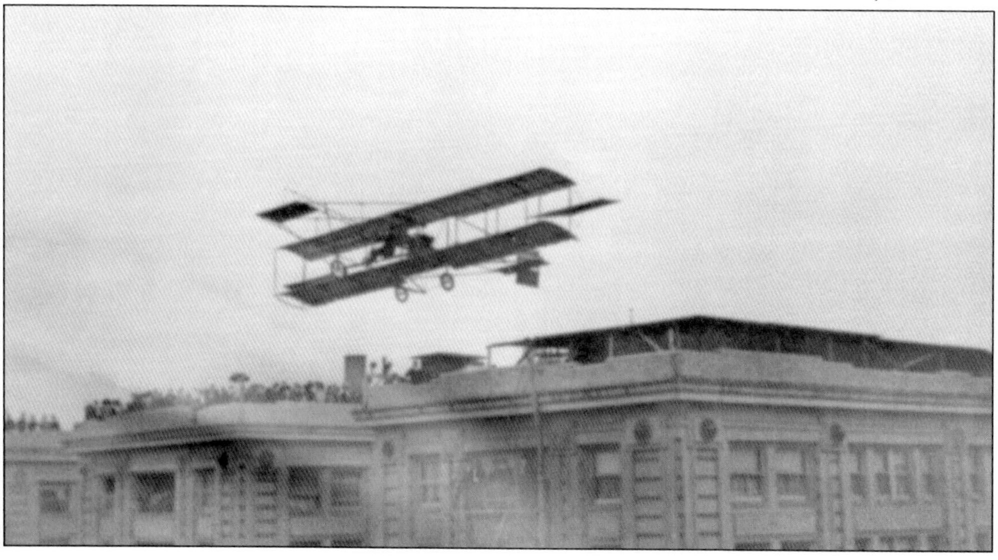

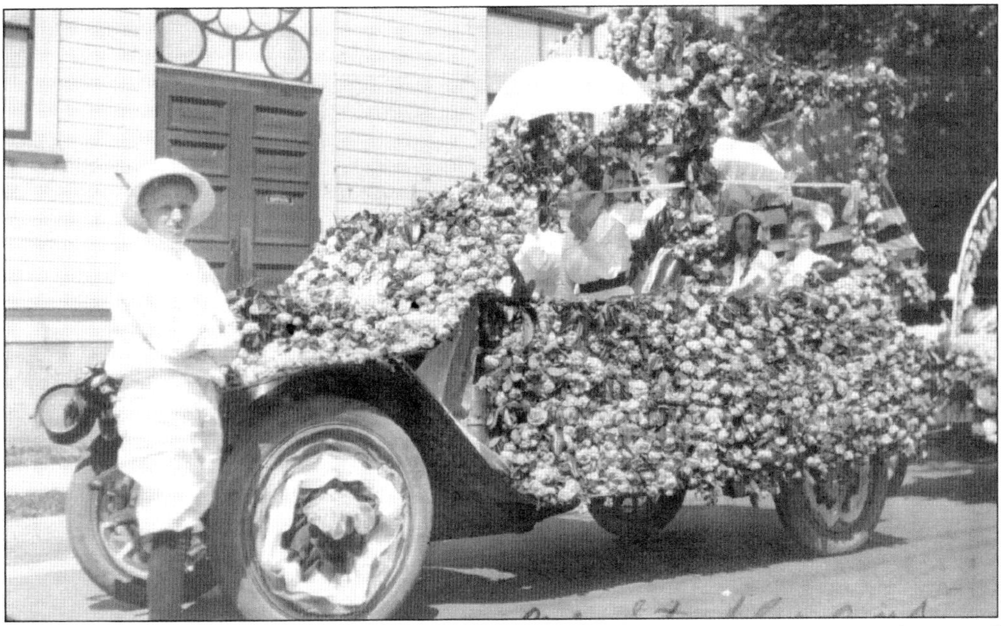

Several parades were scheduled again for the 1913 Rose Festival. Among the entries in the Grand Parade of Decorated Horse and Vehicles on Thursday, June 12 was this car owned by a Mrs. Staples. But it was not the Electric Parade providing the fireworks this year. A fire broke out in the top stories of the J.G. Mack & Co.'s furniture store on Fifth and Stark Streets. Roaring tongues of fire were seen. Some viewers were drenched, not by rain, but by a hose that split in midair, sending torrents of water on the people below and some of the floats passing beneath. (Courtesy Portland Rose Festival Foundation.)

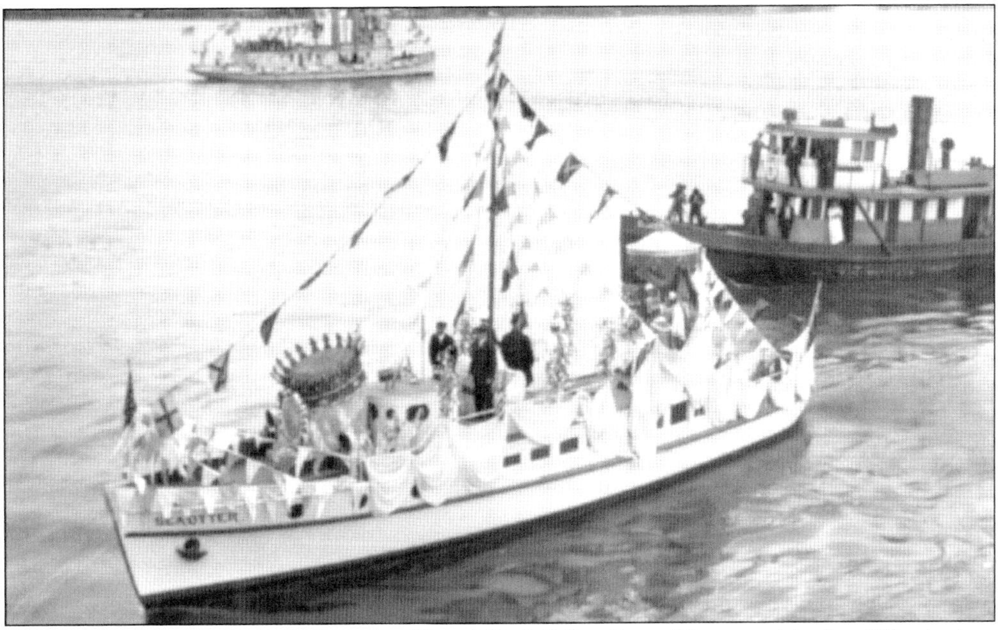

Rex Oregonus arrived in 1913 on the "Royal Yacht" *Sea Otter.* The vessel had a difficult time navigating the swollen Willamette River, and it struggled against the current. Flooding had already begun in some of the downtown businesses. (Courtesy Oregon Historical Society; OrHi45261.)

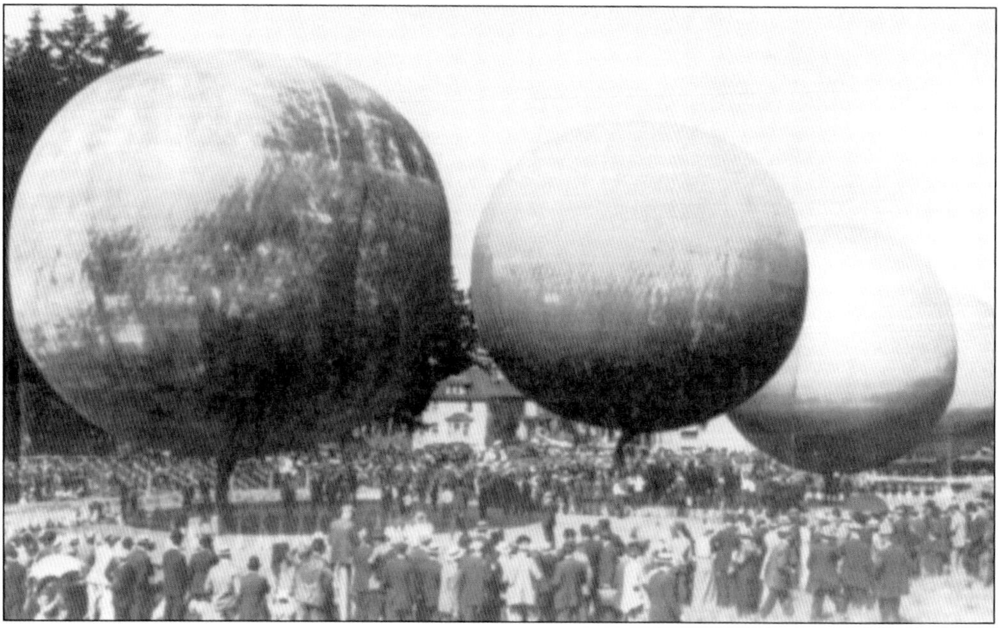

The National Balloon Race was added to the 1914 festival. First prize was $3,000. The *Morning Oregonian* reported on June 9: "This will be a departure from the accustomed festival programs." It certainly would be, as thunderstorms moving into the Portland area scattered the balloons across a wide area after they were aloft. Carrier pigeons released from the balloons brought back news of their locations. (Courtesy Oregon Historical Society)

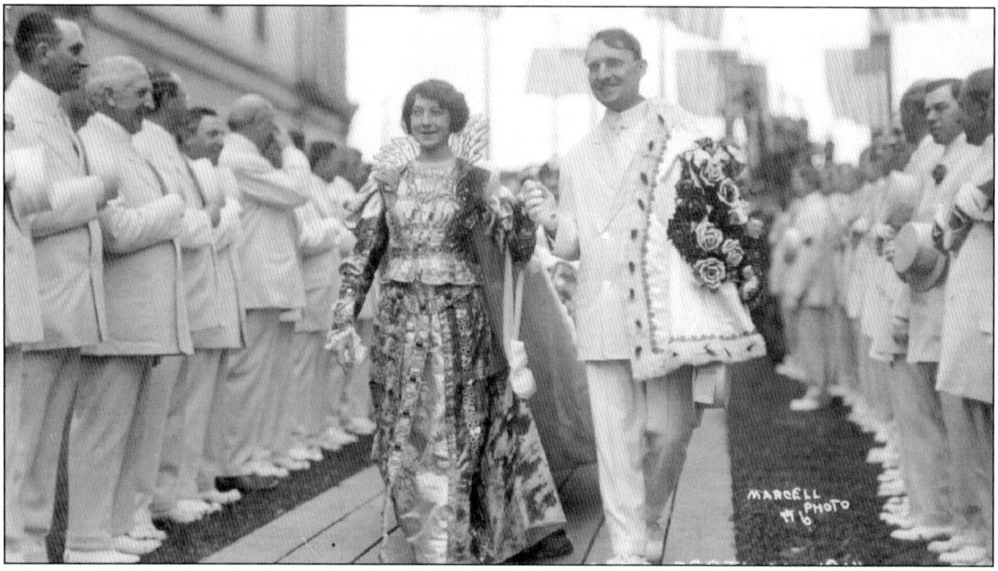

In 1914, a petite clerk named Thelma Hollingsworth became the first elected Rose Festival queen. Citizens purchased votes—10 for a penny—and Thelma won with more than two million; $15,000 was raised by the queen votes, partially used to fund Thelma's train tour around the Western United States. Thelma was escorted by W.J. Hofmann, the first Royal Rosarian prime minister. Hofmann was one of the founders of the Rosarians, formed in 1912 to help support the Rose Festival and to serve as Portland's official greeters. (Courtesy Portland Rose Festival Foundation.)

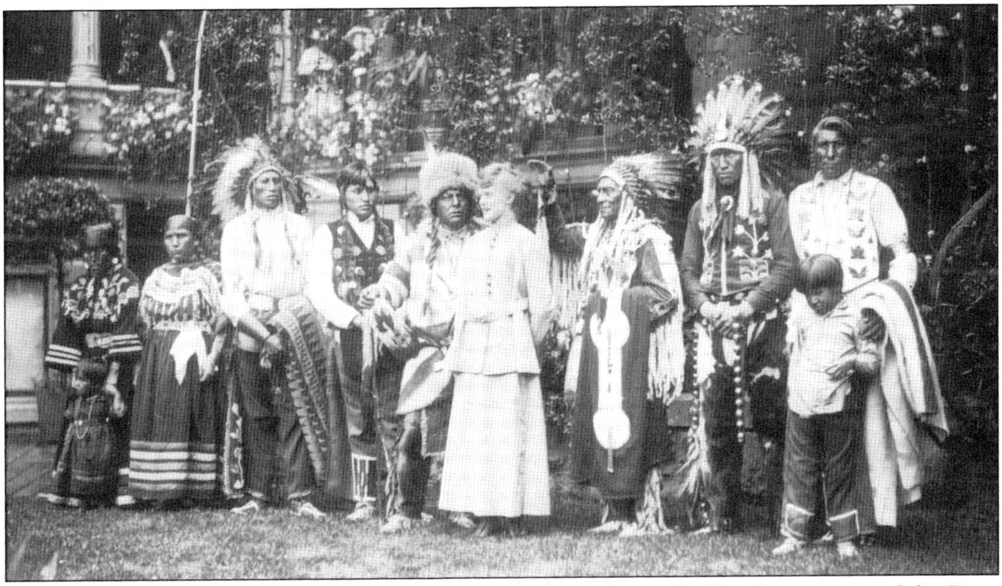

After a wild Rose Festival in 1914, events quieted down for 1915. The Coronation of the Rose Festival queen took place at the Fun Center, which was held in the Park Blocks between Salmon and Madison Streets in front of Ladd School. Queen Sybil was honored as a member of the Blackfoot Nation. (Courtesy Portland Rose Festival Foundation.)

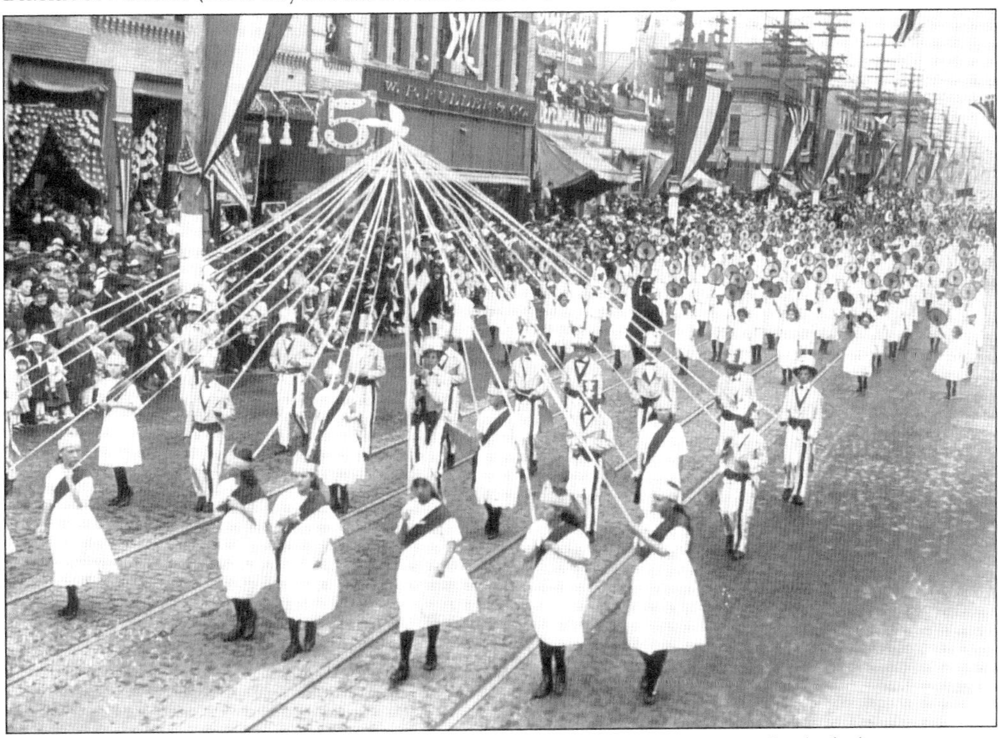

A Human Rosebud Parade was held prior to the Coronation ceremonies. Both daily newspapers lauded the success of the 1915 Rose Festival. Rainstorms did hamper this festival, but across the Atlantic Ocean, a different kind of storm cloud was forming that would have a profound effect on future Rose Festivals. (Courtesy Portland Rose Festival Foundation.)

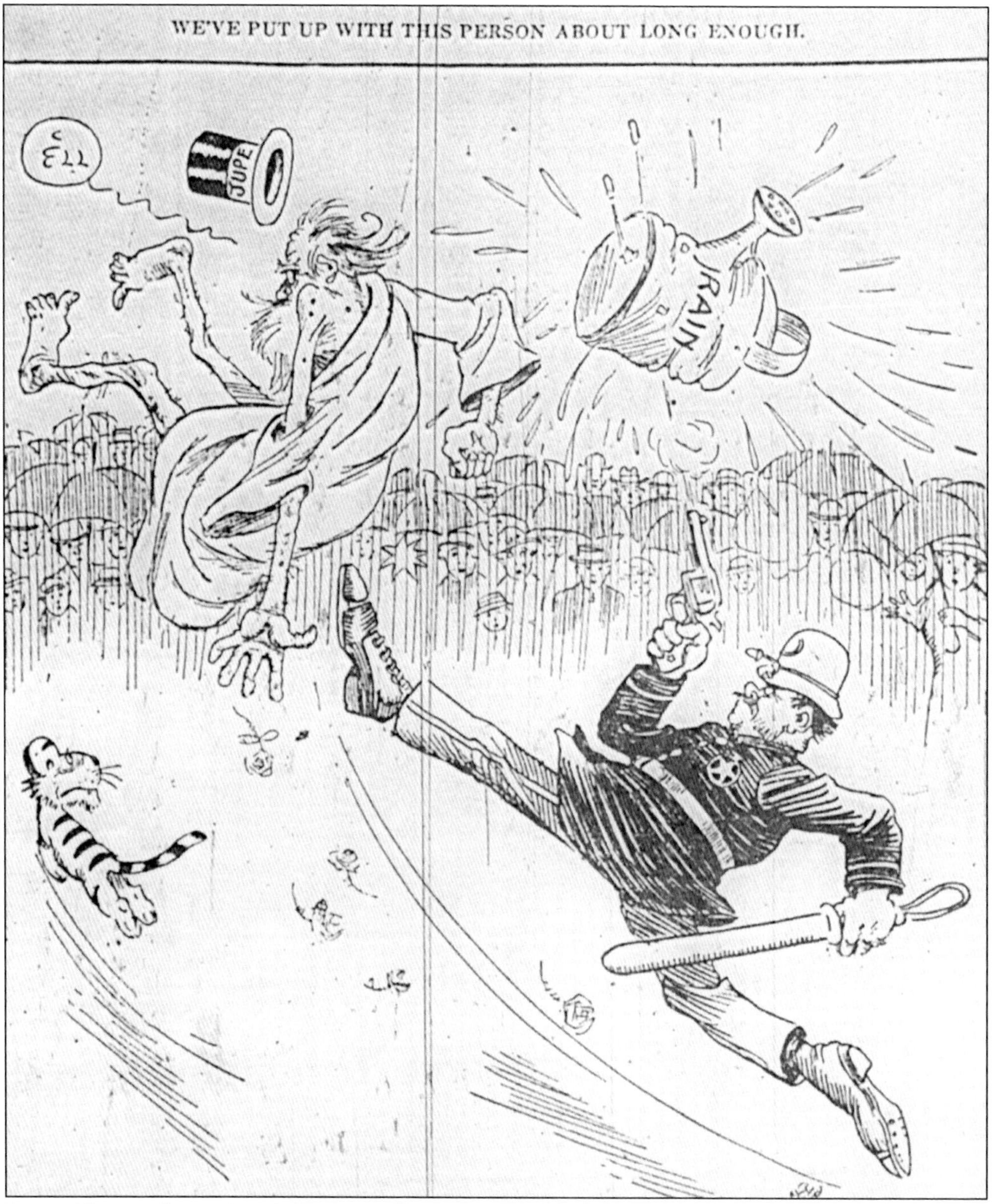

Jupiter Pluvius, the mythical character of rain, was frequently shown in cartoons by local newspapers, especially when rain dampened festival events. In this case, it had rained a quarter inch on June 10, 1915, on the Grand Floral Parade of Motor and Horse-drawn Vehicles. The afternoon high temperature barely reached 62 degrees. The cartoon appeared in the June 11 edition of the *Oregonian*.

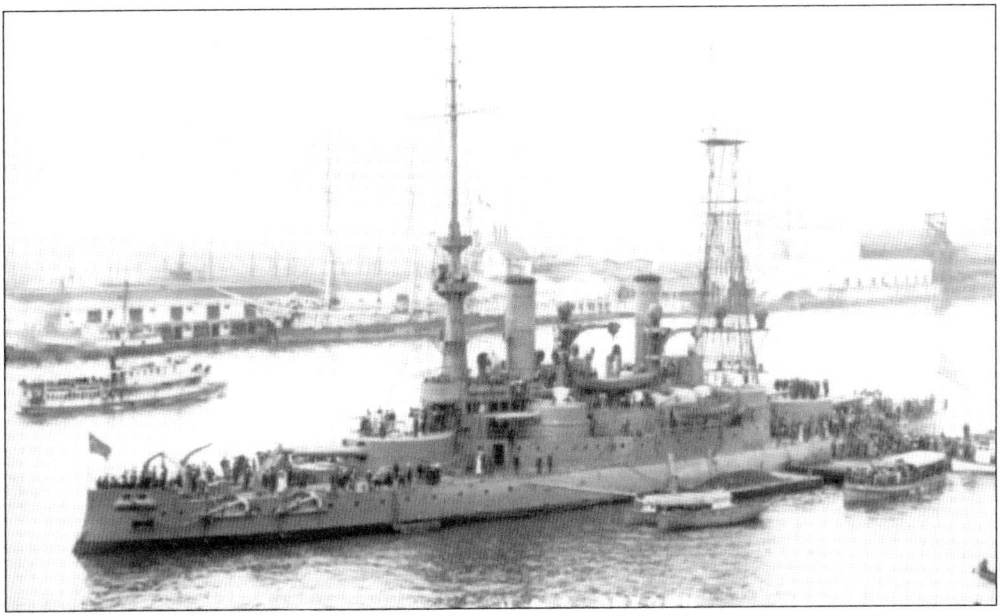

In 1916, German U-boats were menacing the sea lanes, and the United States would soon enter World War I. Numerous Preparedness and patriotic parades were held around the nation. On Saturday, June 3, between 15,000 and 20,000 people participated in one held locally. There was also a Pageant Parade, a Children's Parade, Decorated Automobile and Horse-drawn Vehicle Parade, a Prosperity Parade, and, to close the festival, the Ualtee Carnival Parade. The name of this event was taken from a Chinook word meaning joy and festivities. The battleship *Oregon* docked at the Willamette seawall on the afternoon of June 6 to officially open the Rose Festival. (Both, courtesy Portland Rose Festival Foundation.)

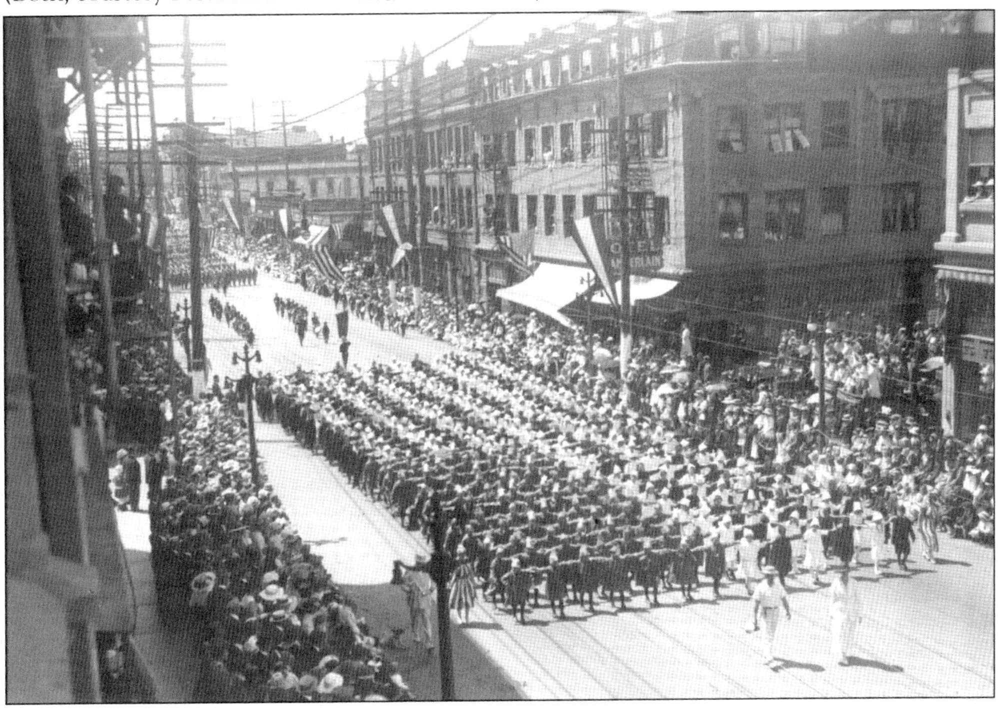

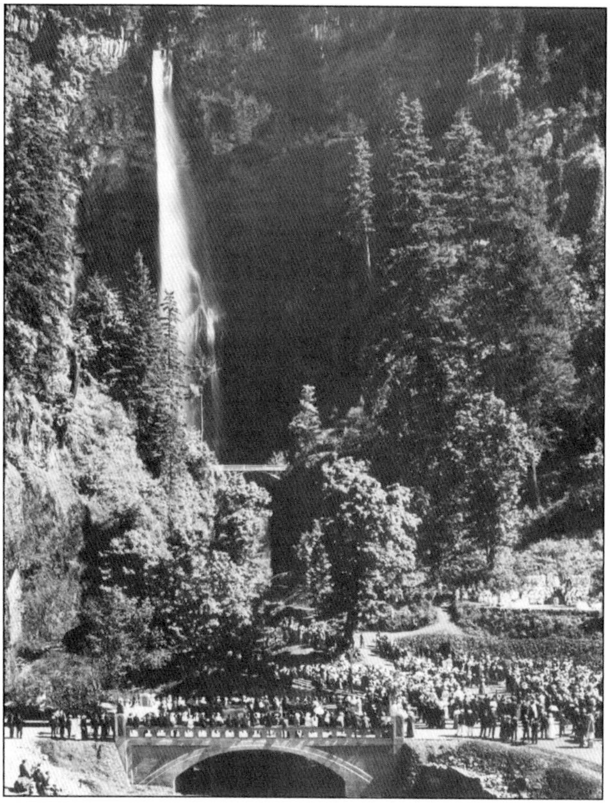

Two other special events occurred in 1916 and were associated with the Rose Festival. Both took place east of Portland in the Columbia River Gorge. One was the dedication of the Columbia River Highway at Multnomah Falls. The Rose Festival queen headed to the dedication ceremonies right after being crowned on June 6. (Courtesy Oregon Historical Society; OrHi11730.)

On June 7, the ground-breaking ceremonies for Vista House at Crown Point occurred, with the new queen participating. Both activities enjoyed sunny skies. In fact, only a trace of rain fell during the entire festival. (Courtesy Oregon Historical Society; OrHi35767.)

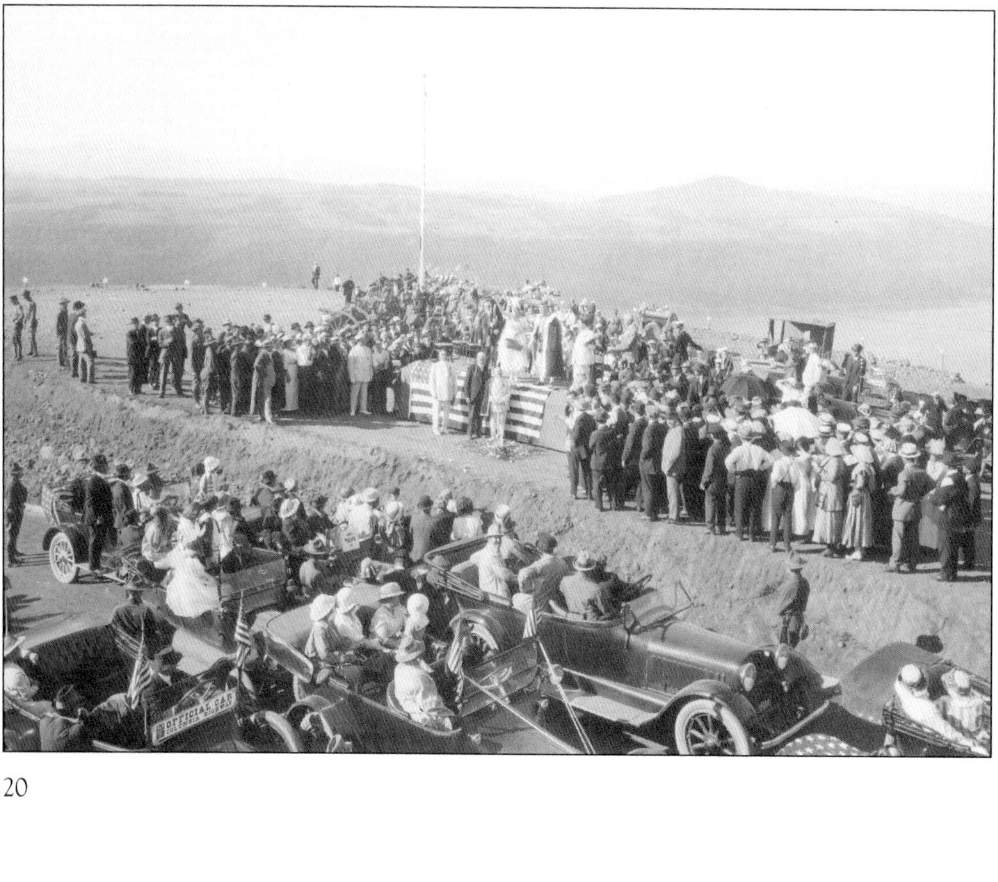

What Every $100 Liberty Bond
Will Buy for the Army

2,000 rounds of ammunition and six standard rifles

Or

16 pairs of blankets and 50 cots;32 shelter tents to accommodate 64 men; 400 pairs of socks; 82 flannel shirts; 36 pairs of marching boots, 16 woolen khaki suits, 42 cotton khaki suits,12 woolen overcoats.

$30 of your $100 Liberty loan bond will buy a Cooking range, which will take care of an entire company of 150 men.

Each $100 Liberty loan bond will equip one Soldier for the front and $500 will keep him a year.

Buy a Liberty Bond today.

Patriotic parades continued to be held throughout the nation in 1917. They took on several displays—from a human shield to flags—as the dark clouds of war in Europe began to cast ominous shadows even on the Rose Festival. Across the nation, people were purchasing Liberty Bonds to finance World War I. Portland was the first city on the West Coast to reach its quota, and the sum was an astounding $8,750,000 as reported by the Federal Reserve Bank. On Wednesday, June 13, from his office in Washington, DC, Pres. Wilson pressed a button, and a signal liberated the shrouds of a striking imitation of New York Harbor's famous monument—the Statue of Liberty—that had been placed at the Festival Center in the Park Blocks. Another famous opening that year was the Interstate Bridge between Oregon and Washington. That same year, the American Rose Society chose Portland to be the new home of an International Rose Test Garden. (Courtesy Portland Rose Festival Foundation.)

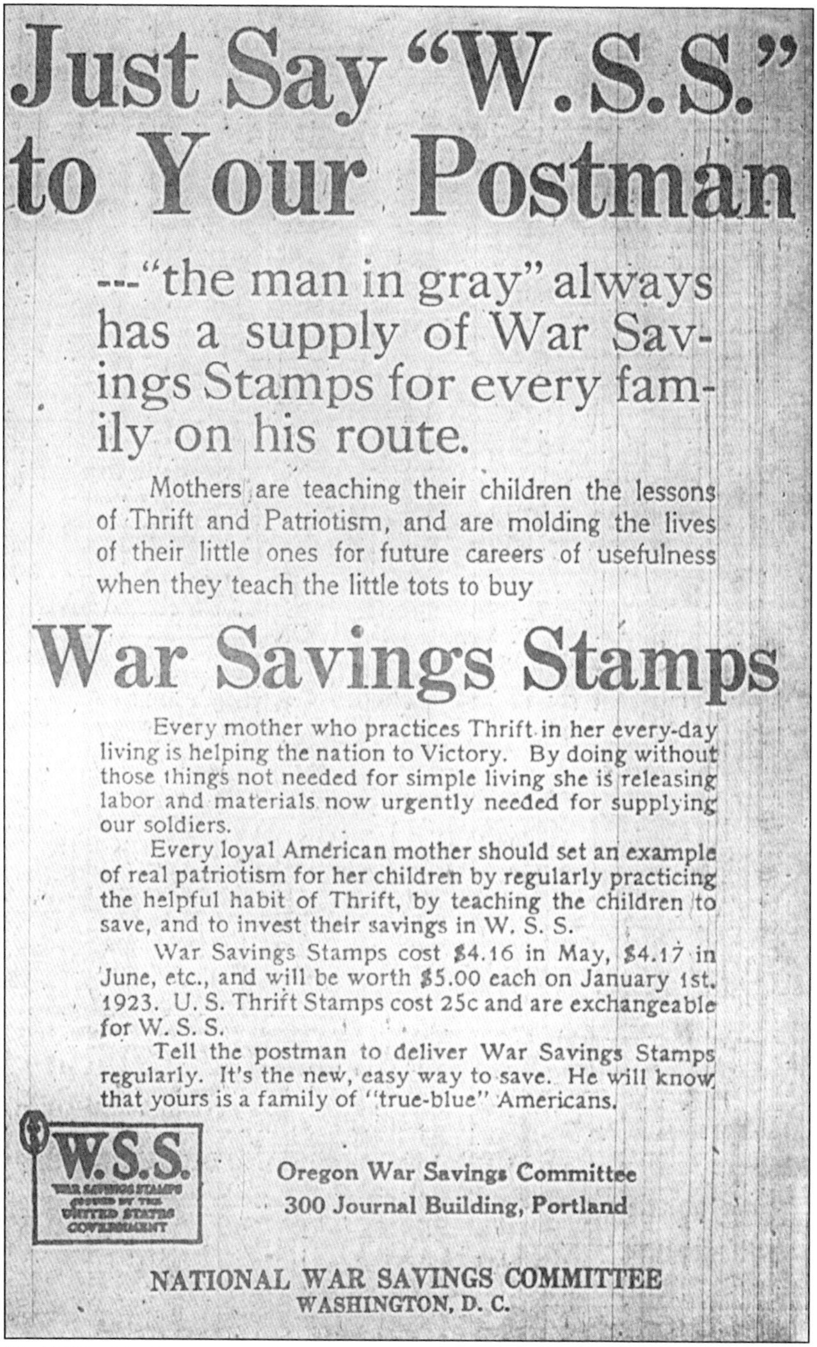

In 1918, World War I in Europe was dominating the news, and for the first year since its conception, Portland would be without a Rose Festival and a Grand Floral Parade. To raise funds to finance the war, people were encouraged to purchase War Savings Stamps as seen in the notice published in the *Oregonian* on June 1; the emphasis was on thrift and patriotism. Thrift certainly would have to be emphasized, as the nation was virtually wheat-less, with wheat supplies down 20 percent. This also resulted in a 30-percent drop in beer production. (Courtesy Portland Rose Festival Foundation.)

Two

1919–1926
Let the Good Times Roll!

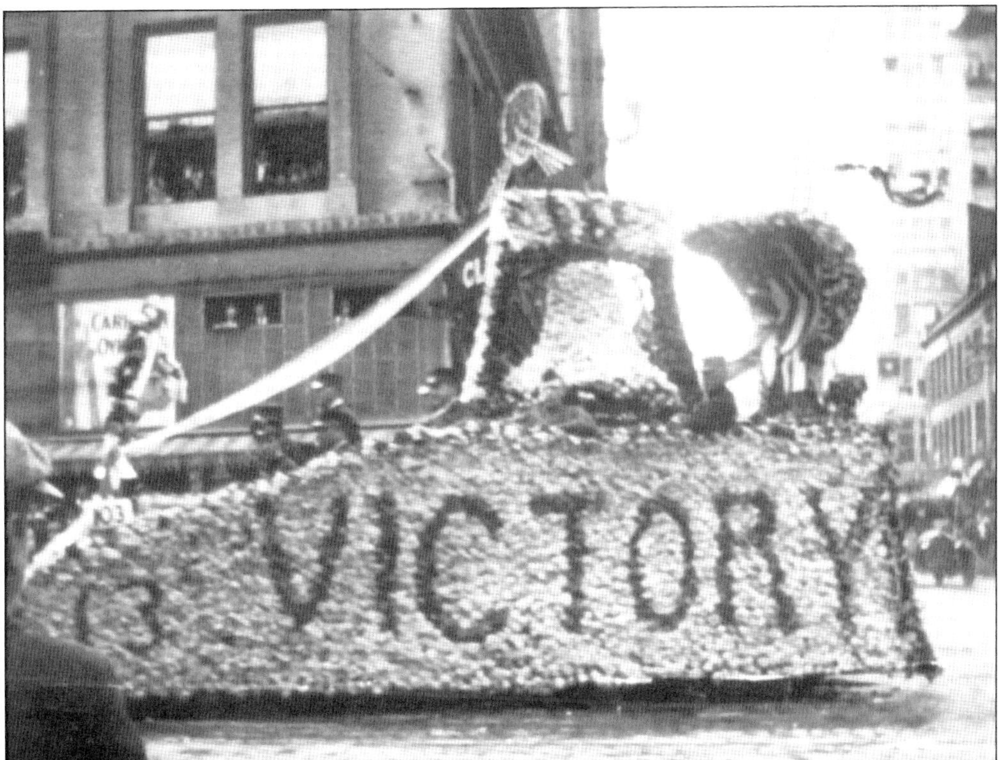

Most Rose Festival events resumed in 1919. A Victory and Industry Parade occurred on Wednesday, June 11 and a Military Parade on June 12 that emphasized victory. An interesting letter to the editor of the *Oregon Journal* appeared on June 12. It read: "Smoking at the dining tables in hotels and restaurants ought to be prohibited. It's very repulsive, annoying, and even insulting to a refined clear person." (Courtesy Oregon Historical Society; OHSFile1910.)

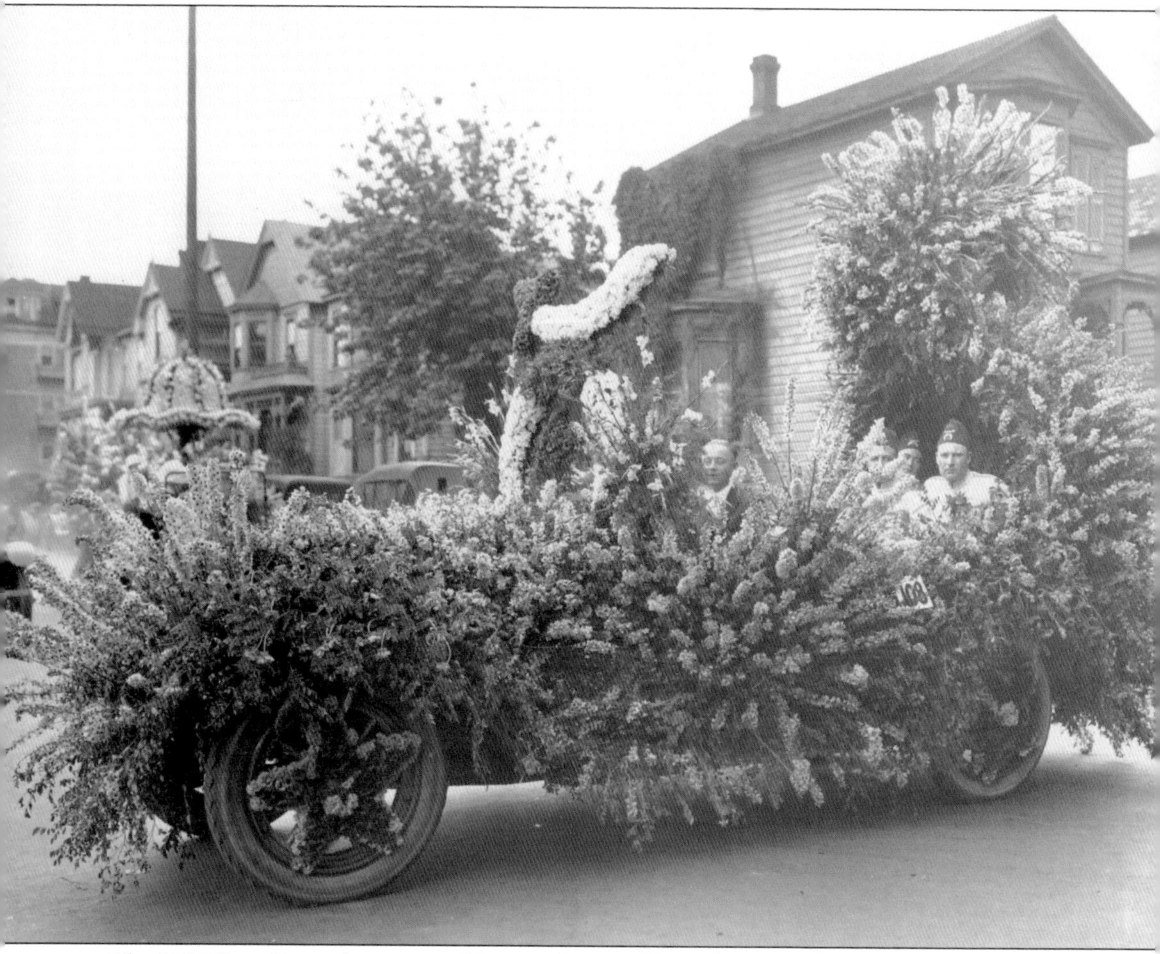

The 1920 Rose Festival was moved later to June 21 through June 26, due to a national Shriners convention. The parade was held under cloudy skies. The *Oregonian* reported on June 21: "Shrine weather all week." That was not to be the case, however. The two Grand Electric parades on Tuesday and Friday escaped the rain. (Courtesy Portland Rose Festival Foundation.)

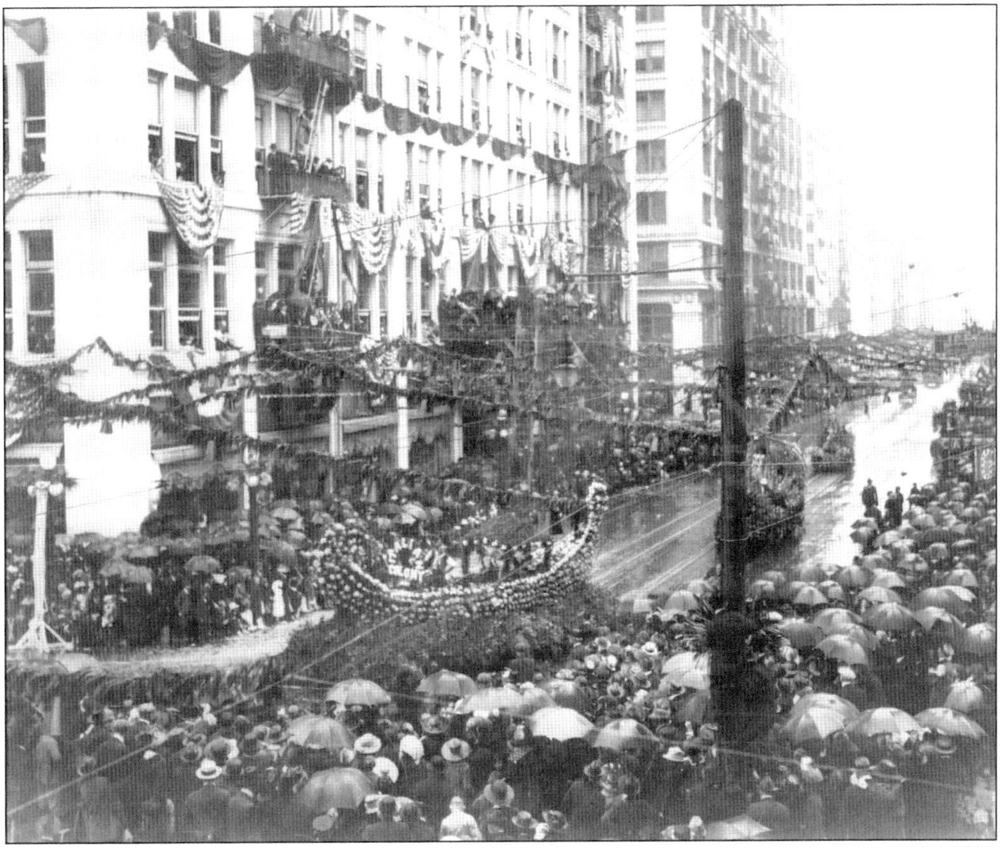

The Grand Floral Parade was not so lucky. As the parade began at 3:00 p.m., rain started to fall, and before a half-mile of the route had been traveled, every participant was drenched by pouring rain. The day's high temperature rose to only 59 degrees. After the shower in 1919 and the rain in 1920, pessimists were beginning to associate rain with the Rose Festival. Decades of history would prove this wrong. (Courtesy Portland Rose Festival Foundation.)

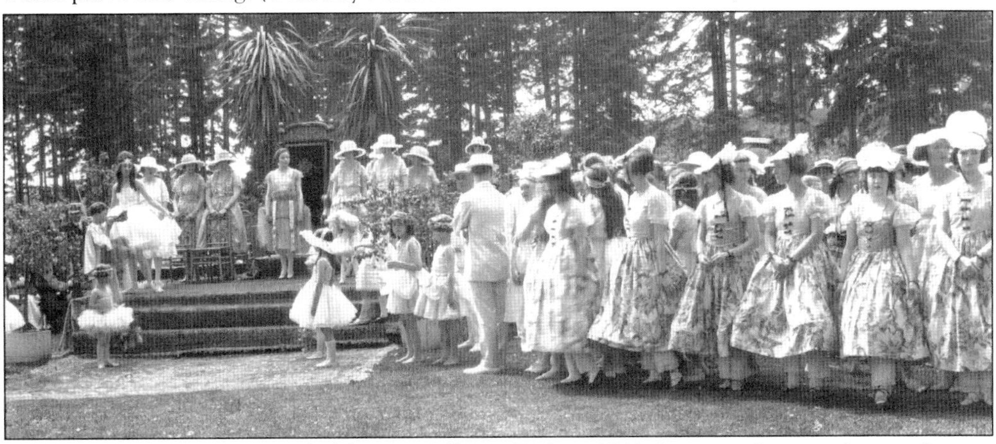

The queen's Coronation was held in Laurelhurst Park in 1921. It enjoyed sunny skies and warm temperatures. And to dress appropriately for that occasion, striped and pleated skirts were selling for $12.50 at Lipman Wolfe & Co., while men's ties were being advertised three for $4.75. (Courtesy Portland Rose Festival Foundation.)

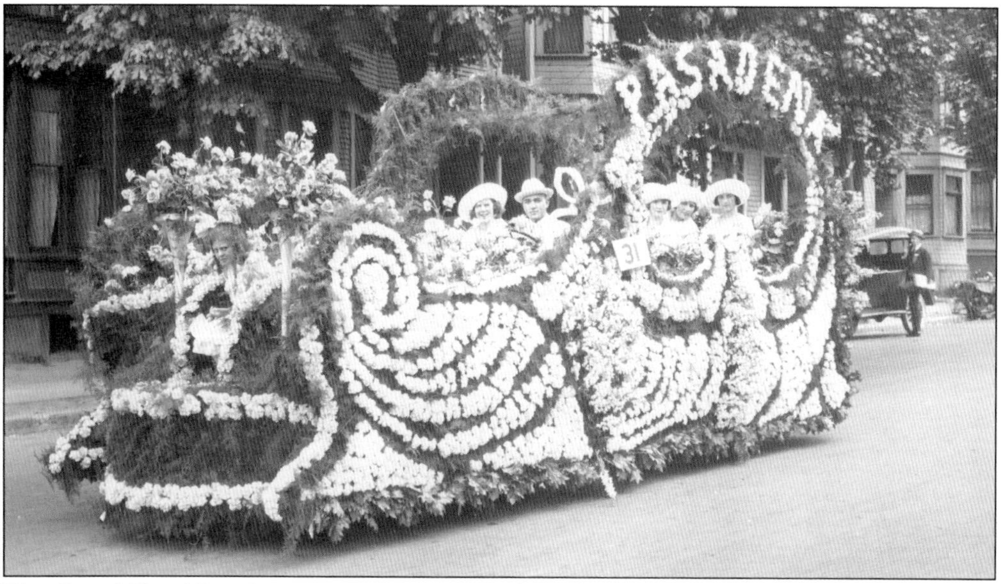

The Grand Floral Parade was gaining attention from the celebrated event held on New Year's Day in Pasadena, another all-floral extravaganza. That city entered a float in the Rose Festival's premier parade, as did various organizations and cities from around Oregon. The festival was once again a success and could be said to have gone out with a bang (or a crash). On Sunday, June 12, crowds at the Rose City Speedway were thrilled by the head-on crash of two locomotives traveling at speeds of 18 to 20 miles an hour. The operators jumped from their respective cabs just as they began converging on the track. (Courtesy Portland Rose Festival Foundation.)

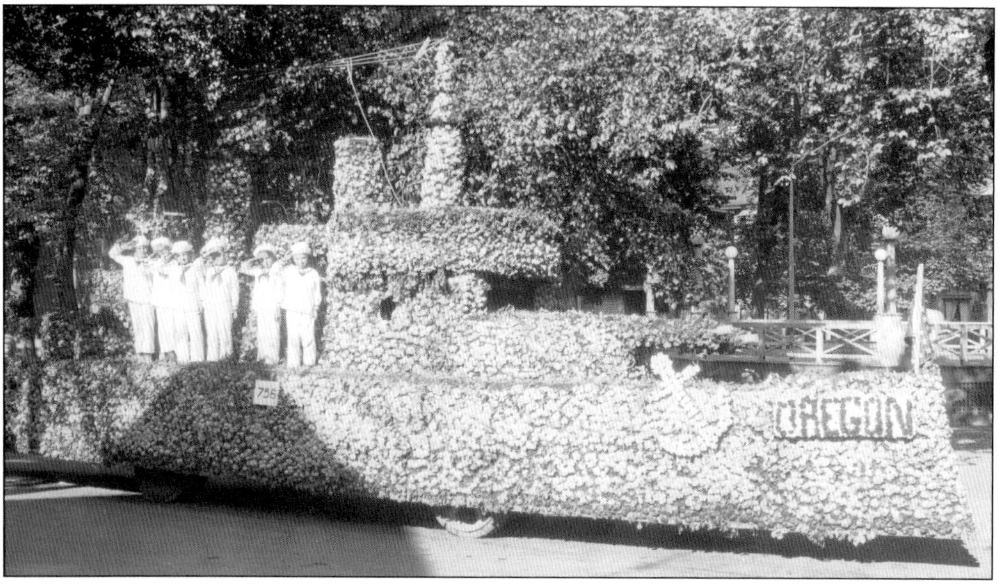

In 1922, an Army-Navy Parade and a Grand Floral Parade were held. A replica of the battleship *Oregon* appeared gaily covered in a plethora of roses. It was a sunny 81 degrees for the Grand Floral Parade. It had been a dry month, with only 0.14 inches of rain, which evidently prompted the erection of several moonshine stills around the area. A 100-gallon still was found along Still Creek near Estacada, and another was discovered just south of the Vista House, east of Portland, as well as in the hills above Scappoose on Scappoose Creek. (Courtesy Portland Rose Festival Foundation.)

Once again, the 1923 Coronation ceremonies were held in Laurelhurst Park. Adm. Hillary P. Jones, commander in chief of the US fleet, approaches the throne with an escort of flower girls. (Courtesy Portland Rose Festival Foundation.)

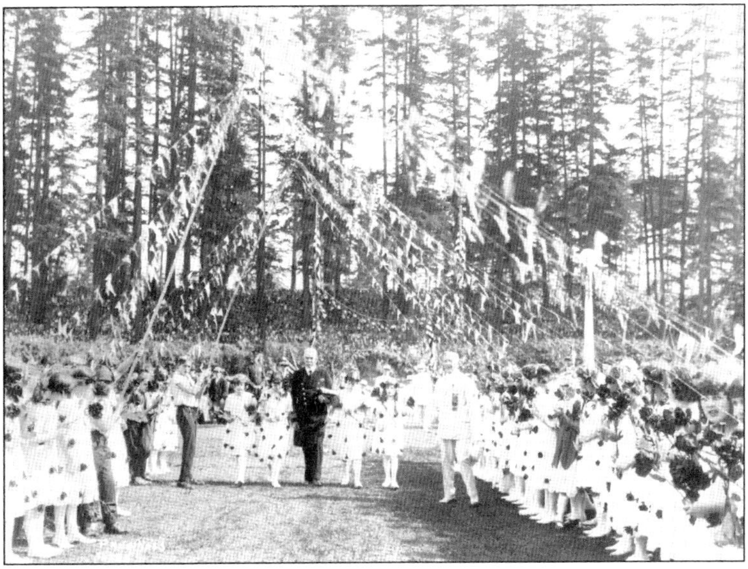

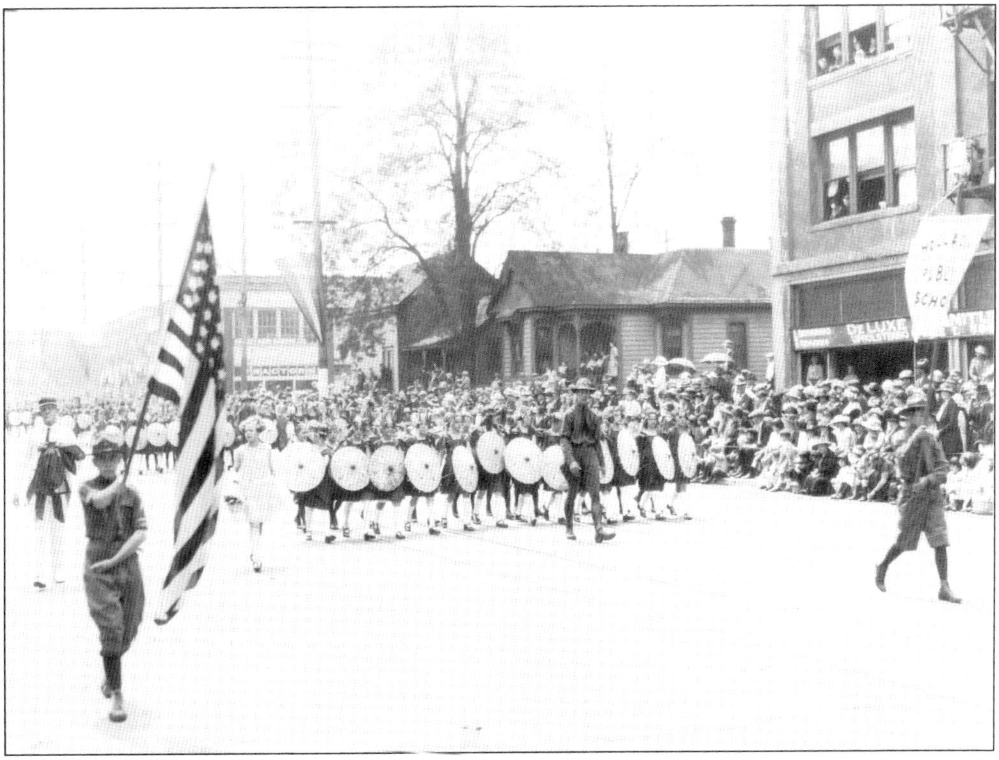

The Rosebud Parade was such a great success in 1923 that it was scheduled to be repeated when President Harding visited the city on July 4. For those who missed attending in person, three Portland theaters—The Peoples, Columbia, and Blue Mouse—would follow every important move of the Rose Festival in motion pictures. For those interested in other entertainment, *Romance Land*, starring Tom Mix, was playing at the Hippodrome movie theater and *She Shock*, starring Lon Chaney, at the Columbia. (Courtesy Portland Rose Festival Foundation.)

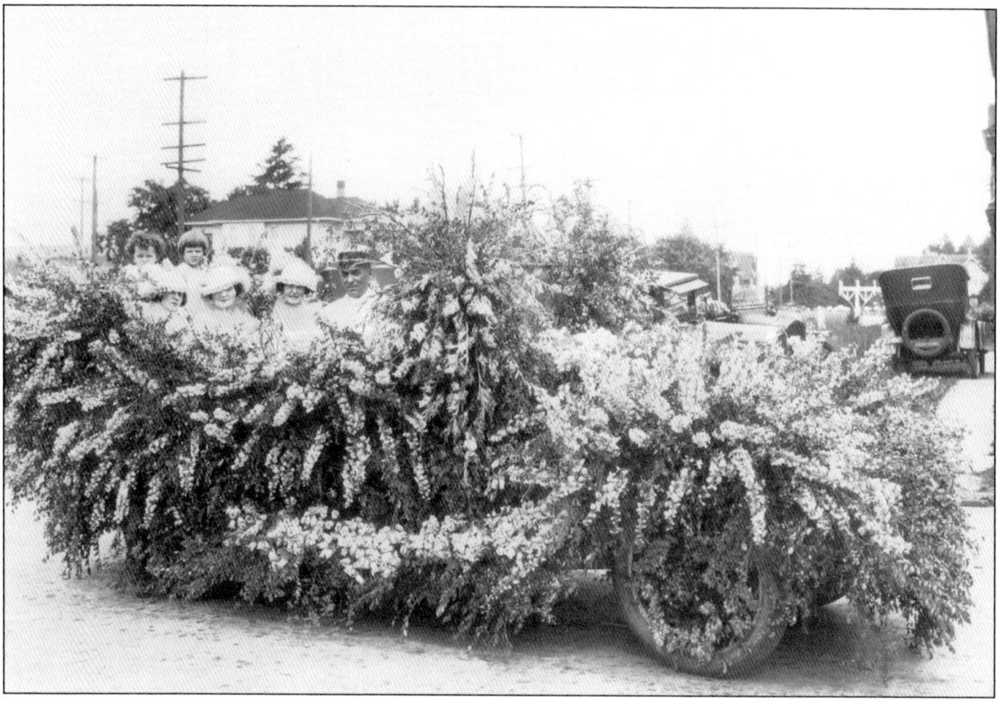

It had been a very dry spring in the Pacific Northwest in 1924. Several forest fires were burning in the area and it was reported that 57 were burning in the national forests of Washington and Oregon. Sunny skies greeted the floats in the Grand Floral Parade on Thursday, June 12. The float in the photograph belonged to Eric Hanson. (Courtesy Portland Rose Festival Foundation.)

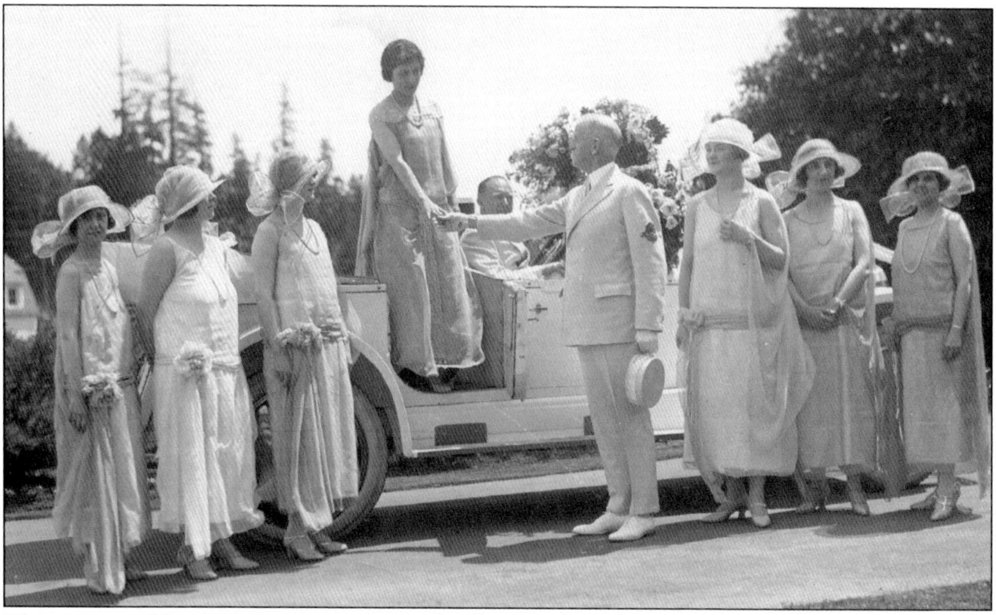

The queen and her court were given a royal welcome when they visited the official Rose Gardens in Washington Park. From left to right are Vineta Hedman, Trena Heerdt, Genevieve George, Queen Edith Dailey, Prime Minister Dr. E.A. Pierce, Doris Joy, Louise Hacker, and Margaret Sullivan. (Courtesy Oregon Historical Society; OrHi72005.)

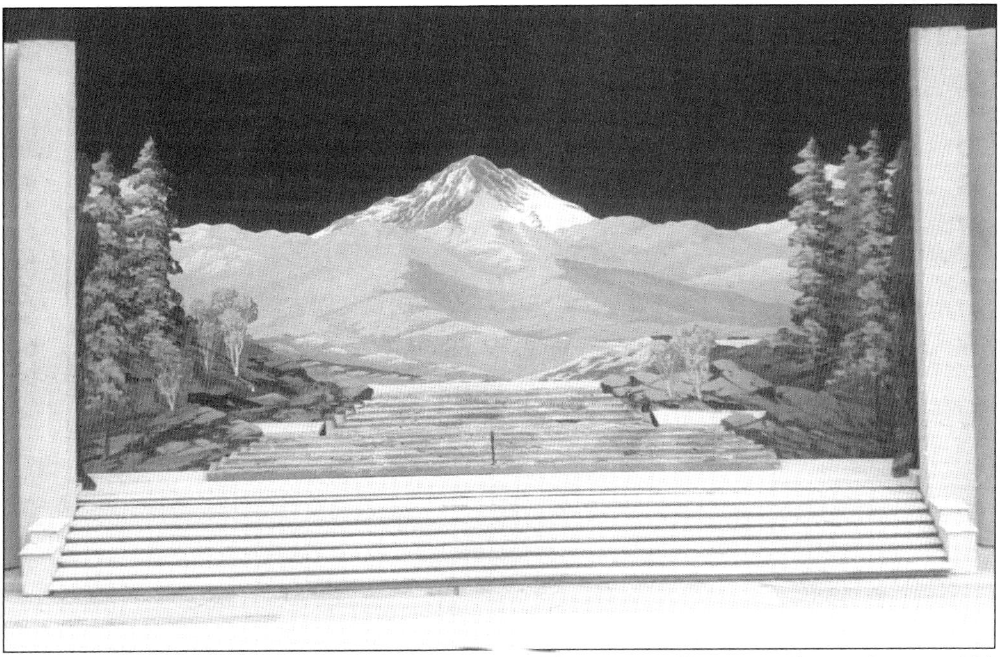

The 1925 Rose Festival offered five performances of the pageant *Rosaria*. It featured a stage 200 feet wide erected on Multnomah Field. The pageant included a cast of 6,000 and a chorus of 2,000, according to the June 16, 1925, Sunday issue of the *Oregon Journal*. It told the "story of the civilizing influence of the rose." Not a drop of rain fell on the pageant, and the fire marshal advised people not to smoke during the performances. The Rose Festival found itself in financial straits trying to pay for the extravagant pageant, so for the first time, it decided to sell advance tickets to make up the difference. (Courtesy Portland Rose Festival Foundation.)

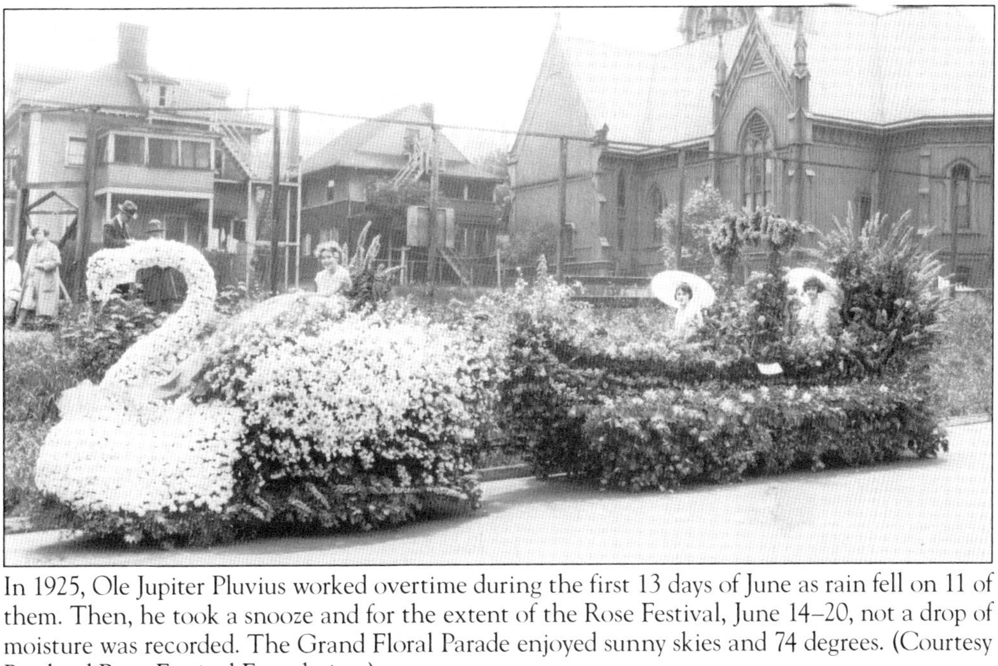

In 1925, Ole Jupiter Pluvius worked overtime during the first 13 days of June as rain fell on 11 of them. Then, he took a snooze and for the extent of the Rose Festival, June 14–20, not a drop of moisture was recorded. The Grand Floral Parade enjoyed sunny skies and 74 degrees. (Courtesy Portland Rose Festival Foundation.)

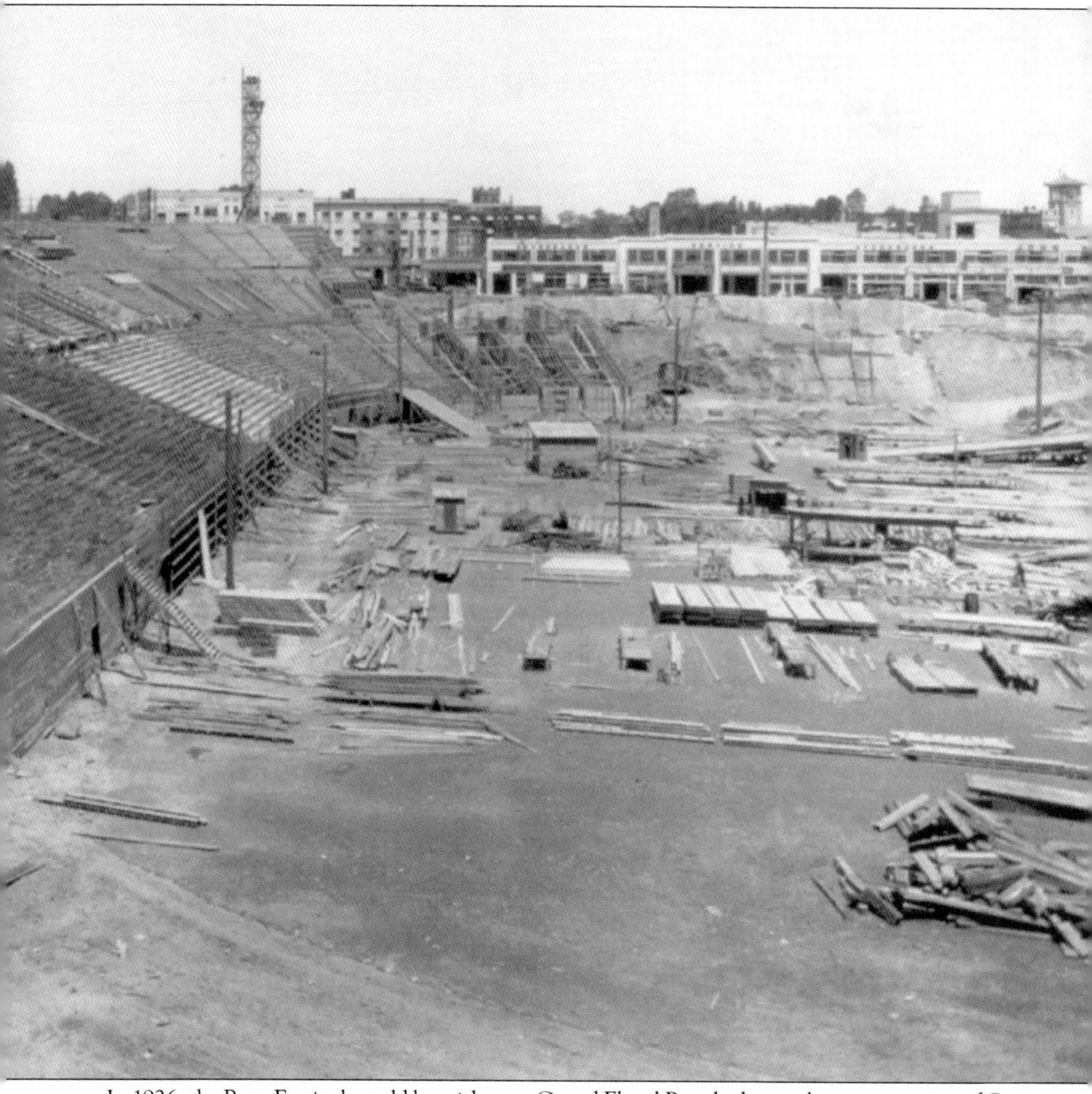

In 1926, the Rose Festival would be without a Grand Floral Parade due to the construction of Civic or Multnomah Stadium. There was one event, however, that was not affected by the construction. It had been a part of Rose Festival activities in the past and would become a permanent feature in years to come. That was the Rose City Park Children's Parade (later called the Rose Festival Junior Parade) that marched along East Fifty-seventh Street to East Forty-second Street. (Courtesy Oregon Historical Society; OrHi66390.)

Three

1927–1936
The Hardy Rose

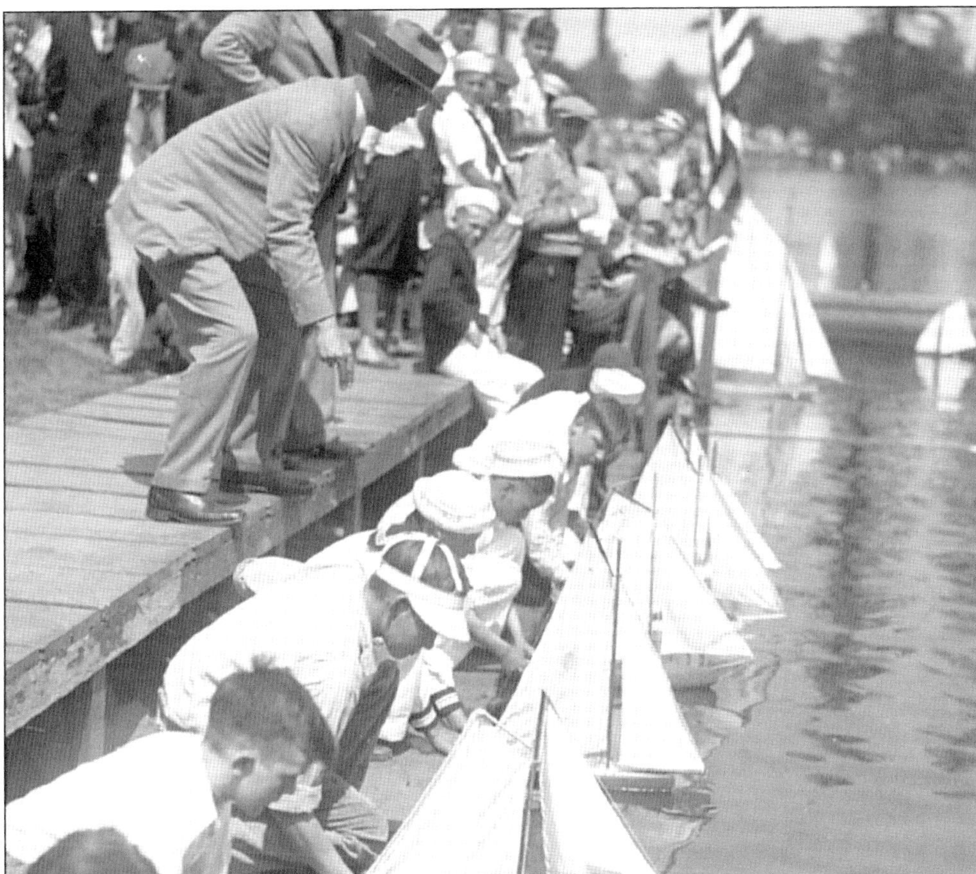

The Rose Festival was greatly expanded in 1927, despite difficulties beginning to appear in the nation's finances. On Tuesday June 14, young sailors could show off their knowledge at the inaugural model boat regatta in Laurelhurst Park. This event soon became an integral part of Rose Festival activities, developing into what would be called the "Milk Carton Boat Races," now held on the casting pond in Westmoreland Park. (Courtesy Oregon Historical Society; OrgLot431,B1,F25.)

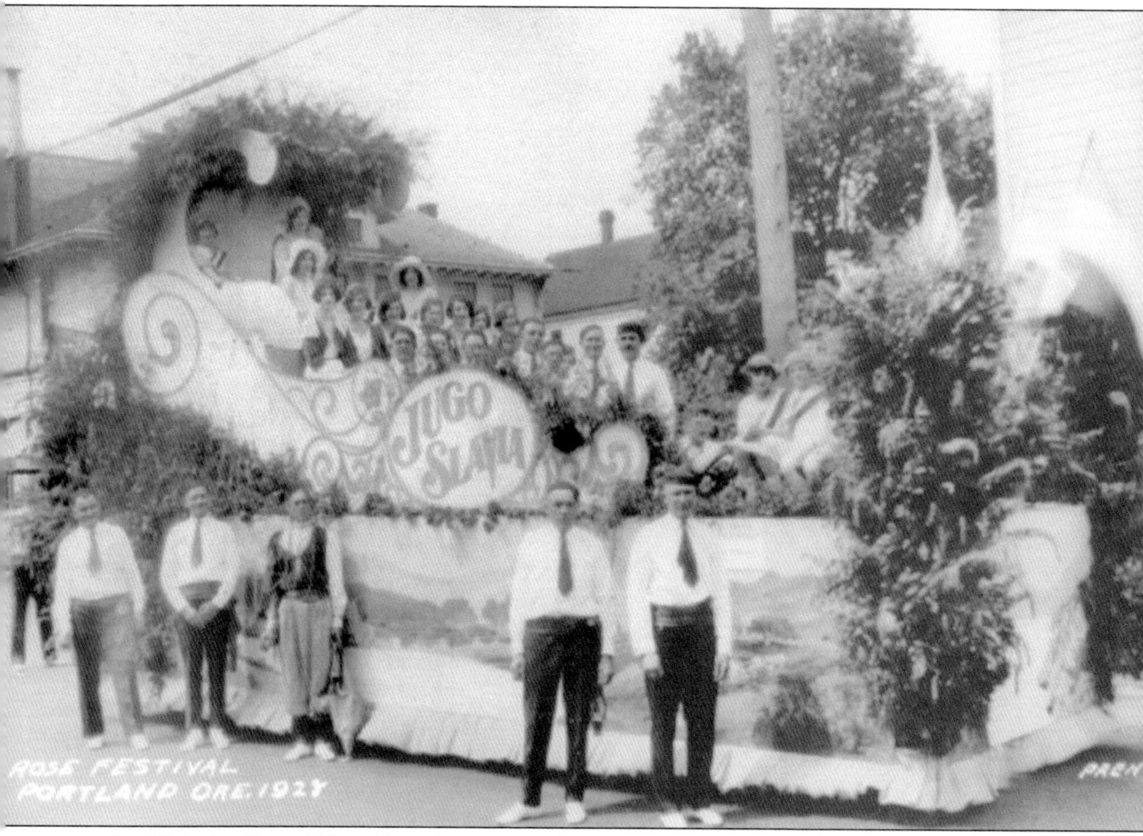

In 1928, the Grand Floral Parade continued to attract many participants. Towns, organizations, businesses, and fraternal groups all contributed well-designed floats. The performance of *Rosaria* was replaced with *Where Rolls the Oregon*. It featured a cast of 3,000, including dancers and pantomime performers portraying the romantic history of the Oregon country from the earliest Native Americans to the pioneers. Directors of the festival were hoping that receipts would equal expenses, totaling a whopping $62,000. Part of the expense ($4,000) was for insurance—rain, liability, and fire. It would not be the last time the Rose Festival would purchase rain insurance. Elsewhere, Lon Chaney appeared on screen in *The Hunchback of Notre Dame*, drawing large crowds at the Peoples Theatre, and Herbert Hoover was nominated for president at the Republican Convention in Kansas City. (Courtesy Portland Rose Festival Foundation.)

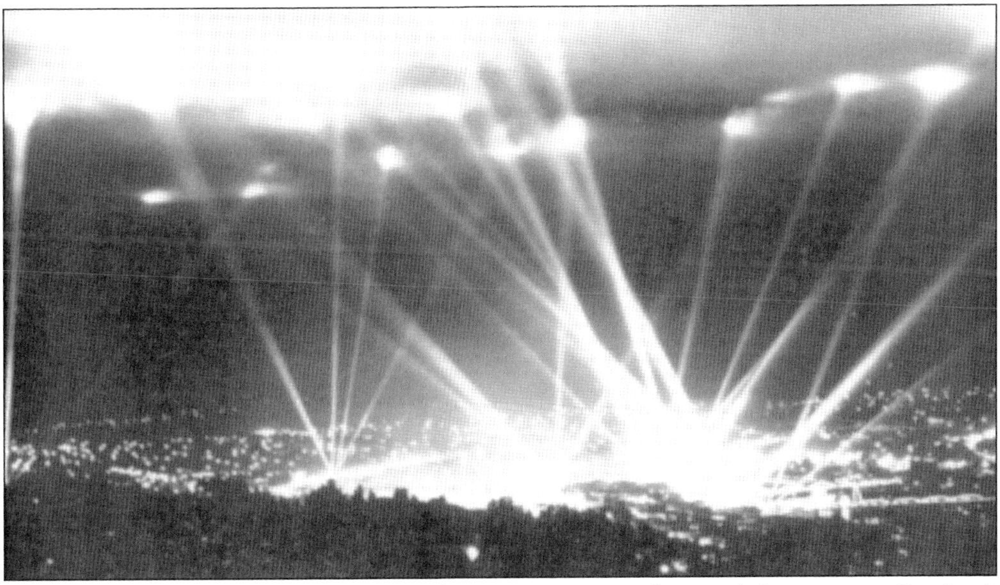

Since the beginning of the Rose Festival, it was customary for naval ships to visit Portland. This c. 1929 photograph shows searchlights from the vessels reflecting off low clouds over the city. The new Portland seawall was completed and dedicated on June 8, 1929, just a day before the Rose Festival Flotilla arrived. Built at a cost of more than $2.5 million, the seawall would become an important part of the annual Rose Festival celebration. (Courtesy Portland Rose Festival Foundation.)

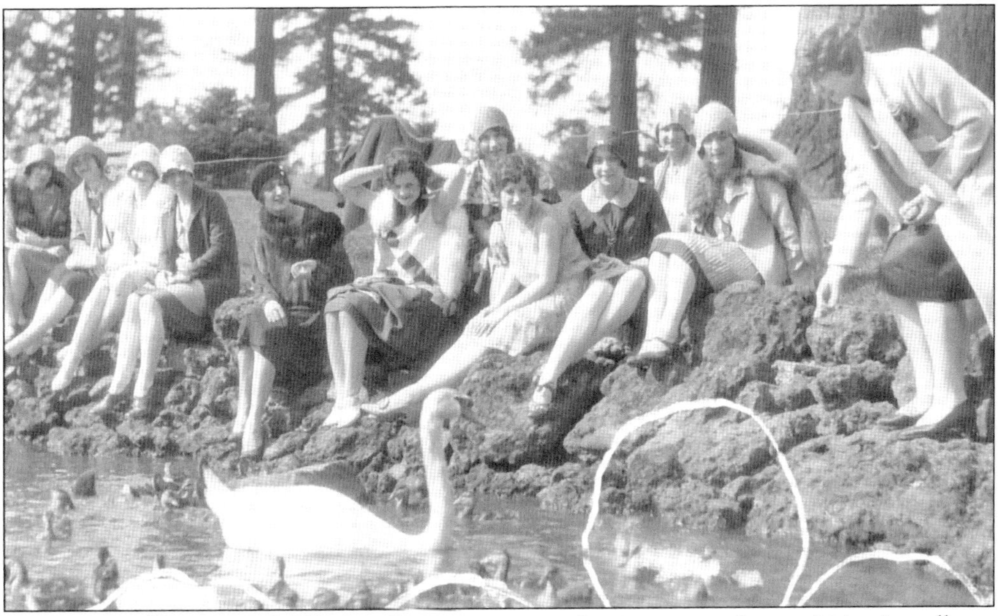

The queen and her court of 1929, as well as some pages and assistants, are shown visiting Laurelhurst Park. Queen Lenore Tamiesie is surrounded by Princesses Jerry Chenoweth, Bertha Wagner, Irene Martin, Hazel Hess, Sunnye Daye, Agnes Cameron Graham, Claribel Seigner, Dewey May Yates, Lucille Leland, and chaperones. During festival week, Meier & Frank Company announced plans for the construction of a 14-story, $2-million addition at Sixth and Morrison Streets that would cover an entire block. (Courtesy Oregon Historical Society; OrHibb002330.)

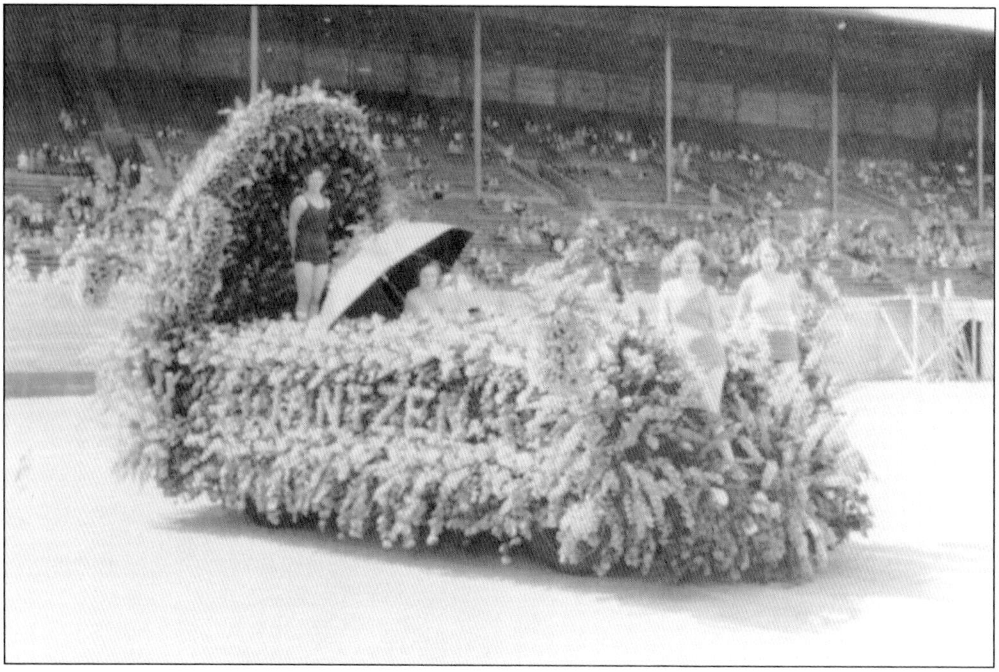

After its construction, Multnomah Stadium became the focal point for the Grand Floral Parade. Large crowds sat in the grandstands to see the parade entries in 1930 before they exited up a steep ramp to continue along the parade route through downtown Portland. Thirty years later, Portland's new indoor arena, the Veterans Memorial Coliseum, would take the place of the stadium seating. Oregon's population had reached the 1,000,000 mark, and in England, Albert Einstein said he was on the eve of a startling discovery of a new relation between space and matter. (Above, courtesy Oregon Historical Society OrHi77861; below, courtesy Oregon Historical Society, OrgLot431,B1,F35.)

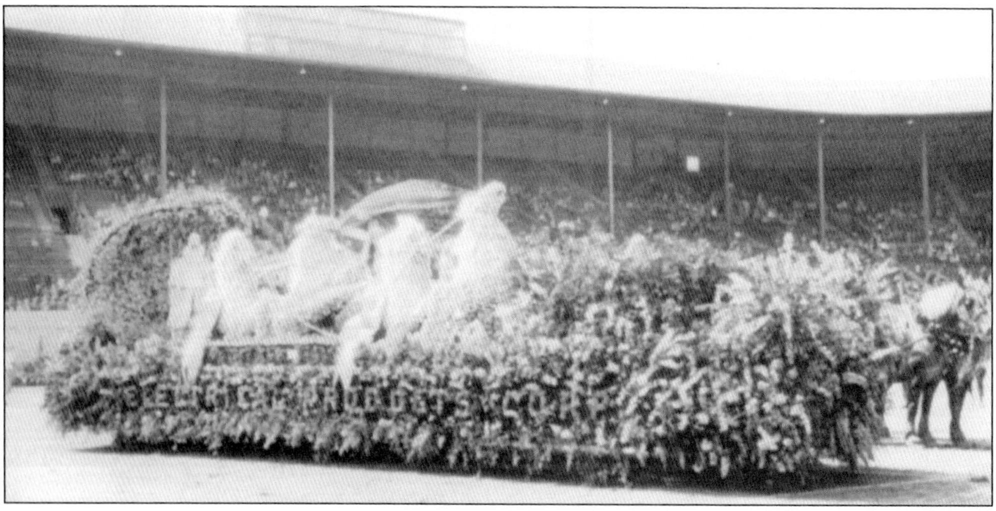

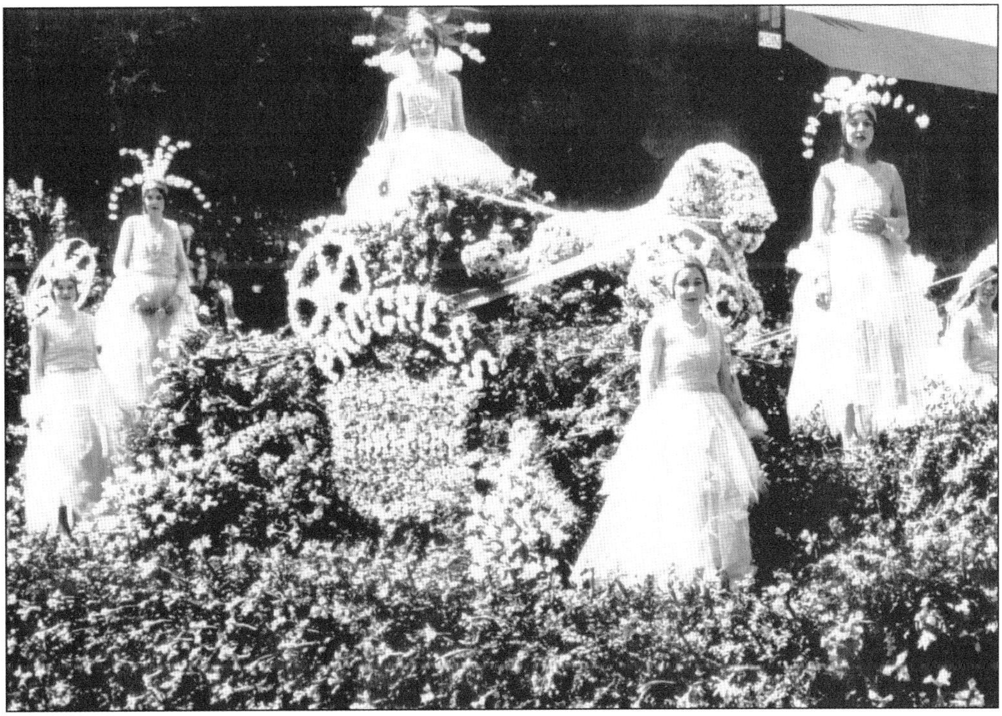

The Grand Floral Parade was held on Friday, June 12, 1931. The photograph shows Queen Rachel's float, "Progress." Admission into Multnomah Stadium to watch the formation of the parade was 50¢. The second-annual Rose Festival Air Show and Exhibit was held at Swan Island. (Courtesy Portland Rose Festival Foundation.)

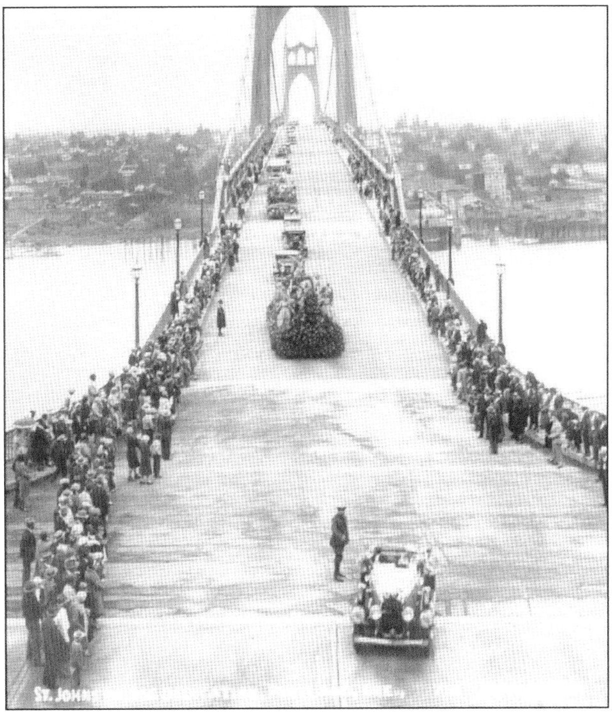

On Saturday, June 13, 1931, the new St. Johns Bridge across the Willamette River was dedicated. The parade to commemorate this event featured floats held over from that year's Grand Floral Parade. It began on the east side of the Willamette River at Grand Avenue and Hawthorne Streets and headed northwest to the east side of the bridge, where ribbon-cutting ceremonies were conducted by Queen Rachel Atkinson. The bridge was built for $4 million. In the mid-1800s, Oregon pioneer James John (known as "Saint John" to many Portlanders) operated a ferry service from the neighborhood now known as St. Johns to Linnton on the west side of the Willamette. (Courtesy Oregon Historical Society; OrHi26296.)

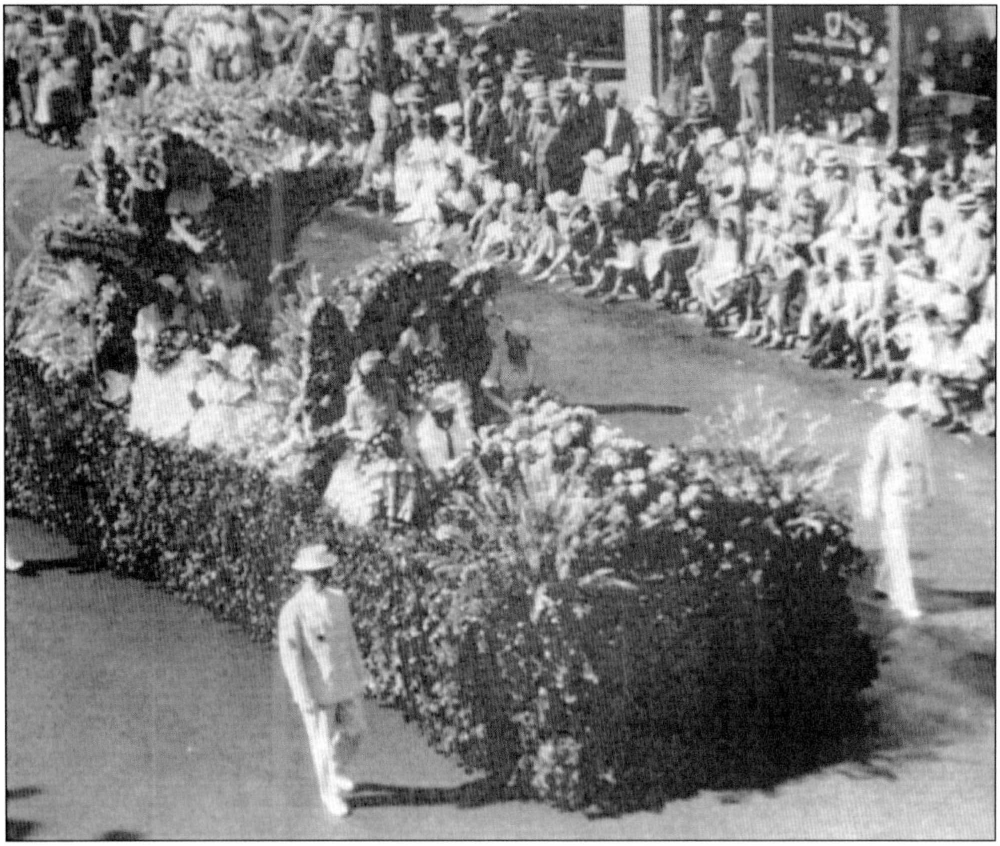

If festival officials wanted a Rose Festival filled with sunshine and warm temperatures, 1932 was the year. Only 0.07 inches was recorded all month, and that fell on June 2. The Grand Floral Parade is shown with Queen Frances Kanzler and her court basking in the sunshine on their float on Friday, June 17. The Merrykhana Parade, also called the Costume and Mardi Gras Parade, enjoyed clear skies as thousands gathered before it began that evening. The Republican National Convention was held in Chicago in late June, calling for some forward-thinking policies in its platform: "The wise use of natural resources freed from monopolistic control; also the conservation of oil by co-ordination effort through the states, the producers and the federal government." (Above, courtesy Oregon Historical Society, OrgLot431,B1,F1; below, courtesy Oregon Historical Society, OrLot431,B1,F40.)

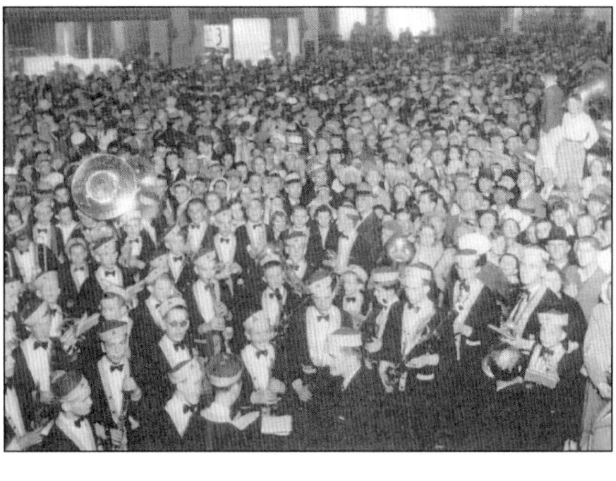

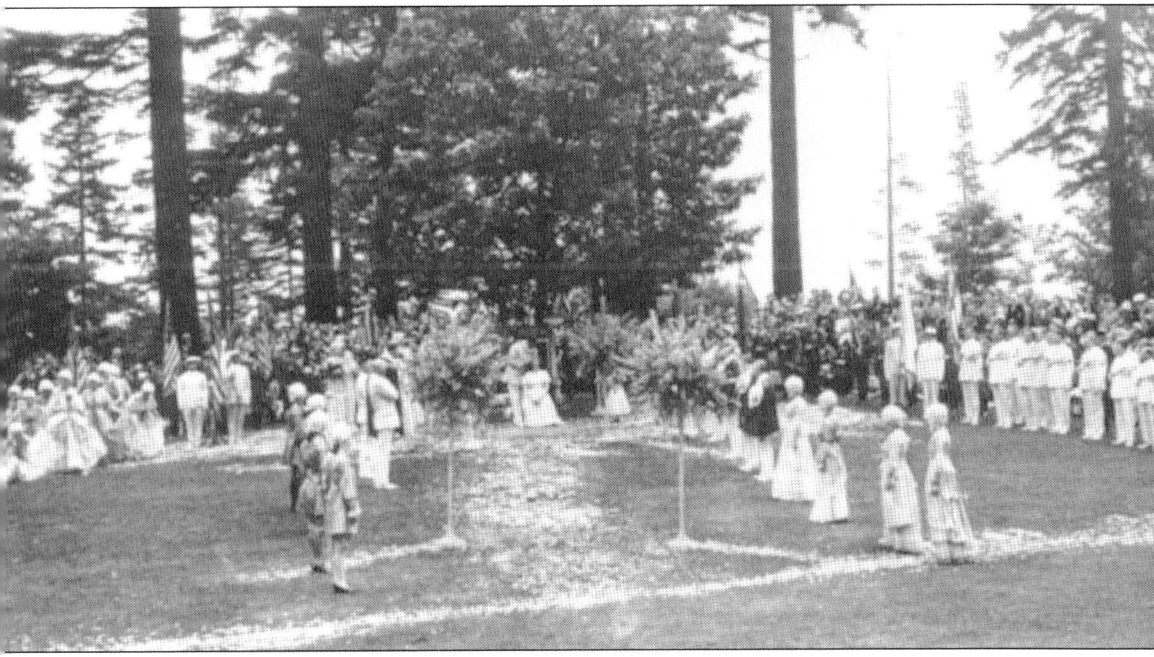

The queen's Coronation, frequently held in the lush Laurelhurst Park in southeast Portland, was always a well-attended affair. Such was the case in 1932 when Queen Frances Kanzler was crowned on Thursday morning, June 16. Roses were plentiful that year. The Women's Advertising Club of Portland had a motto: "A rose for every festival visitor." For three days, they were stationed on downtown corners with baskets of flowers to be given away. Not everything was rosy in Portland that year. In an angry city council session, Mayor George Baker delivered two uppercuts to the jaw of liberal Portland attorney Harry L. Gross after Gross called him a liar, as reported in the *Oregonian* on June 9. Baker served 16 years as mayor, leaving office in 1933. (Courtesy Oregon Historical Society; OrHi89457.)

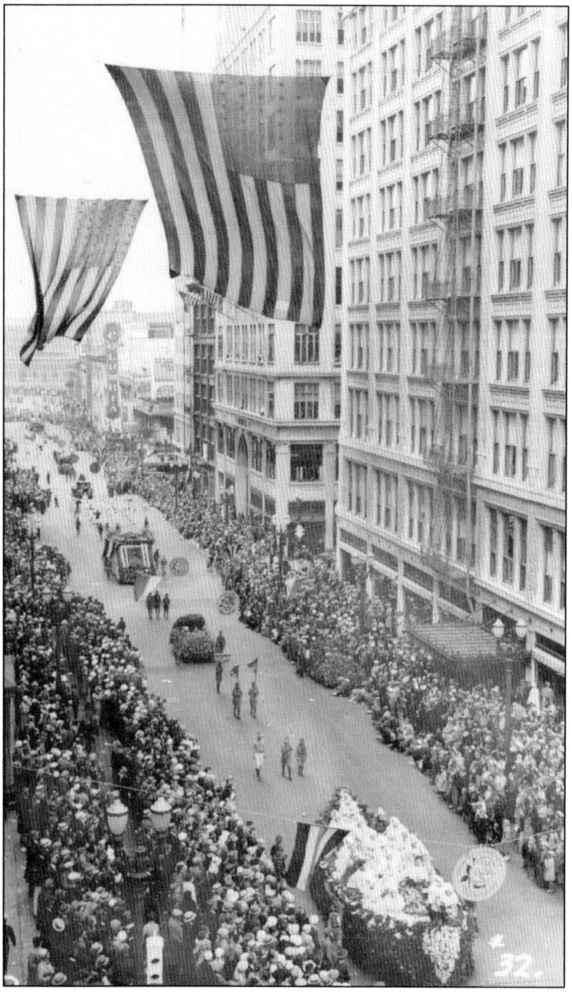

In 1933, the Rose Festival reached its Silver Jubilee; it was 25 years old and going strong. Crowds continued to line the Grand Floral Parade route, as well as the Junior Parade, with its array of pet-drawn floats. The South Park blocks were turned into a veritable fairyland, where 10 performances of *Alice in Wonderland* were held. On Sunday, June 11, Queen Jean Stevenson inaugurated United Airlines's 21.5-hour flight to New York City. Olds & King's Department Store advertised a silk stocking that was perfect for parade-going; it was absolutely guaranteed against garter runs for only 85¢—or three pair for $2.40. (Courtesy Portland Rose Festival Foundation.)

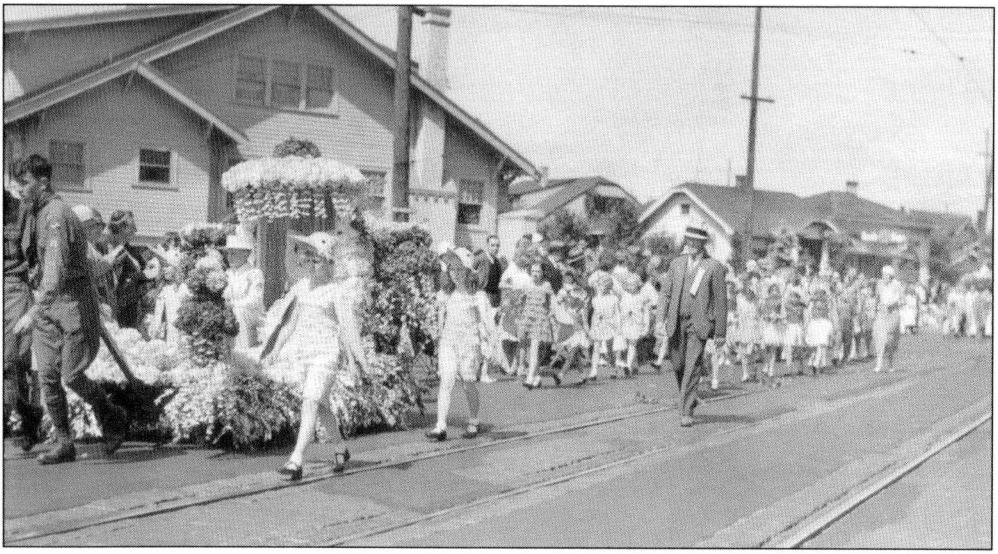

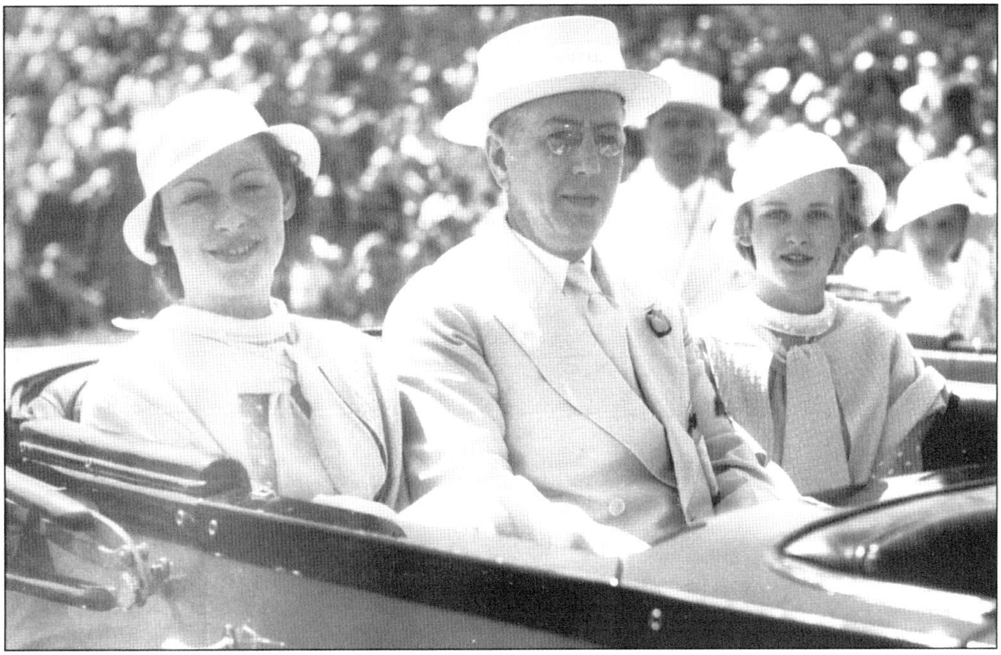

From left to right, Princess Mary Agnes Grigsby, Rosarian Fred L. Wegner, and Princess Marian Dryer rode together in the 1933 Grand Floral Parade. The decision was made to put the Rose Festival Court in convertibles instead of on a float because of threatening rain. (Courtesy Portland Rose Festival Foundation.)

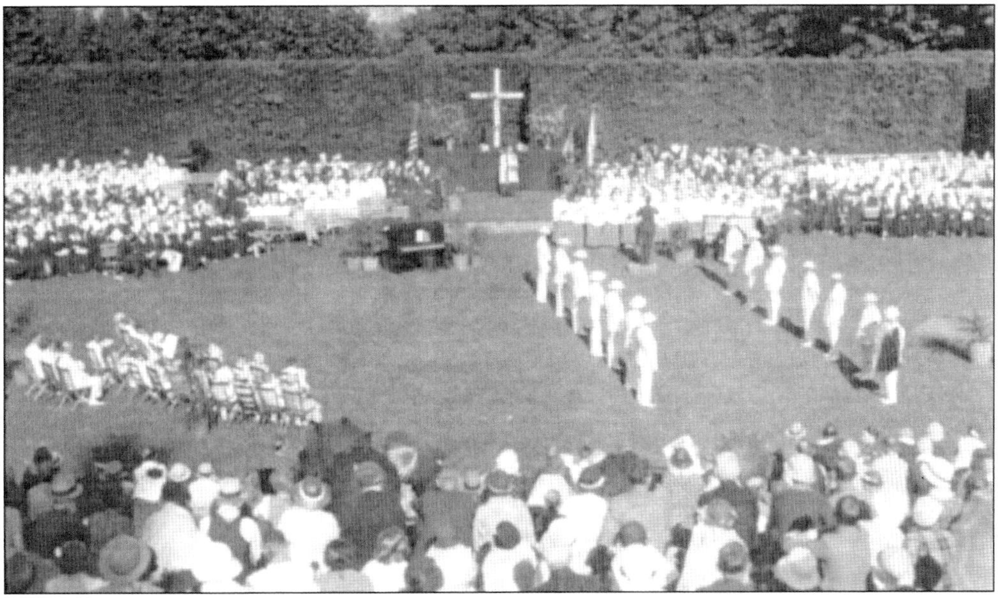

To close the 1933 Silver Jubilee Rose Festival on Sunday, several events were scheduled. Motorboat races were held on the Willamette River, a fly-casting tournament was at Laurelhurst Park's Firwood Lake, and a presentation of *Alice in Wonderland* was given at the festival center in the downtown park blocks. Vesper services were held in the beautiful Rose Bowl in Washington Park, under the sponsorship of the Portland Council of Churches and the Rose Festival. It was a program of song and pageantry in exaltation of the rose. (Courtesy Oregon Historical Society; OrgLot431,B2,F1.)

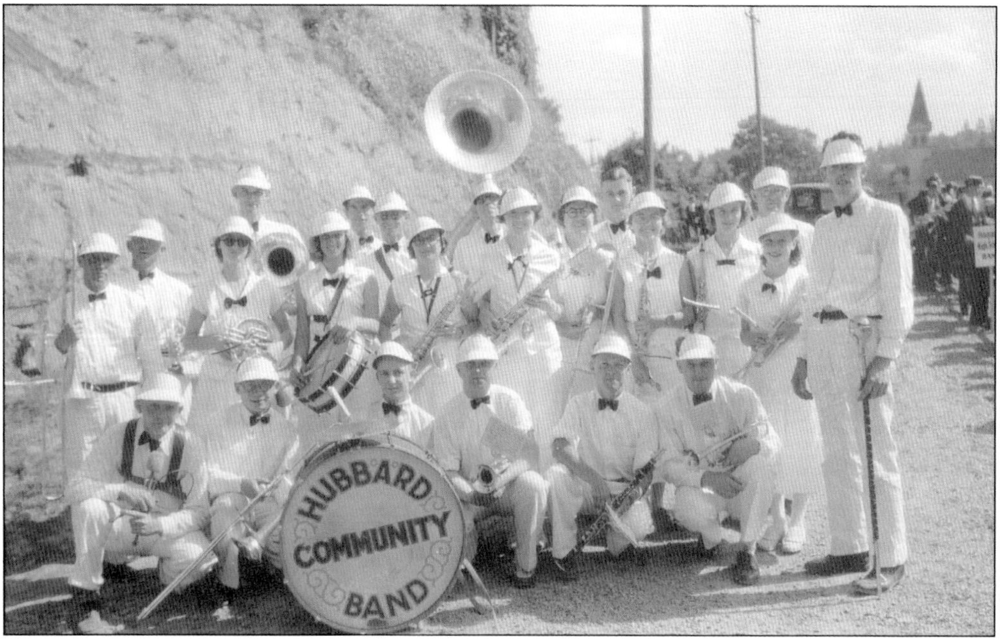

A band was a lively addition to the Grand Floral Parade on Thursday, June 14, 1934. Communities from around Portland entered both floats and marching units in the parade. Units not appearing in the Grand Floral Parade often appeared in the Junior Parade, which formed in Grant Park off Sandy Boulevard. On Portland movie screens, Clark Gable and Claudette Colbert were starring in Frank Capra's screwball comedy, *It Happened One Night*, and film buffs could enjoy the future Oscar winner at the Capitol movie theater for 15¢ before 6:00 p.m. At the Broadway Theatre, Myrna Loy and William Powell appeared in *The Thin Man* with Maureen O'Sullivan. (Both, courtesy Portland Rose Festival Foundation.)

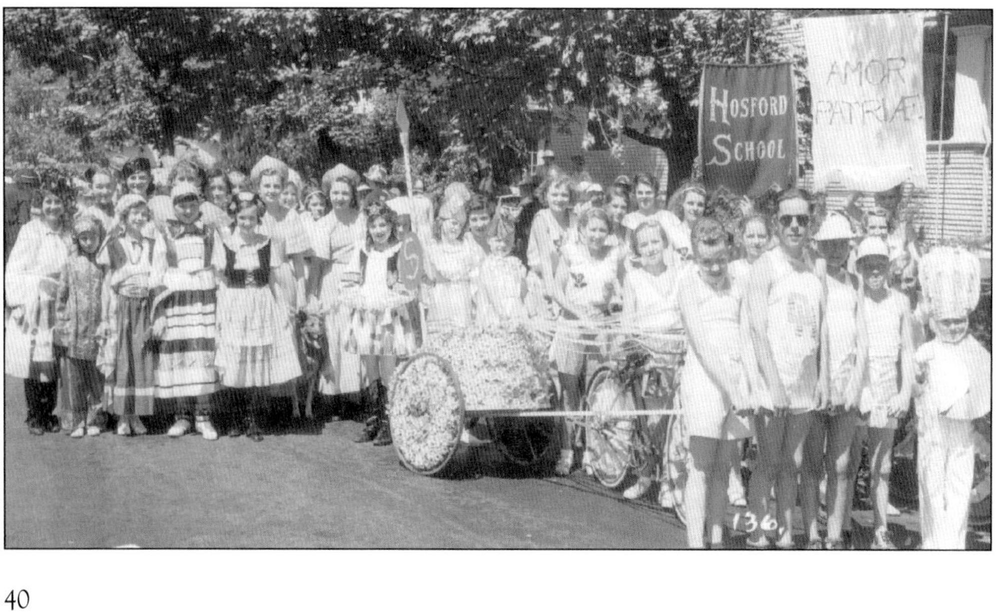

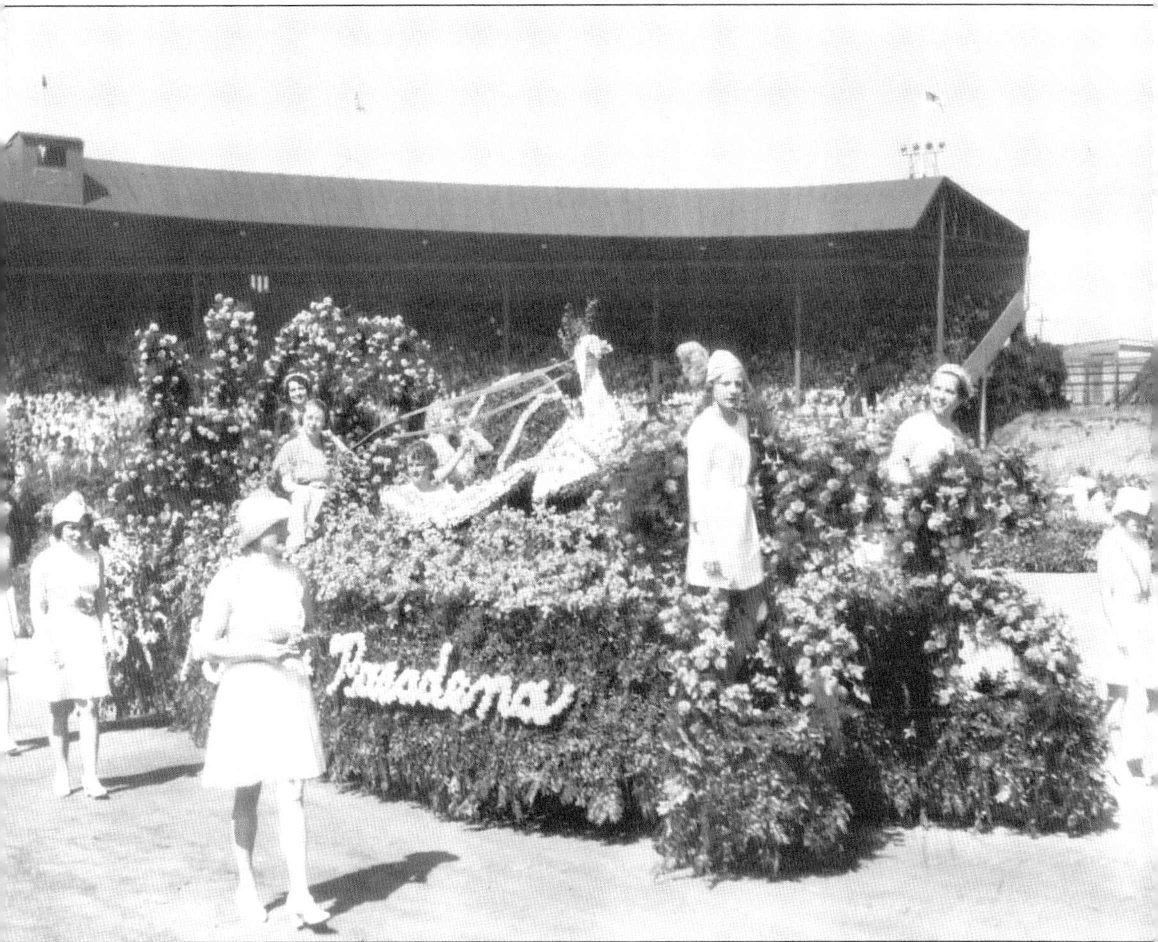

The Rose Festival's kissing cousin from Southern California, the Tournament of Roses, often appeared with a float in the Grand Floral Parade. Here, a Pasadena entry is shown preparing to leave Multnomah Stadium at the start of the Grand Floral Parade in 1934. (Courtesy Oregon Historical Society File1912.)

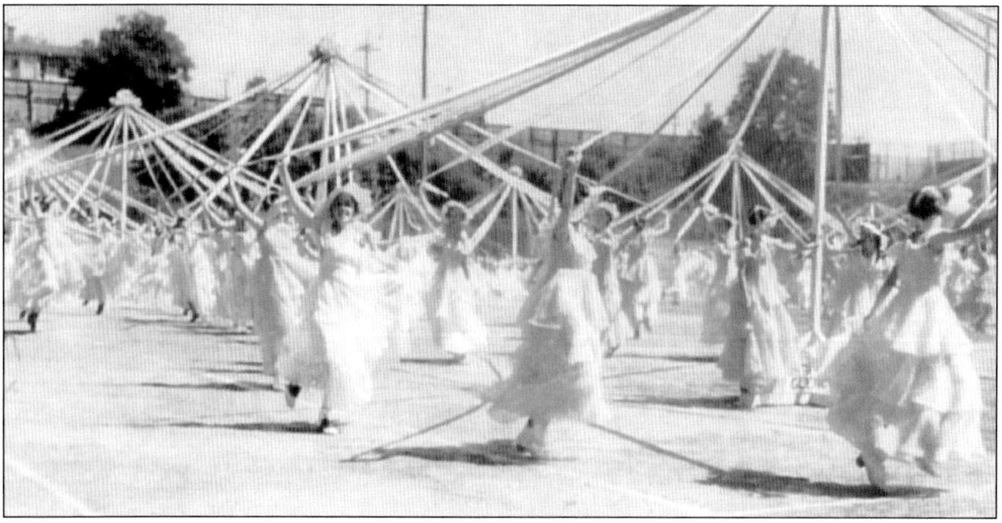

Nearly 500 primary school girls in fluffy pink and blue dresses took part in the maypole dance in Multnomah Stadium, preceding the 1935 queen's Coronation. The thermometer reached a sizzling 96 degrees on Thursday, June 6, causing many high school girls participating in the ceremonies to faint. Luckily, no one was seriously hurt. (Courtesy Portland Rose Festival Foundation.)

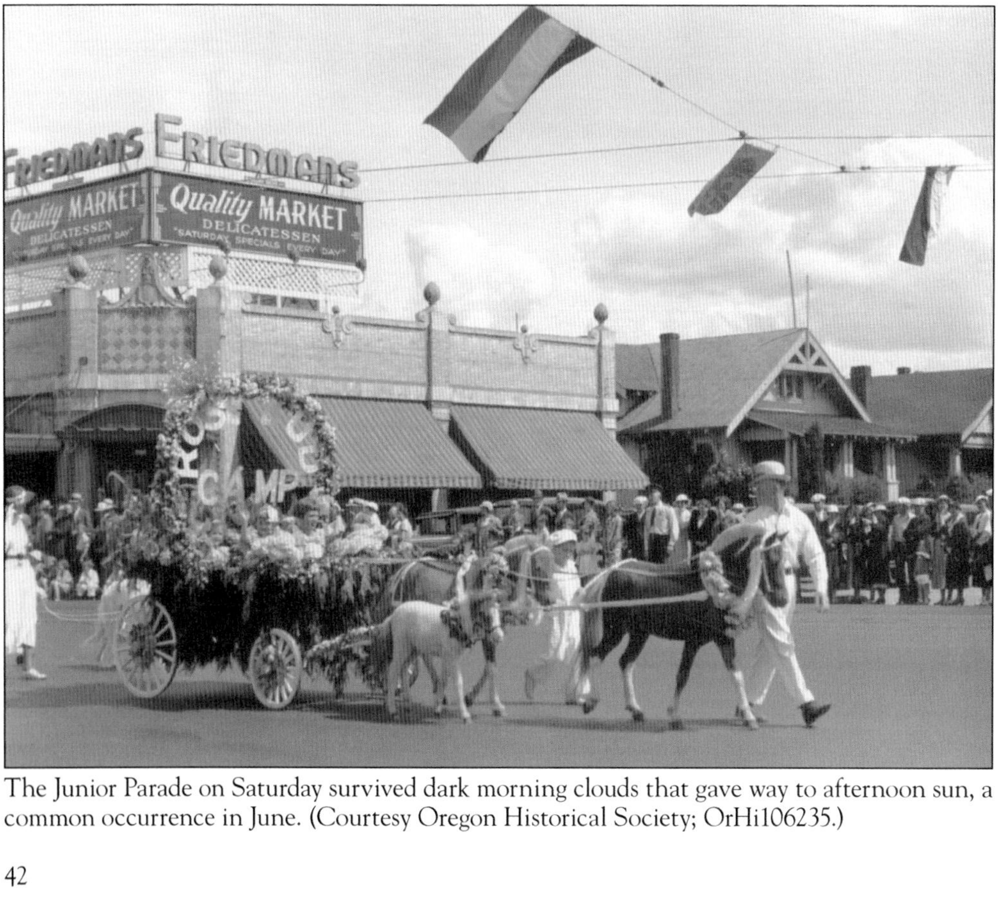

The Junior Parade on Saturday survived dark morning clouds that gave way to afternoon sun, a common occurrence in June. (Courtesy Oregon Historical Society; OrHi106235.)

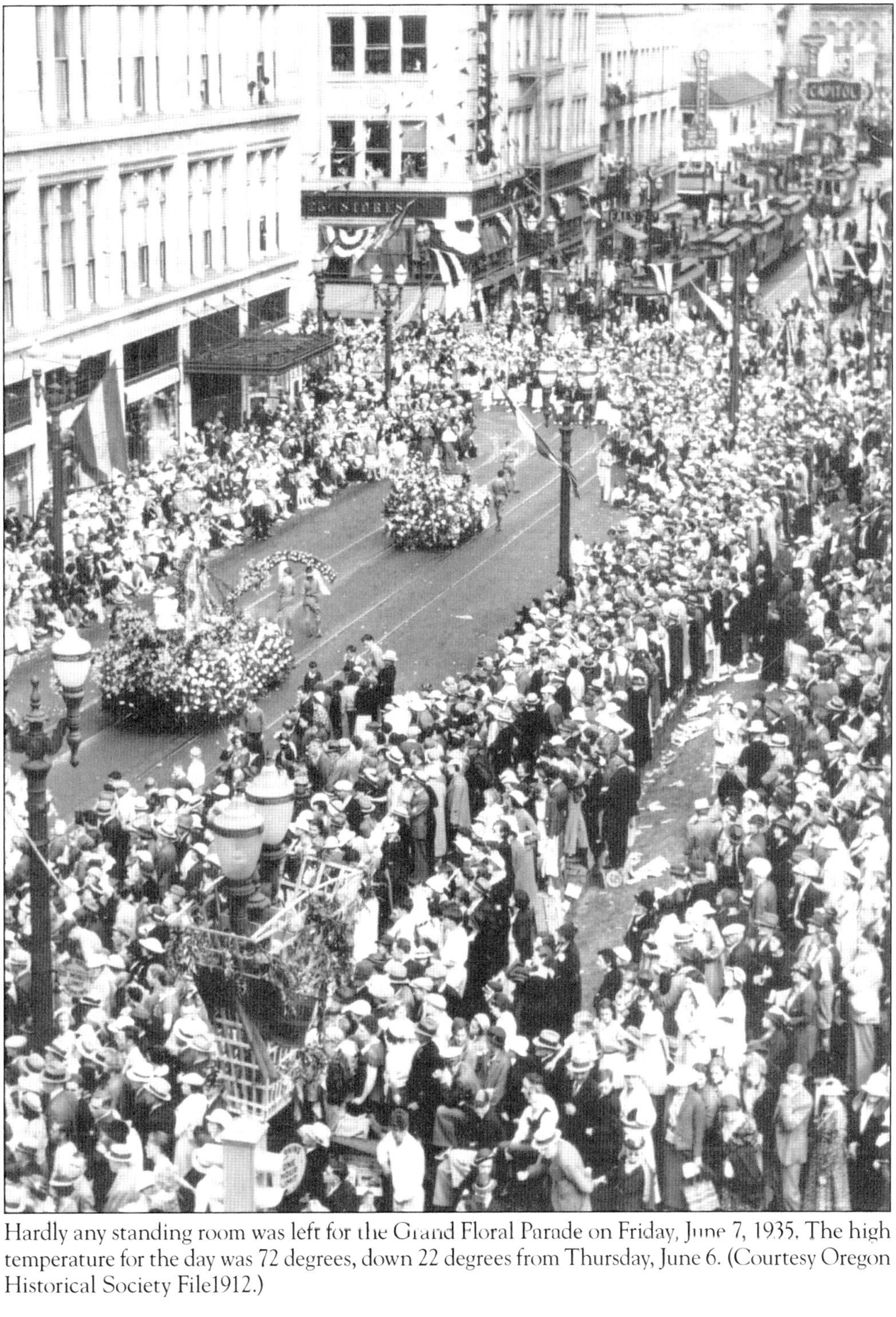

Hardly any standing room was left for the Grand Floral Parade on Friday, June 7, 1935. The high temperature for the day was 72 degrees, down 22 degrees from Thursday, June 6. (Courtesy Oregon Historical Society File1912.)

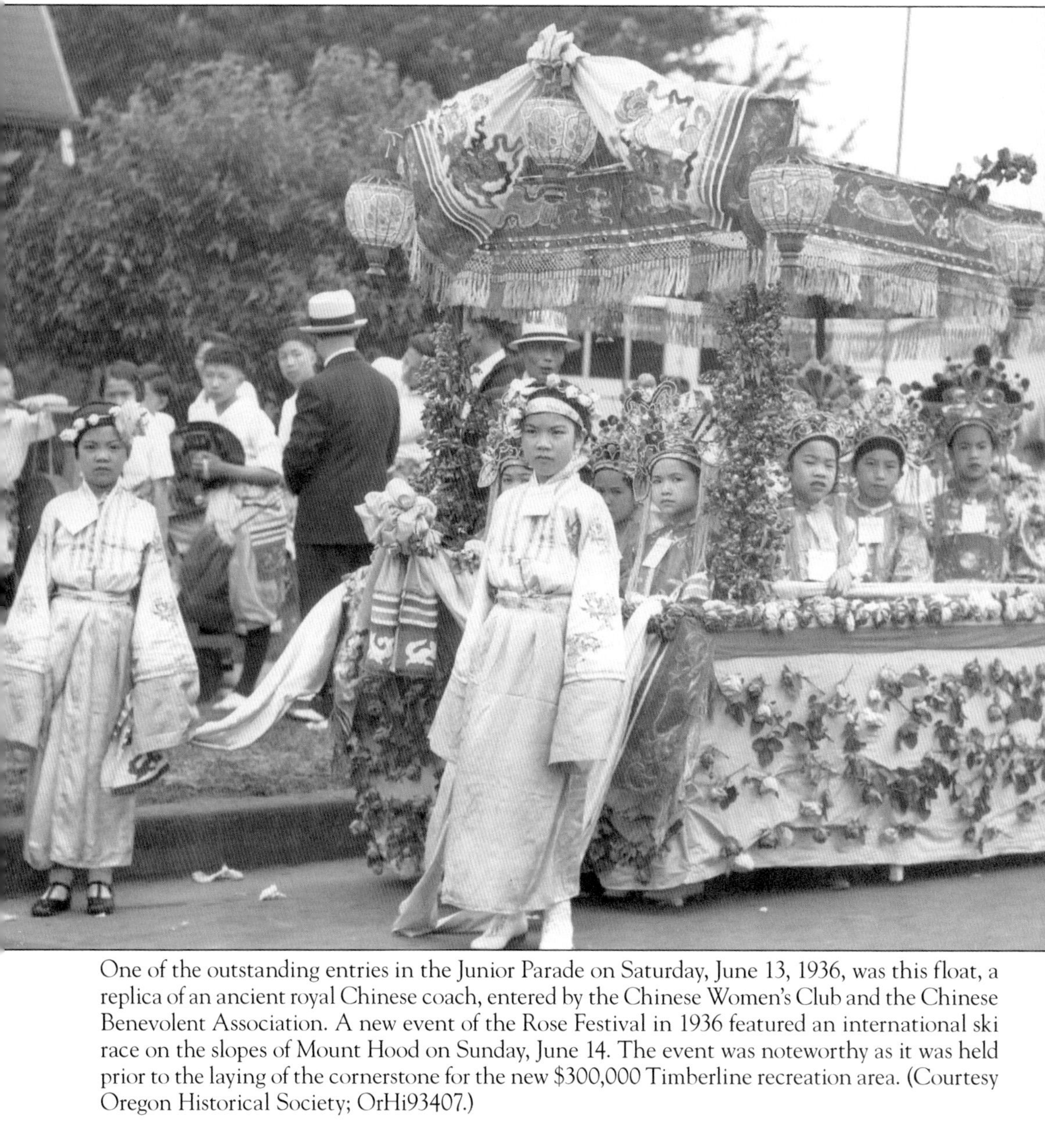

One of the outstanding entries in the Junior Parade on Saturday, June 13, 1936, was this float, a replica of an ancient royal Chinese coach, entered by the Chinese Women's Club and the Chinese Benevolent Association. A new event of the Rose Festival in 1936 featured an international ski race on the slopes of Mount Hood on Sunday, June 14. The event was noteworthy as it was held prior to the laying of the cornerstone for the new $300,000 Timberline recreation area. (Courtesy Oregon Historical Society; OrHi93407.)

Four

1937–1945
World War II—Keep the Home Fires Burning

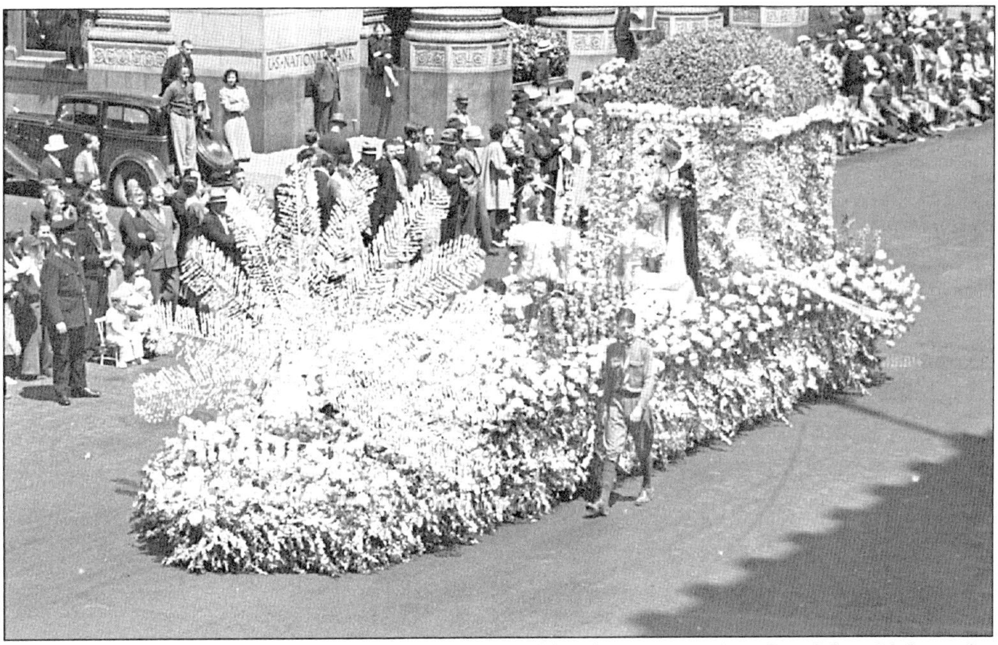

"Paradise" was the name of the lovely float entered by the Oregon City Breakfast Club in the Grand Floral Parade on Friday, June 11, 1937. It captured first prize in the division for "Oregon Cities Outside Portland." Almost all Portland retail stores were closed for the duration of the parade. On June 1, Amelia Earhart took off from Miami, Florida, for the first leg of her attempt to fly around the world. (Courtesy Oregon Historical Society File1912.)

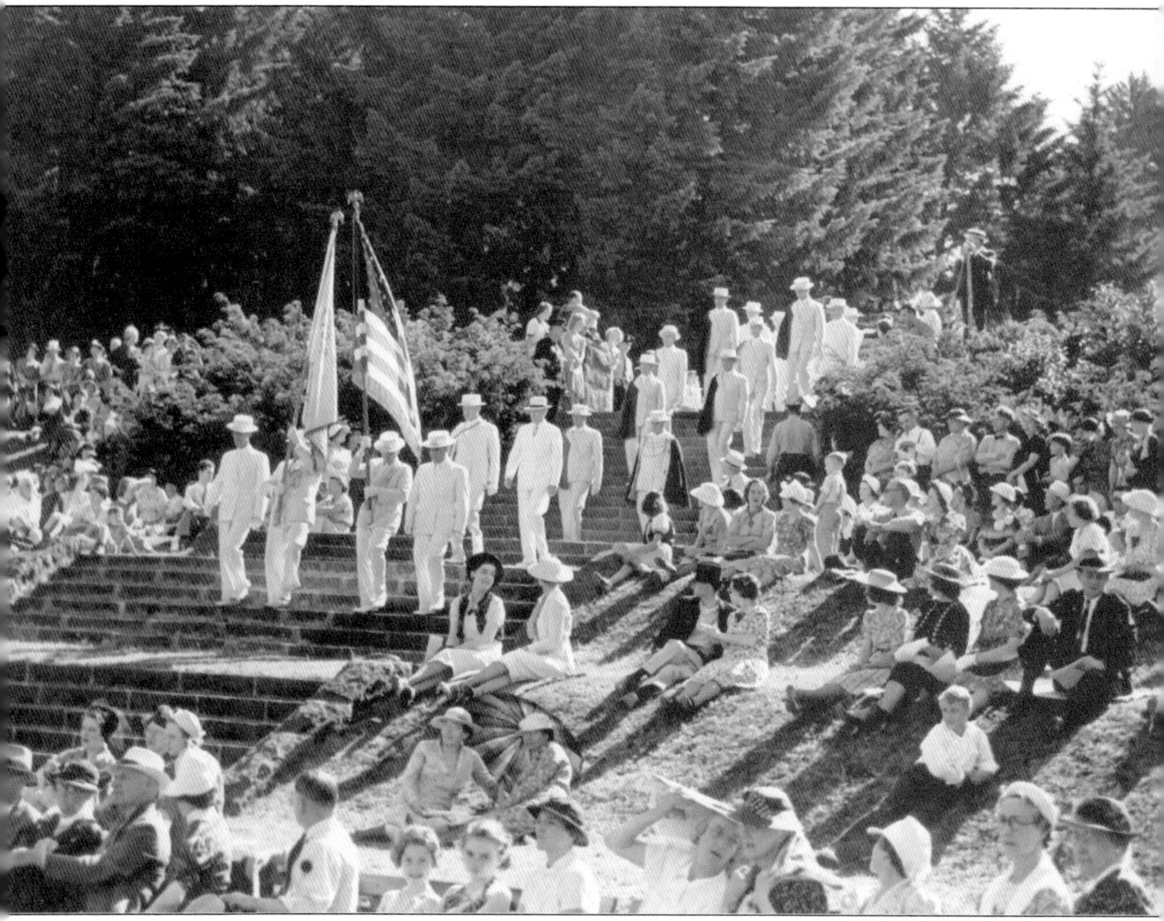

In 1938, the Royal Rosarians led the procession down the steps in Washington Park at a ceremonial opening of the Rose Festival on Sunday, June 5. More than 5,000 people were in attendance. Admission to the Rose Festival Dog Races at Multnomah Stadium was 25¢, but ladies attended for free. (Courtesy Oregon Historical Society; OrHi83703.)

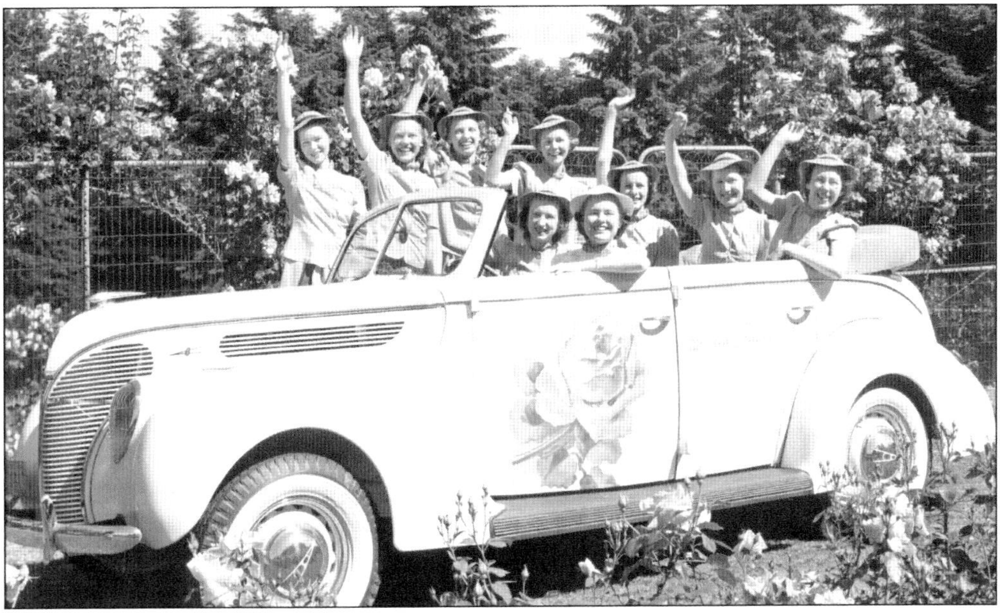

Later, Queen Frances Hulse and her court visited the Washington Park Rose Garden. The Portland Rose Festival Association had a fleet of these Ford convertibles used to carry queen and court in the Grand Floral Parade. (From the *Oregon Journal,* June 12, 1938.)

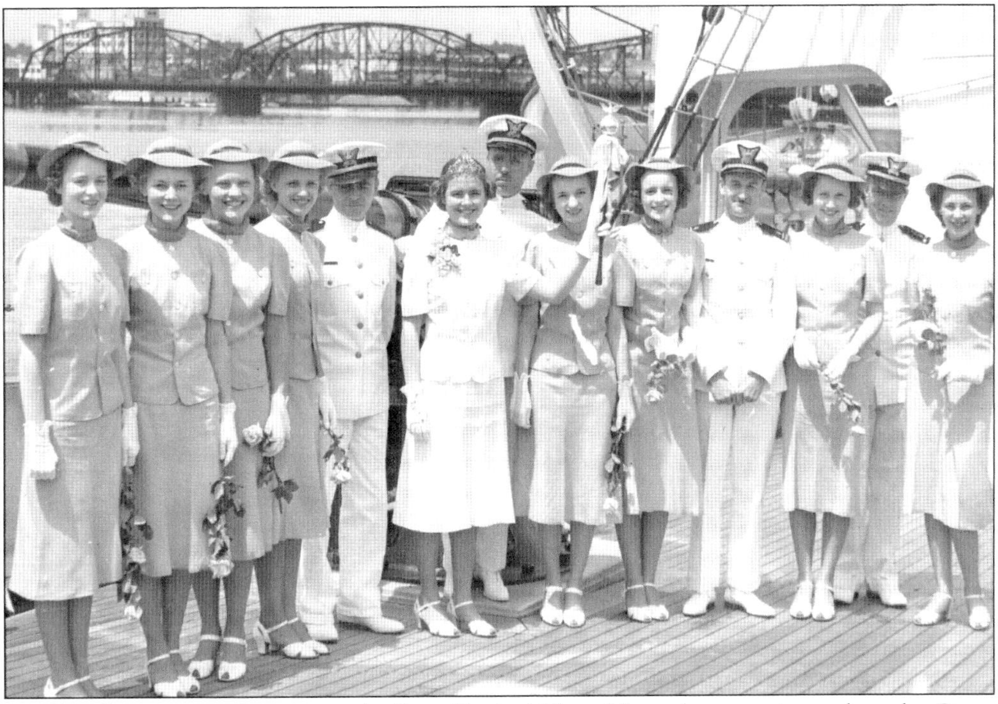

In 1938, the court paid a visit to the Rose Festival Fleet. Here, they are pictured on the Coast Guard cutter *Onondaga.* From right to left are Princess Virginia, Princess Dagney, Princess Marjorie, Princess Marie, Lt. R.E. Morrell, Queen Frances, Capt. Frank D. Higbee; Princess Norma; Princess Bettie; Lt. J.T. Stanley; Princess Beatrice; Chief Machinist A.J.K. Wallace, and Princess Ethel.(Courtesy Oregon Historical Society; OrHi83722.)

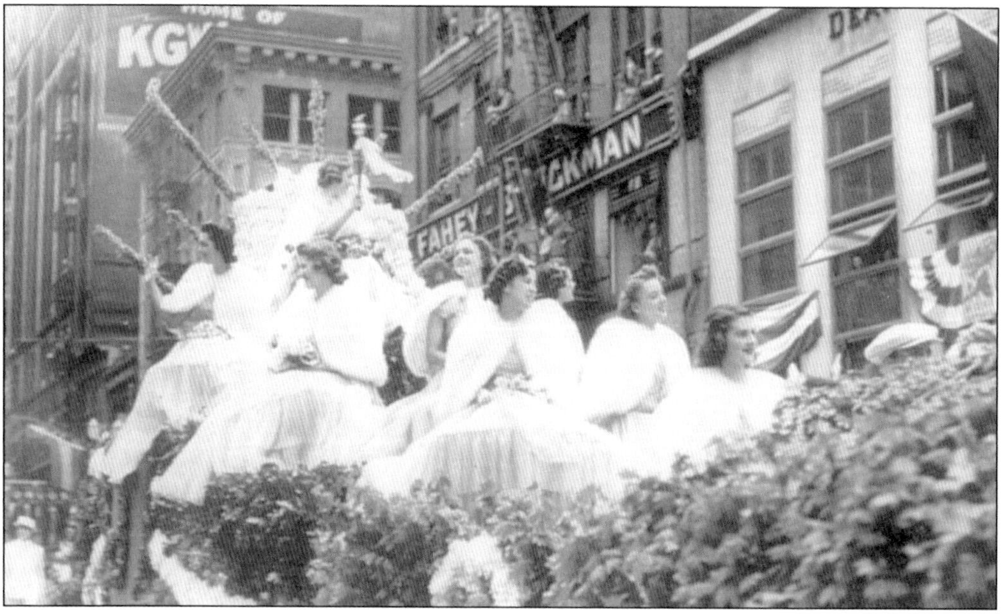

This photograph shows Queen Jean Hoover (holding the scepter) and her court as they progressed along the parade route during the Grand Floral Parade on Friday, June 9, 1939. One of the entries in the parade was from Bixby's Coffee Shop. It was a first-prize winner in the merchant division. Mrs. Bixby's slogan was, "Mrs. Bixby Does the Cooking." In May 1939, the first scheduled television programming went on the air in New York City, an event that would eventually revolutionize the way people would watch the parade. Sets cost $200 to $600, and images were small and indistinct. The age of television had arrived, but it would be 14 years before the Grand Floral Parade itself would be televised in June 1953. (Above, courtesy Portland Rose Festival Foundation; below, courtesy Oregon Historical Society; OrHi65485.)

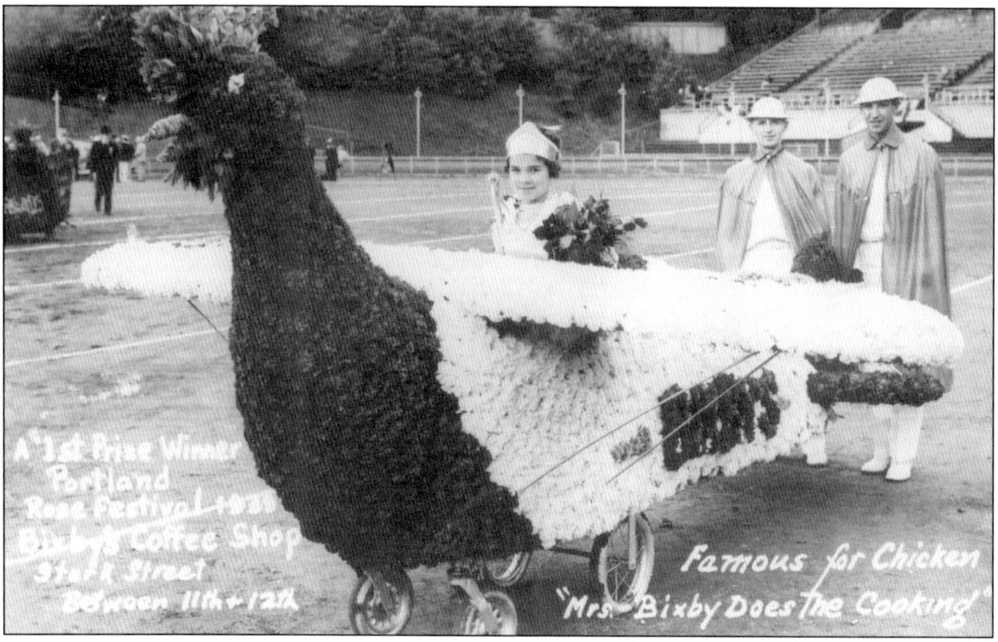

In 1940, the Grand Floral Parade drew entries from a large number of places. This float was from the City of San Francisco, with a replica of the Tower of the Sun. (Courtesy Oregon Historical Society File 1913.)

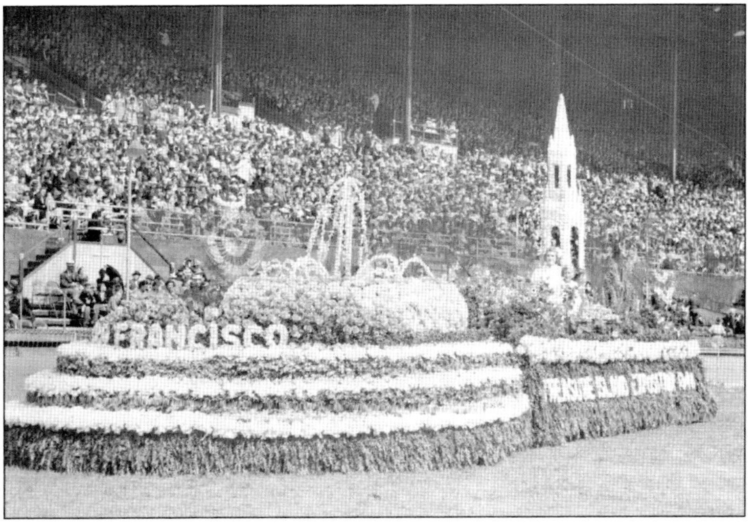

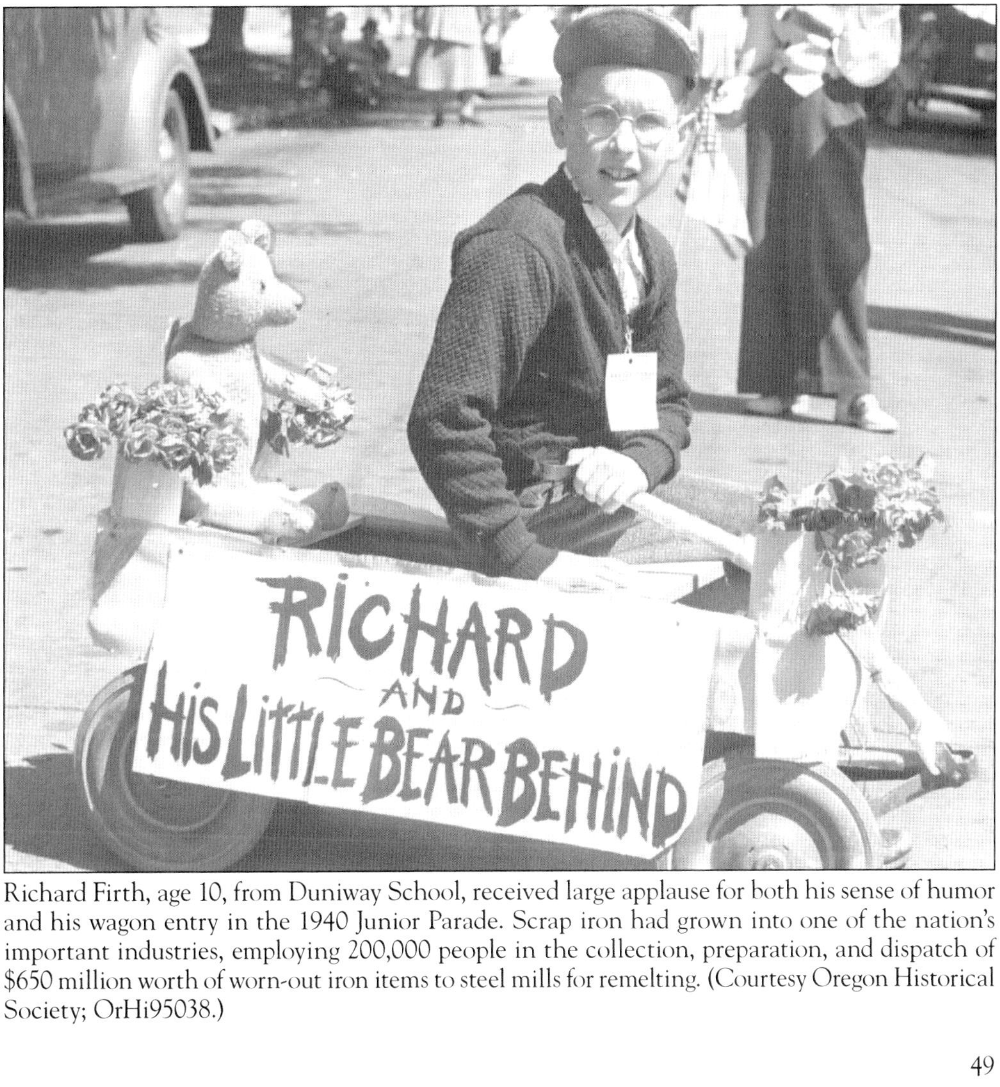

Richard Firth, age 10, from Duniway School, received large applause for both his sense of humor and his wagon entry in the 1940 Junior Parade. Scrap iron had grown into one of the nation's important industries, employing 200,000 people in the collection, preparation, and dispatch of $650 million worth of worn-out iron items to steel mills for remelting. (Courtesy Oregon Historical Society; OrHi95038.)

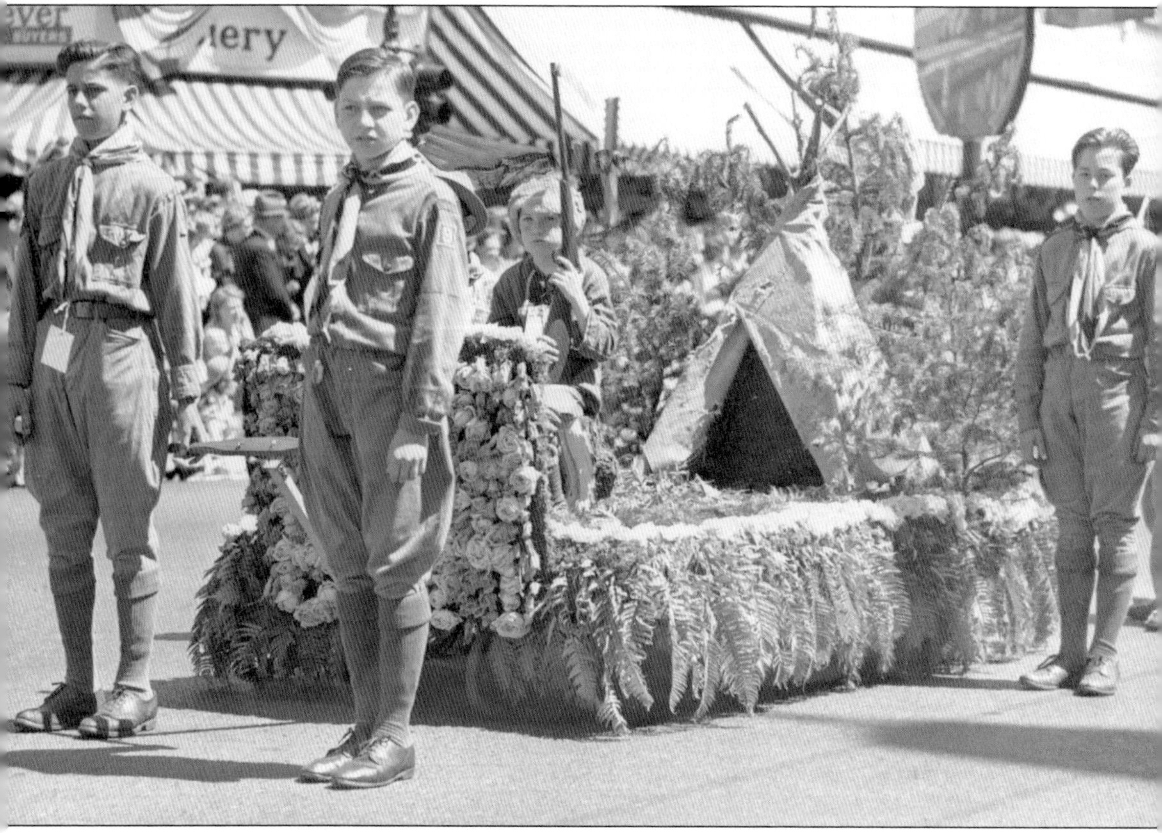

This entry in the Junior Parade in 1940 by Boy Scout Troops Nos. 9 and 131 won first prize. Robert Daly (troop No. 9) impersonated Daniel Boone. Northwest Airlines was advertising flights to Chicago for $99, and the Supreme Court ruled on Monday, June 3, that schoolchildren could be legally compelled to salute the American flag to promote patriotism. (Courtesy Oregon Historical Society; OrgLot431,B3,F17.)

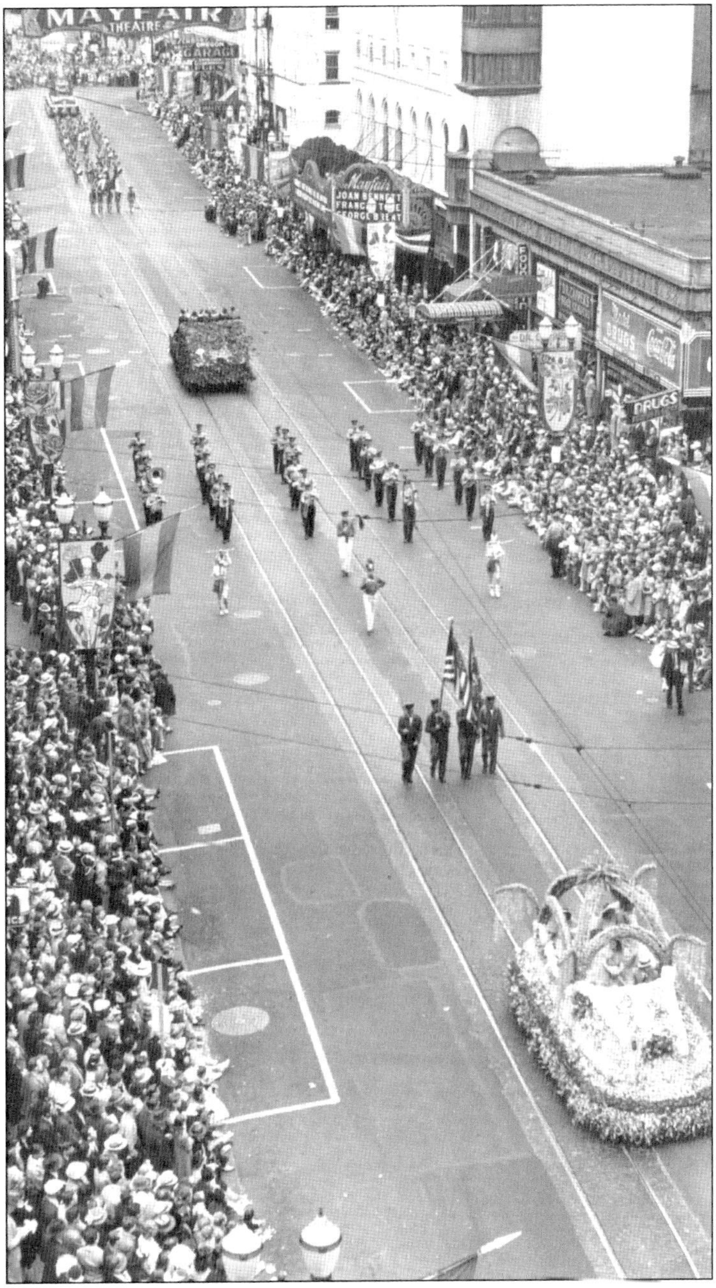

With the theme "patriotism," the 1941 Rose Festival was held despite reports of the war raging in Europe. The US Navy steamer *Robin Moore* had been sunk by a U-boat torpedo just weeks earlier in the North Atlantic. The Grand Floral Parade on Friday, June 13, contained several military units and at least one decorated tank. It was cloudy for many 1941 festival events, but the clouds overseas would soon have more effect than those at home. Events were more dramatic south of Portland in California. On June 9, three thousand Army soldiers with bayonets and machine guns took over the strike-bound North American Aviation Plant in Inglewood, California, by executive order of Pres. Franklin Roosevelt, claiming the strike was "seriously detrimental to the defense of the United States." (Courtesy Oregon Historical Society.)

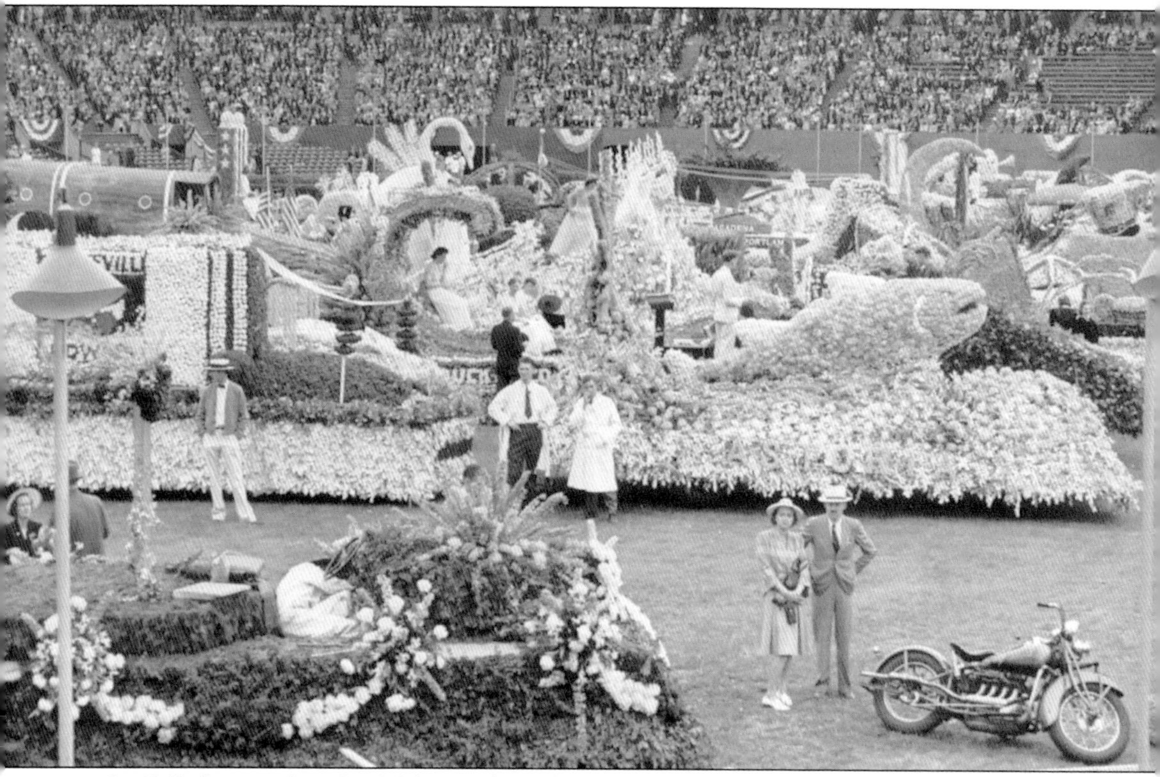

In 1941, floats gathered in Multnomah Stadium prior to the Grand Floral Parade. Then, parades were absent from the festival for several years. The Rose Festival concluded that year, under the heavy, dark clouds of war. Not everywhere was the scene dismal, as the *Oregon Journal* reported in an editorial June 12: "Over on the East Side, at the approach to the Morrison Bridge but below the level of the deck, there is a litter of carelessly piled boards and planks. In earlier days, maritime industry, docks and moving life may have commanded the scene. And there is, beyond the water's edge, a well-conducted terminal of small boats. But the planks that once composed the sturdy structure of marine enterprise have so long lain untended that they are deeply touched by decay. Yet, beauty is there. Beauty, because a rose vine—who knows who hand planted it or when?—began growing deep under the disorderly heap." Yes, the rose is hardy! (Courtesy Portland Rose Festival Foundation.)

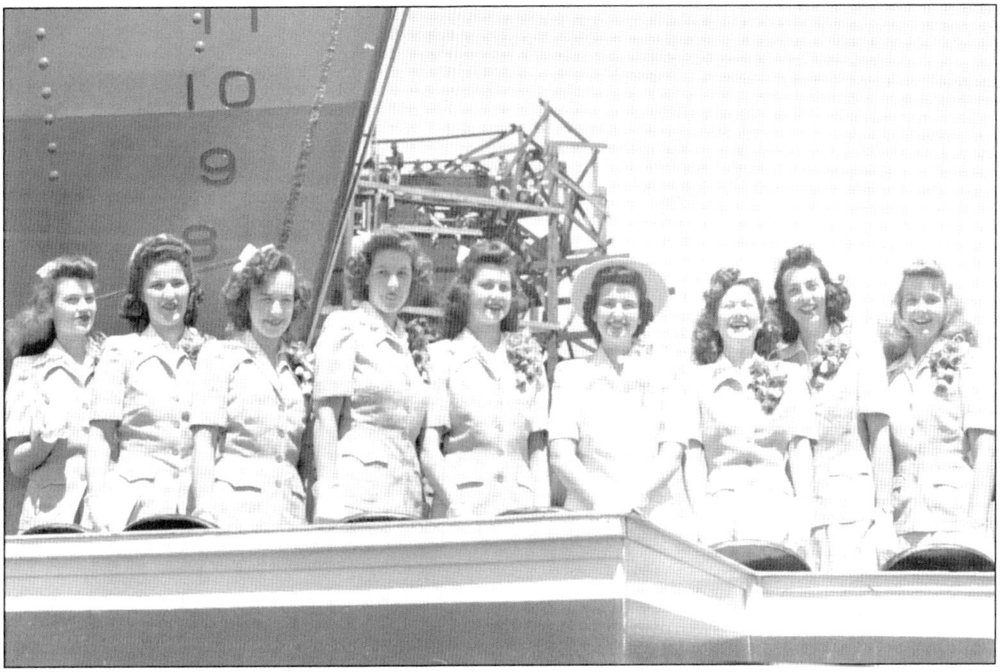

World War II had a drastic effect on the 1942 Rose Festival. Parades and all large outdoor events were canceled at the order of the US government. The princesses took part in the christening of the Liberty Ship *John Howard* on Thursday, June 4. Queen Shirley Fowler (wearing a hat) is shown with her court. (Courtesy Oregon Historical Society Negbb002357.)

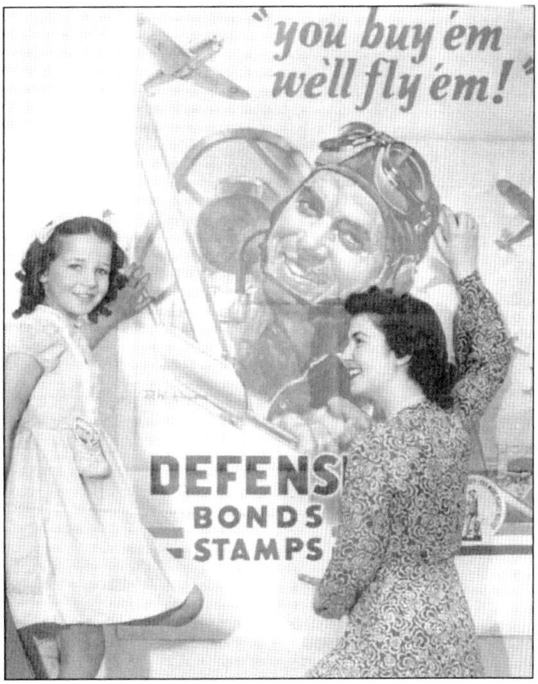

Instead of parades, entertainers would provide shows to raise money to buy Defense Bonds and Stamps. Among the entertainers to visit Portland were Duke Ellington and Lana Turner. Turner sold kisses to raise money for Defense Bonds and was made an honorary member of the Rose Festival Court. Advertisements appeared daily in newspapers around the country. On Saturday, May 30, the War Production Board ordered production of all musical instruments stopped after June 30. No critical materials—such as metals, cork, plastics, and rubber—could be used in the production of musical instruments other than pianos and organs. In November, the public housing project being constructed for the workers at Kaiser Shipyards was christened "Vanport." Vanport would figure prominently in the 1948 Rose Festival. (Courtesy Portland Rose Festival Foundation.)

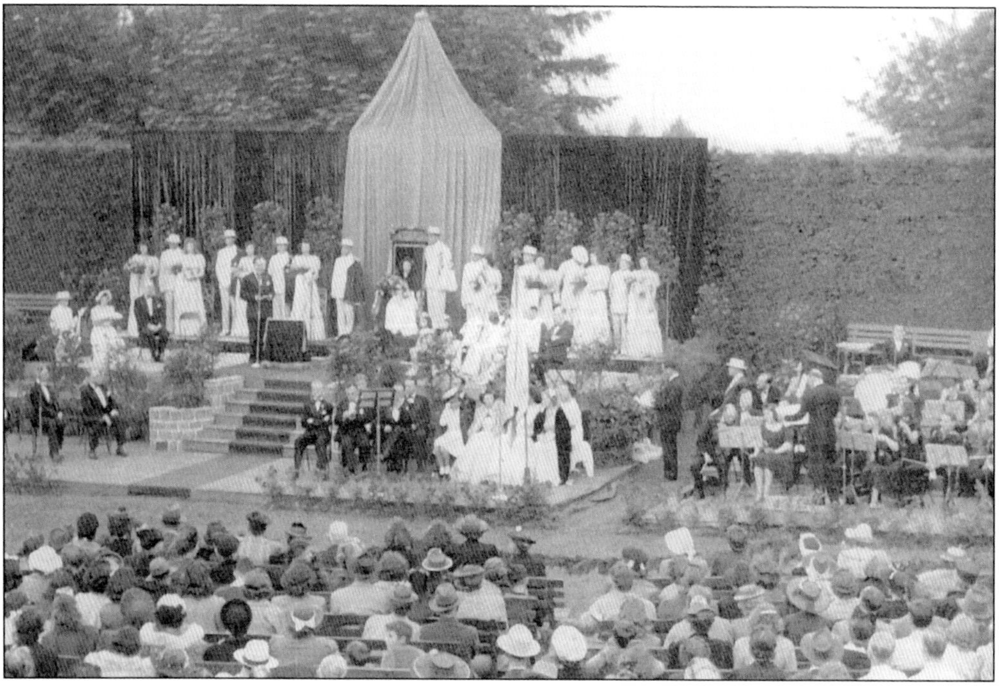

The world continued to wage war in 1943, so the ban on large parades stayed in effect. However, that did not stop the Rose Festival from holding Coronation ceremonies, during which Queen Shirley Howard was crowned. A junior queen and court were also selected. A June 1 advertisement in the *Oregonian* pleaded with ladies to "please bring down every pair of old, laundered silk hose you can round up and deposit in one of the red, white, and blue boxes on the street floor." Gas was also rationed and mileage was limited. The *Oregonian* reported on June 12 that a driver forfeited his driving privileges in municipal court for speeding 65 miles per hour. (Above, courtesy Portland Rose Festival Foundation; below, courtesy Oregon Historical Society; OrHi58297.)

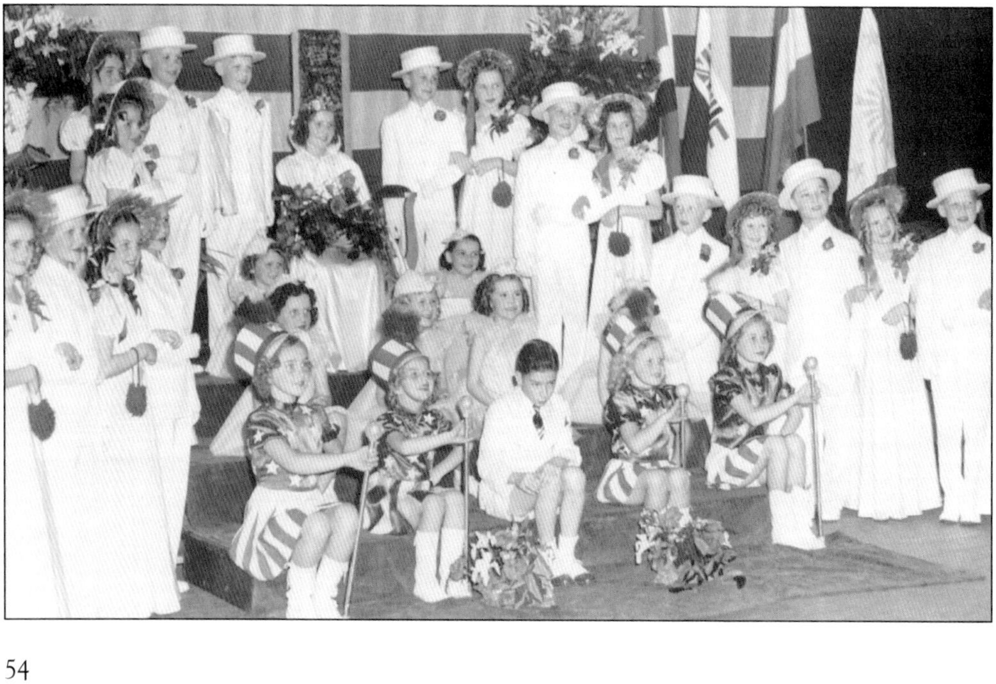

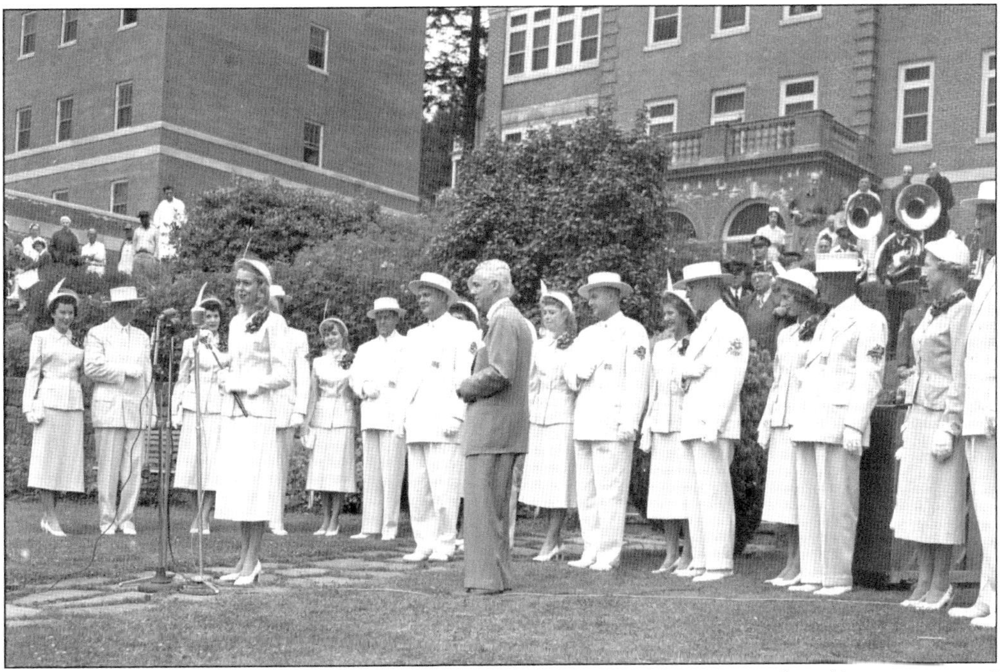

With servicemen returning home with injuries from the war, Queen Jo Anne Bush and her court visited the Veterans Hospital, shown here in 1944. (Courtesy Portland Rose Festival Foundation.)

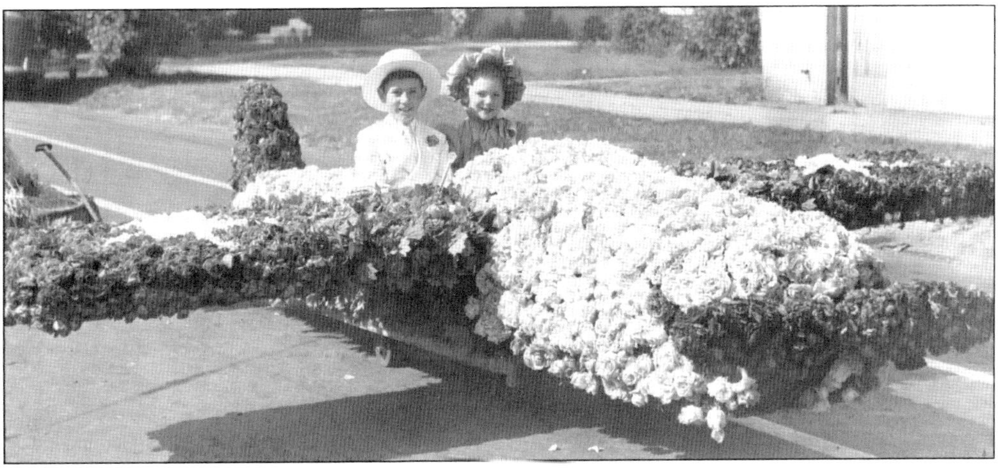

Across the Atlantic Ocean, American, Canadian, and British forces landed in northwest France on the beaches of Normandy on June 6. Again, there was no Grand Floral Parade, but despite the war, a Junior Parade was held on Saturday, June 10, 1944. Shown in their airplane float are Princess Virginia McKee, Holy Redeemer School, and Prince Jerry Sibelia, Peninsula School. That same year, Portland elected its first woman to city council, Dorothy McCollough Lee. (Courtesy Oregon Historical Society; OrHi83723.)

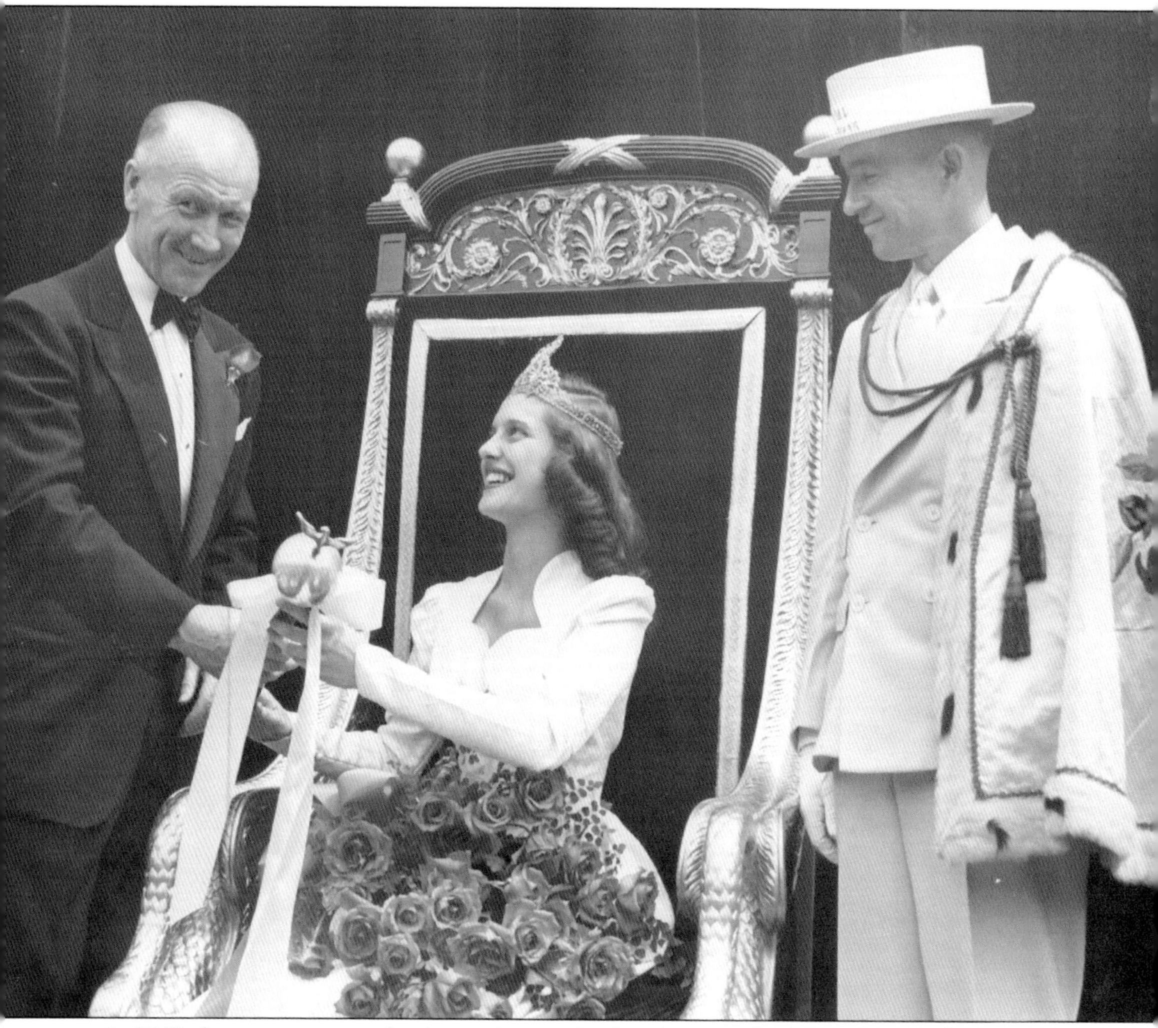

In 1945, there were no parades due to the war. In this photograph, Queen Joan Williams is shown receiving her silver scepter from Milo K. McIver, Rose Festival president, while Prime Minister William Ruggles watches. The war in the Pacific had brought tragedy to Southern Oregon when a Japanese balloon carrying explosives detonated near the town of Bly, killing six people. Other reports of these balloons had been sighted in Washington, Michigan, California, Canada, and Mexico. Many products were still being rationed, including gasoline and sugar. Eggs were also scarce, but Fred Meyer was advertising Cuban pineapple for 19¢ a pound and Safeway was selling asparagus for 16¢ a pound. Wednesday, June 6, was a "Free Movie Day" for purchasers of E Bonds across the United States. (Courtesy Oregon Historical Society; OrHi28339.)

Five

1946–1955
The Country Booms, The Festival Blooms

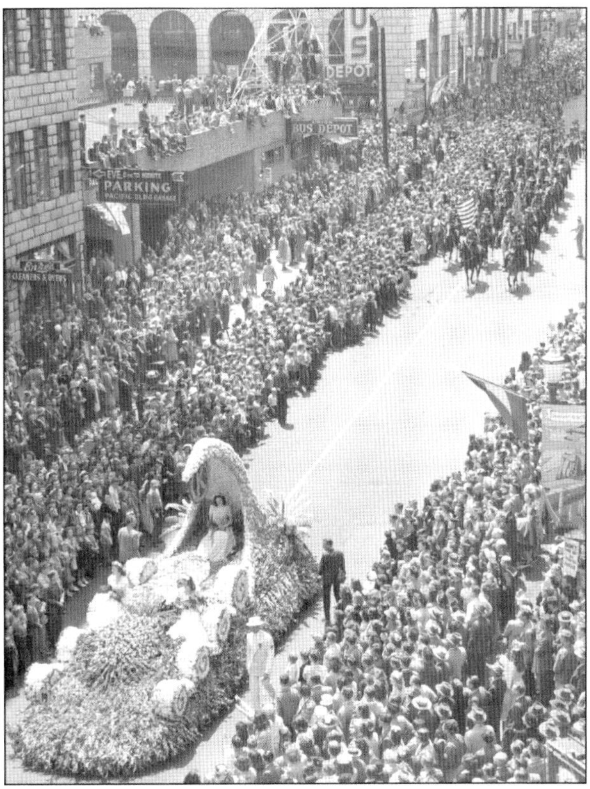

The war had ended, and Portlanders were anticipating a wonderful Rose Festival in 1946. They were not disappointed. So many people watched the Grand Floral Parade that crowd control methods would be put in place the following year. Jane Powell was on hand for the Rose Festival. Comedian Bob Hope also had a show in Multnomah Stadium on Sunday, June 9. Hope's comments on the weather in Portland appeared in the *Oregon Journal* on June 10, 1946: "I'm very happy to be here in this deep freeze locker," he quipped. "I had a nice swim out at the golf course this afternoon." It had been a cool day with the high temperature only at 60 degrees with a bit of precipitation. The war had slightly dampened the Rose Festival, but like the rest of the country, it persevered. (Courtesy Oregon Historical Society; OrHi67091.)

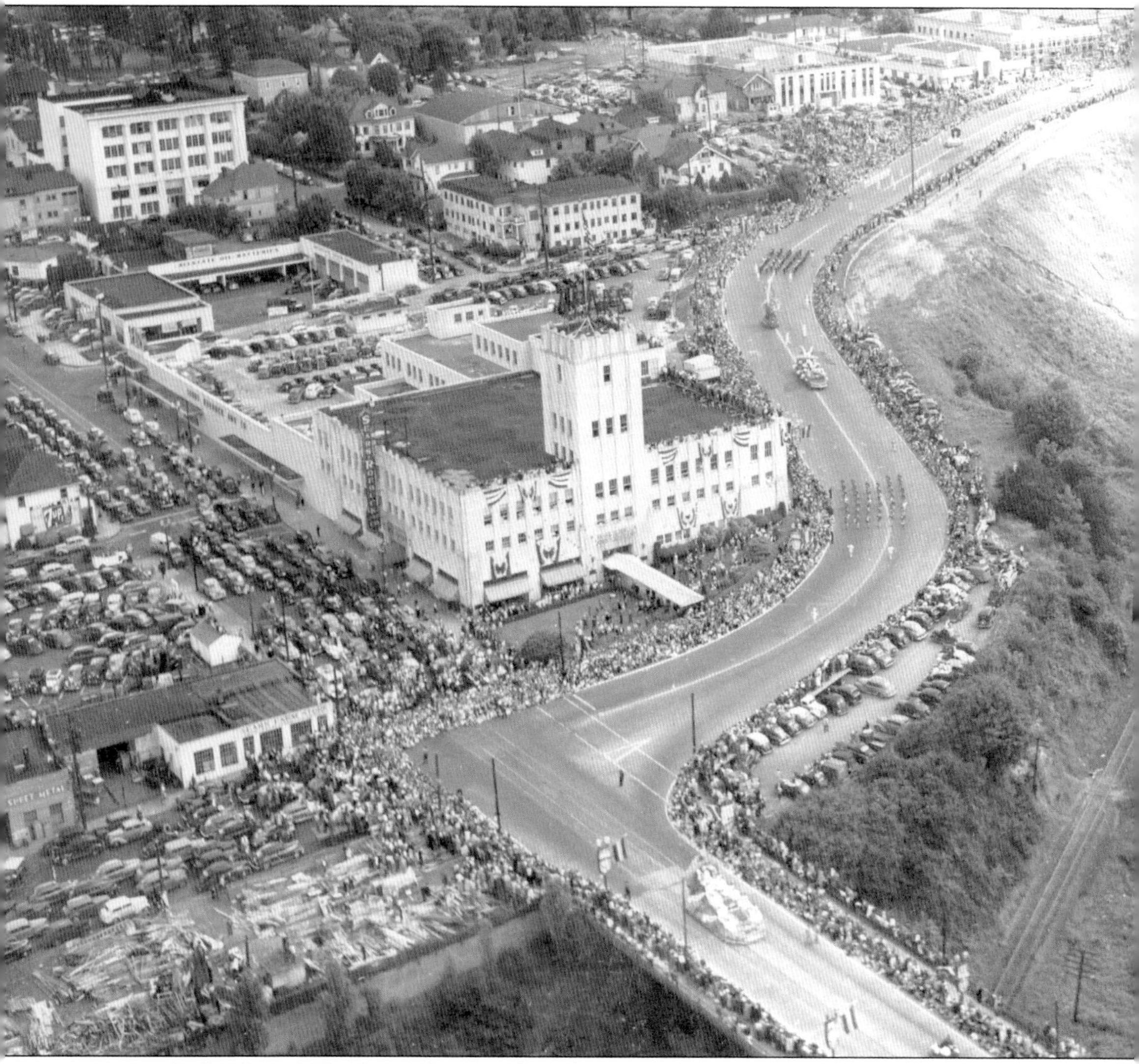

In 1947, the Grand Floral Parade started on the east side of the Willamette River in Holladay Park. It proceeded west on Lloyd Boulevard and then across the Burnside Bridge. As it did, a shower marred the parade and drenched the queen's float. It was the only rain recorded that day. (Courtesy Oregon Historical Society; OrHi93454.)

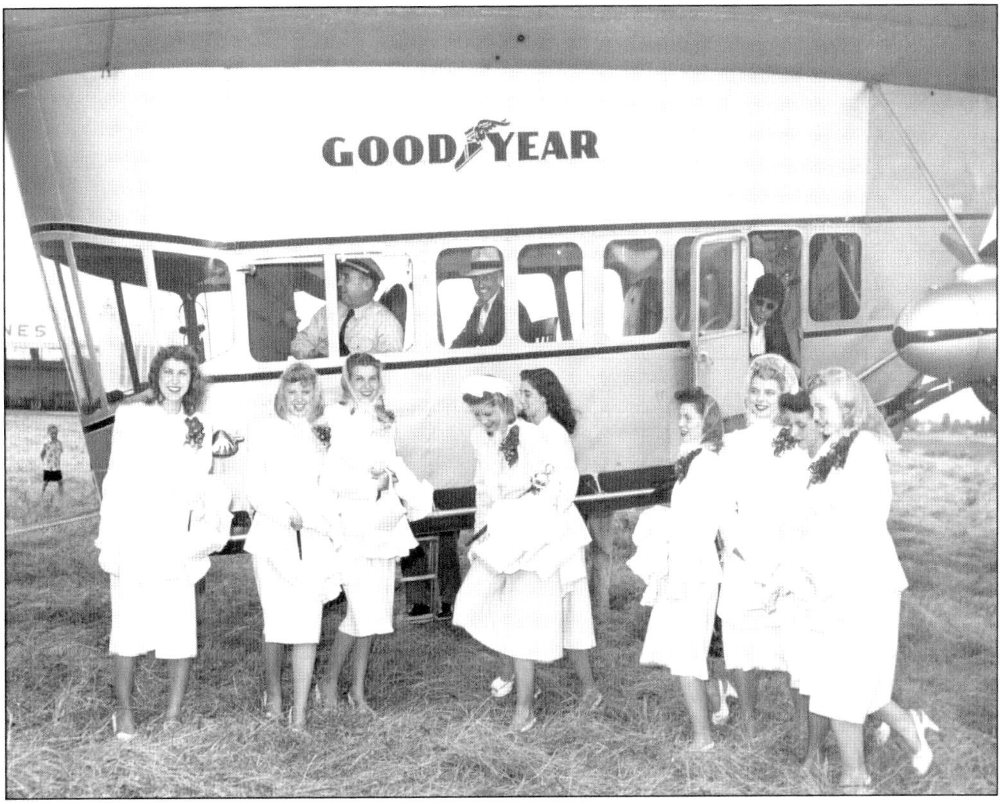

Queen Georgene Ormston and her court are shown the day they received a ride in the Goodyear Blimp at the 1947 Rose Festival. (Courtesy Portland Rose Festival Foundation.)

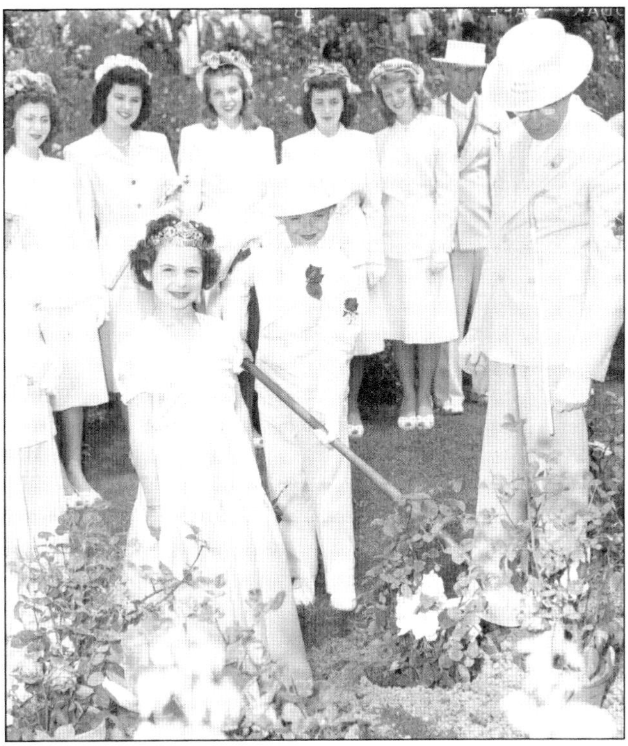

The final event of the 1947 Rose Festival was the planting of roses in Peninsula Park by the Junior Court. Here, Junior Prime Minister Bruce Stinnett wields the shovel after Queen Sharon Barnes consigned the bush to its place. Rosarian C.P. Keyser sees that everything is done properly. Queen Georgene and her court were official spectators at the ceremony. (Courtesy Oregon Historical Society; OrgLot431,B4,F14.)

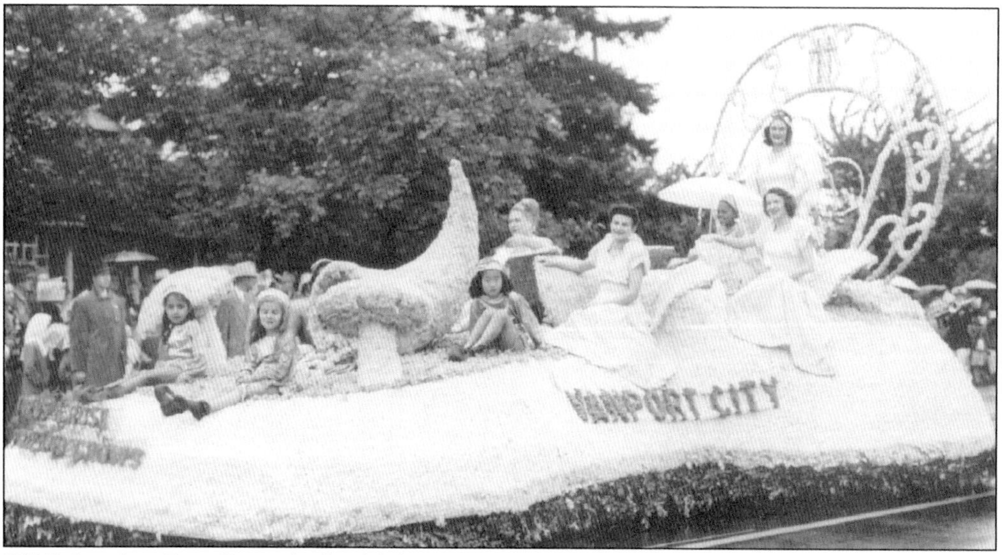

"Will there be a Rose Festival? Should there be a Rose Festival?" Those were questions that plagued Rose Festival officials in 1948. In late May, a break in a dike flooded and destroyed Vanport, the second-largest city in Oregon. Vanport had been built to house people working in the shipyards in North Portland. Several people drowned, and thousands lost their homes. The city council voted three to two to allow the Grand Floral Parade to continue that year, with Portland Mayor Earl Riley voting no. The Portland Fire Bureau built this float to honor the spirit of the people of Vanport. (Courtesy Portland Rose Festival Foundation.)

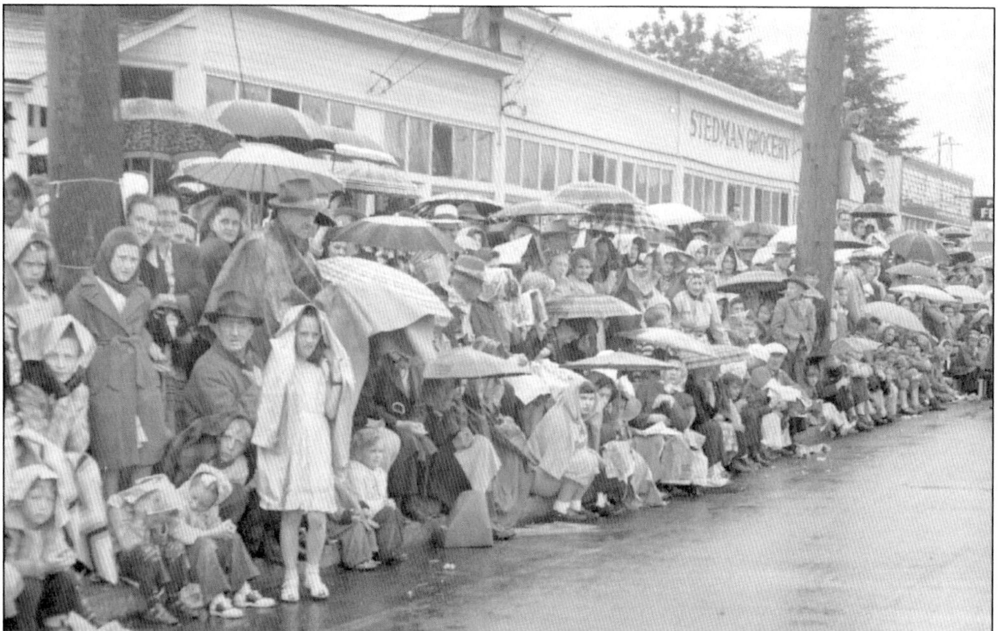

The Grand Floral Parade went on as planned on Saturday, June 12, but moved to the east side of the Willamette River. It was one of the few years that rain dampened most of the parade. Rain, however, does not discourage parade viewers in Portland. They simply huddle under umbrellas and plastic. (Courtesy Oregon Historical Society; OrgLot431,B4,F22.)

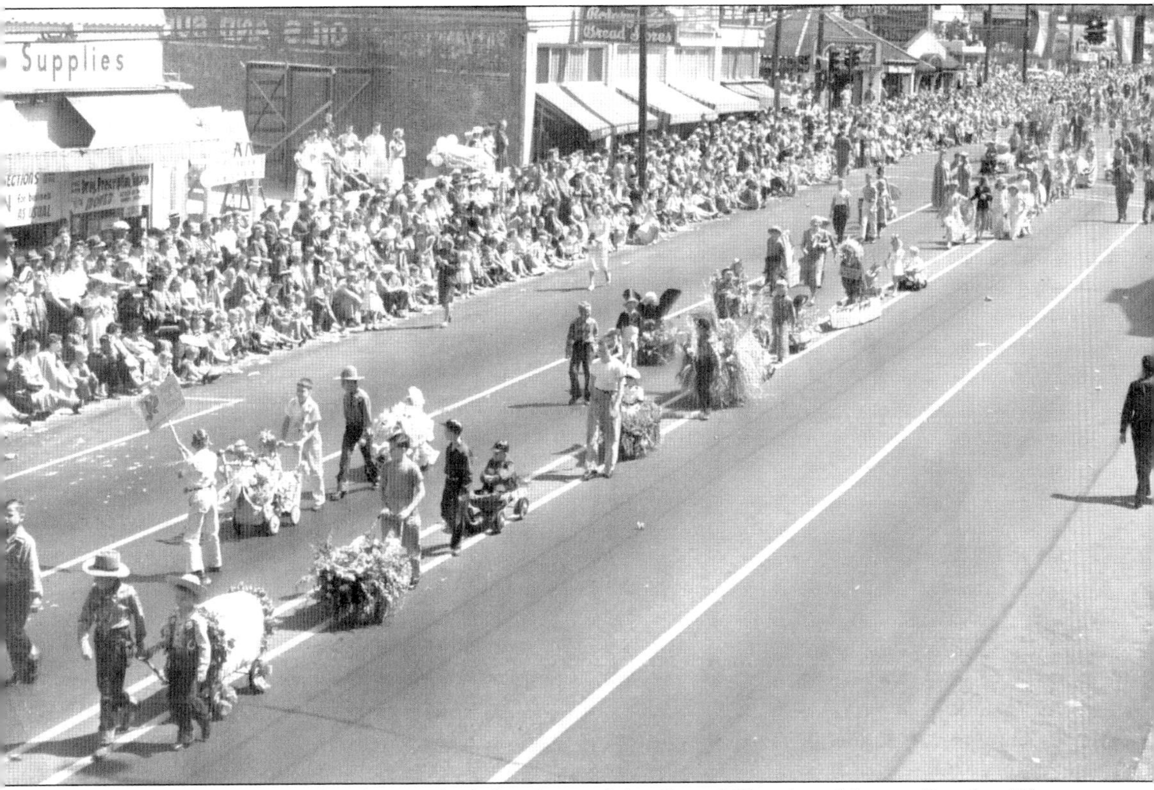

In 1949, Rose Festival officials switched the dates of the Grand Floral and Junior Parades. The Grand Floral Parade was held on Friday, June 10, and the Junior Parade was held on Saturday, June 11. Both parades enjoyed sunny weather, in contrast to 1948. Portland's first female mayor, Dorothy McCollough Lee, took office on January 1, 1949. For musical entertainment, one could listen to Gene Autry's records on a radio and phonograph combination that was selling for $159.72 at Jennings. Safeway grocery stores had whole or half spring Chinook salmon selling for 45¢ a pound. (Courtesy Oregon Historical Society; OrHi67094.)

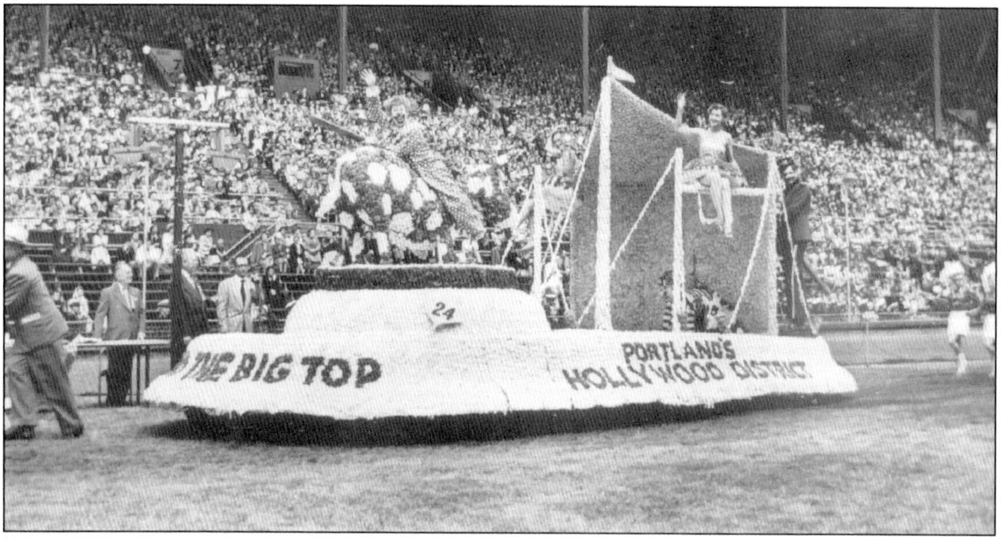

During the sever winter of 1949–1950, Portland's all-time low temperature was minus three degrees on February 2, 1950. There was worry that the area's rose bushes would suffer. Such was not the case. By the time the Grand Floral Parade floats gathered in Multnomah Stadium in June, the roses were in full bloom. (Courtesy Portland Rose Festival Foundation.)

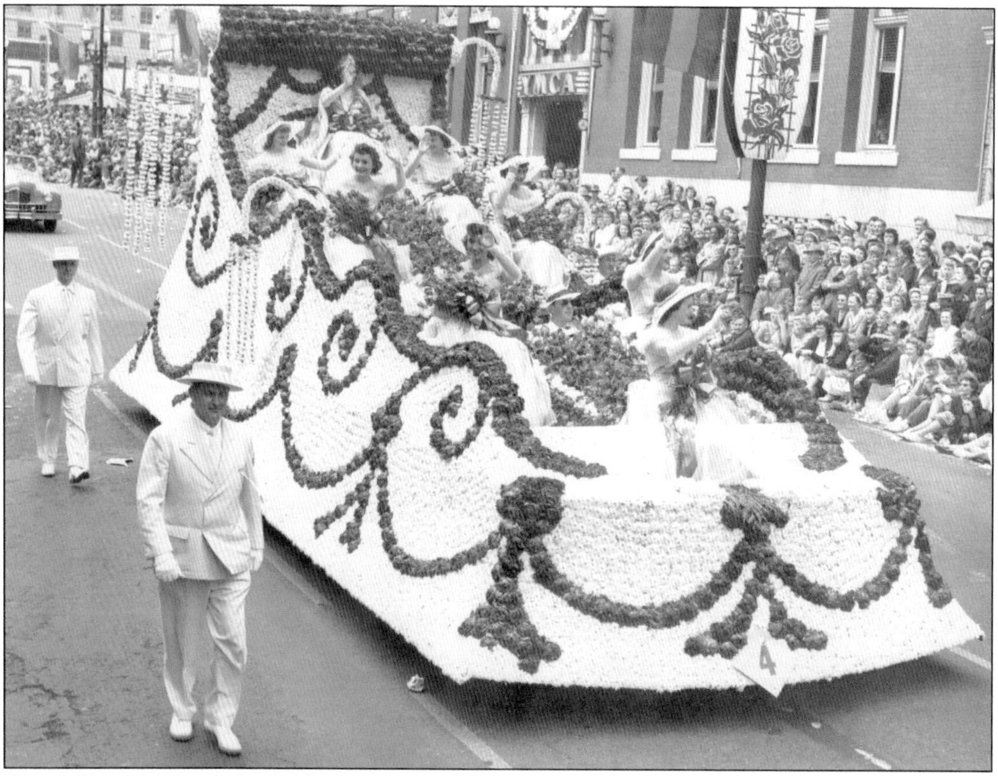

Queen Dorothy Anderle and her court are shown in the 1950 Grand Floral Parade. The Albany Jaycees brought their city's float to the Rose Festival via the Willamette River that year, the first time it had happened in festival history. And high on Mount Hood, racers cut through icy fog during the Golden Rose Ski Tournament. (Courtesy Oregon Historical Society; OHSbb01559.)

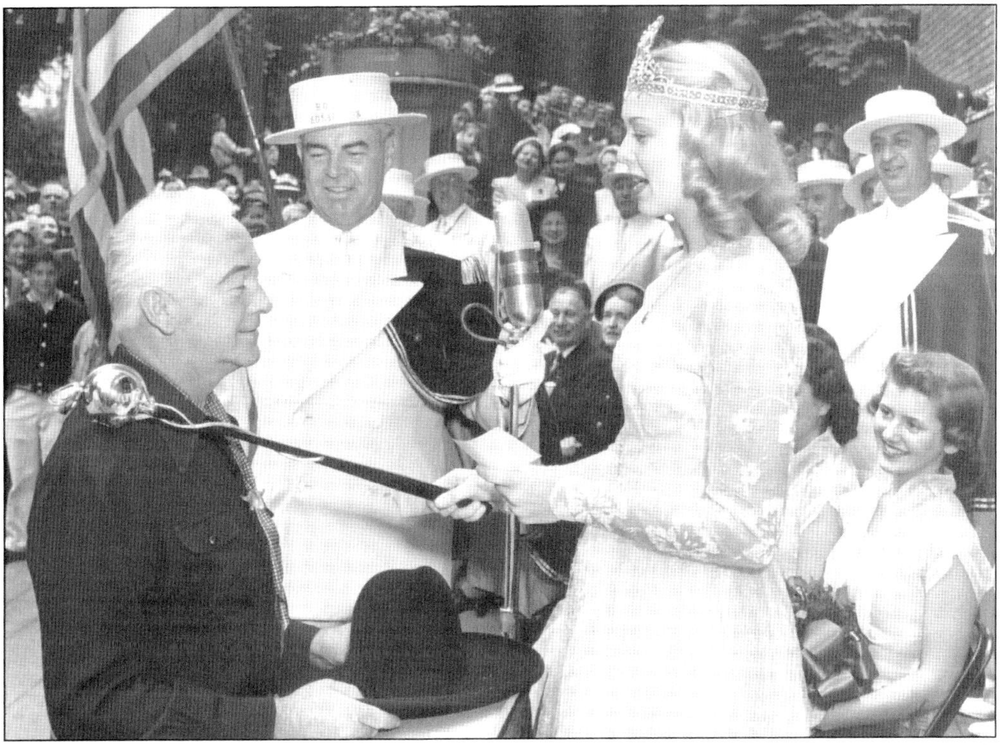

William Boyd "Hopalong" Cassidy was grand marshal of the 1951 Grand Floral Parade, in which he rode his horse Topper. He is shown dressed in his signature black, being knighted by Queen Gloria Krieger. Honorary knighting ceremonies became part of the Rose Festival after the formation of the Royal Rosarians in 1912. The princesses of the Portland Rose Festival served as goodwill ambassadors, visiting numerous cities in Oregon. Here, they are shown visiting the Oregon Coast with Hopalong Cassidy. Rollie Truitt, the voice of the Portland Beaver baseball team, announced the Junior Parade. (Above, courtesy Oregon Historical Society; OrHi74646; below, courtesy Portland Rose Festival Foundation.)

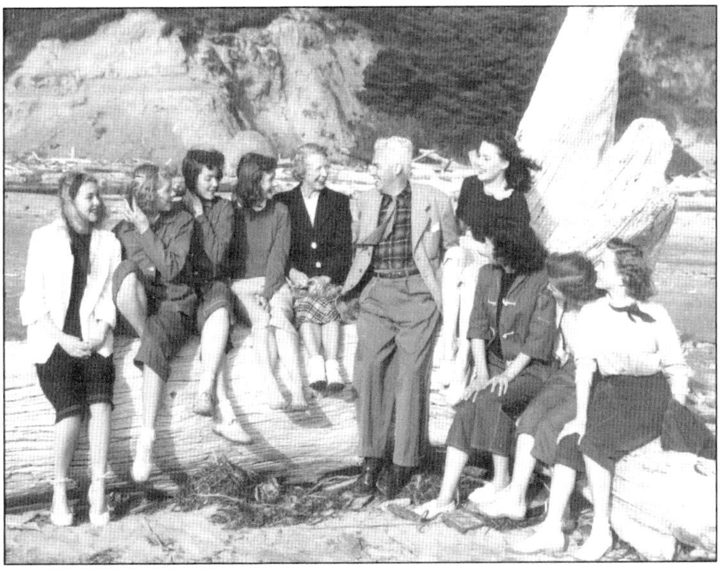

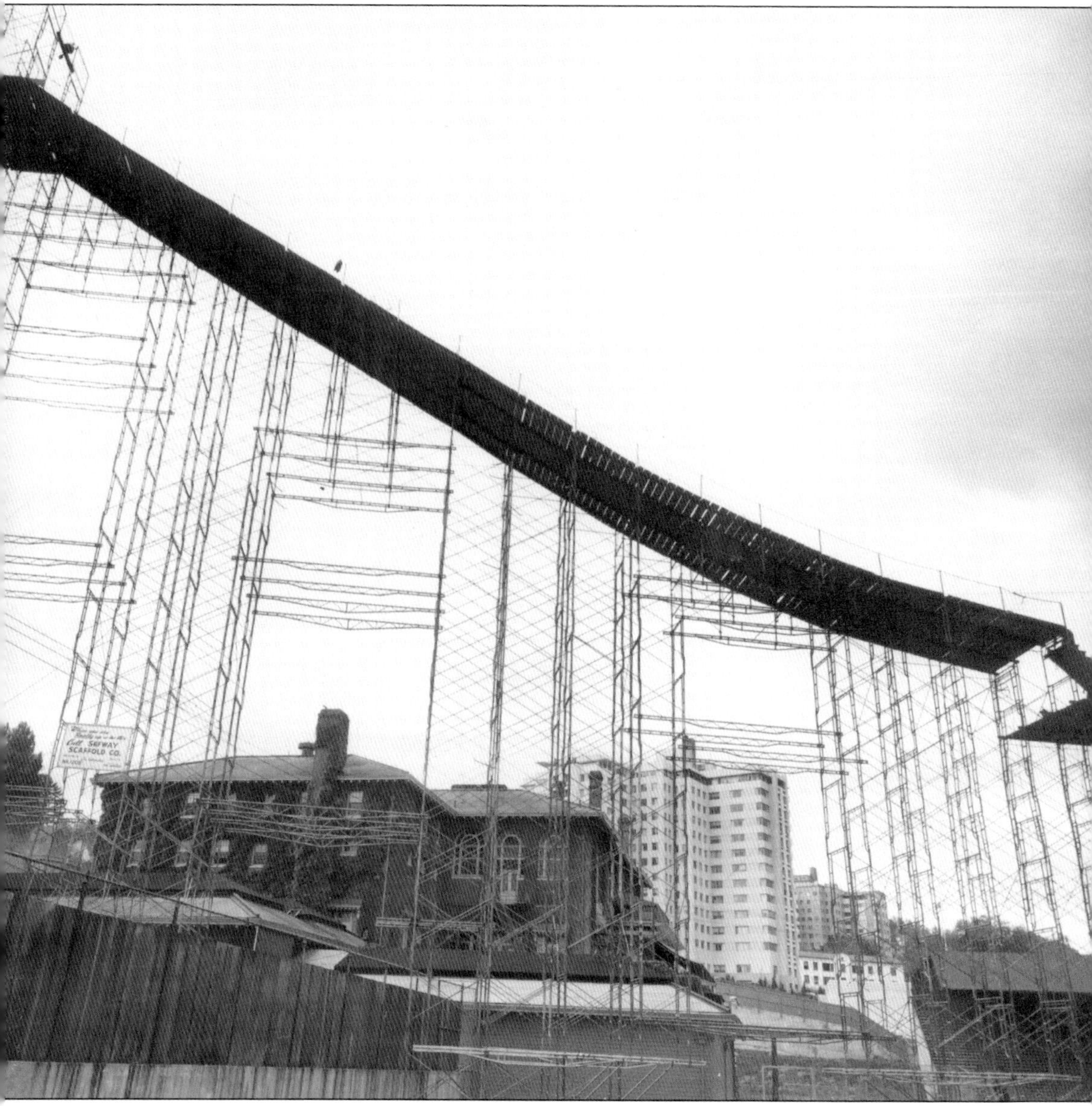

The Rose Festival, always looking for new and exciting features, brought the mountains to Multnomah Stadium in 1951. A ski-jumping event was scheduled. It did not actually snow, but tons of crushed ice and snow were blown onto the track. (Courtesy Oregon Historical Society; OrHi91675.)

In this photograph, Queen Jeanne Wallace was crowned the 44th Rose Festival queen in Coronation ceremonies held Wednesday evening, June 11, 1952, in Multnomah Stadium. Queen Jeanne is pictured with Rose Festival president Chester Duncan and Royal Rosarian prime minister Harold A. York. (Courtesy Portland Rose Festival Foundation.)

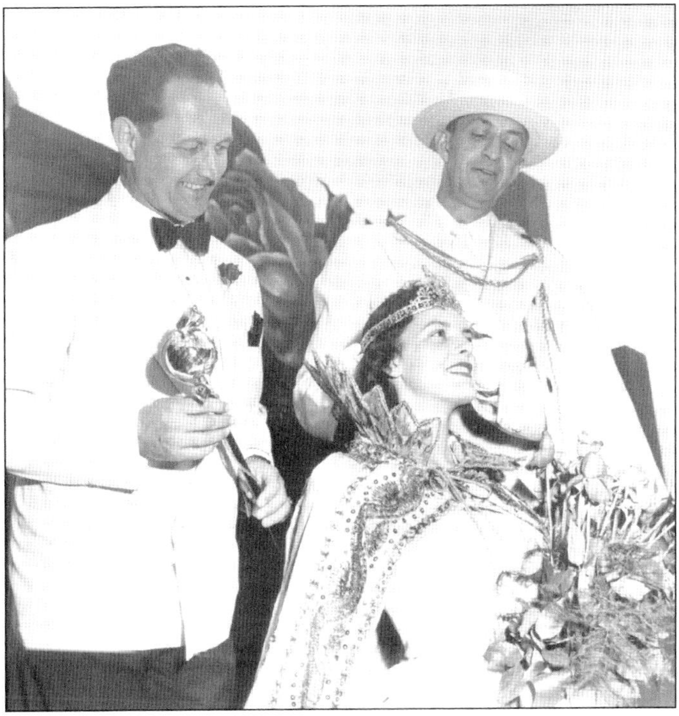

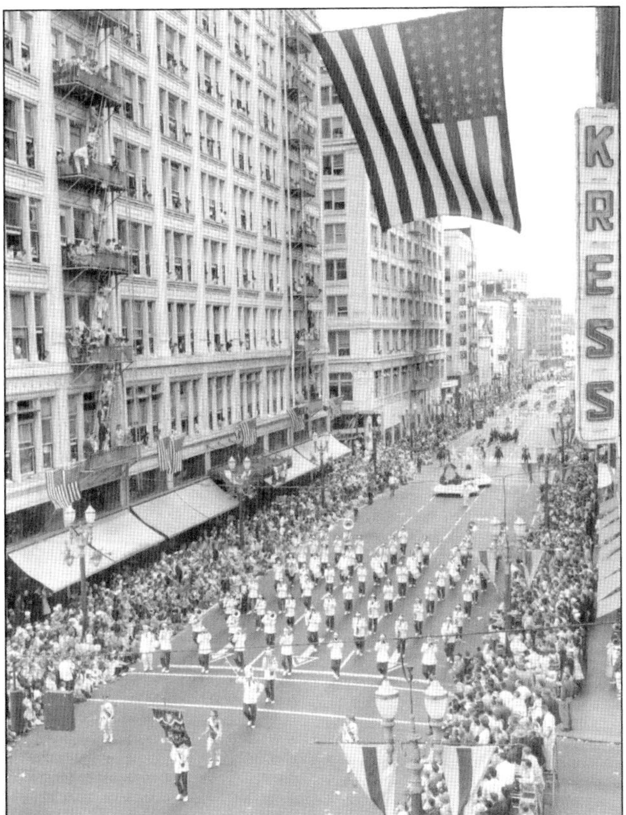

The Lincoln High School Band is shown marching in the Grand Floral Parade on Friday, June 13, 1952. The huge American flag stretching from Meier & Frank Company across Sixth Avenue was a fixture in downtown Portland for years during Rose Festivals. Shoppers could go to J.K. Gill Company to purchase a 1952 De Luxe Streamliner Olympia typewriter for a hefty $69.50. (Courtesy Portland Rose Festival Foundation.)

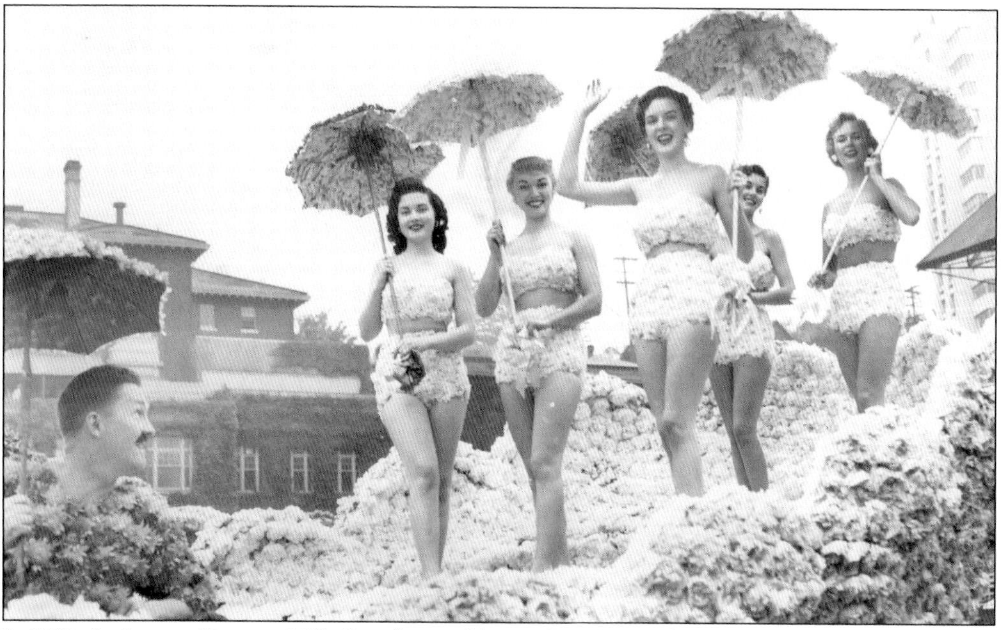

In 1953, the Jantzen Knitting Mills float featured former Rose Festival Queen Jeanne Wallace and 1953 Miss Oregon, Patti Throop. Others on the float are Lois Pope, Pat Carmen, and Harriette O'Halloran. The gentleman is John Zehntbauer Jr. (Courtesy Oregon Historical Society; OrHi67115.)

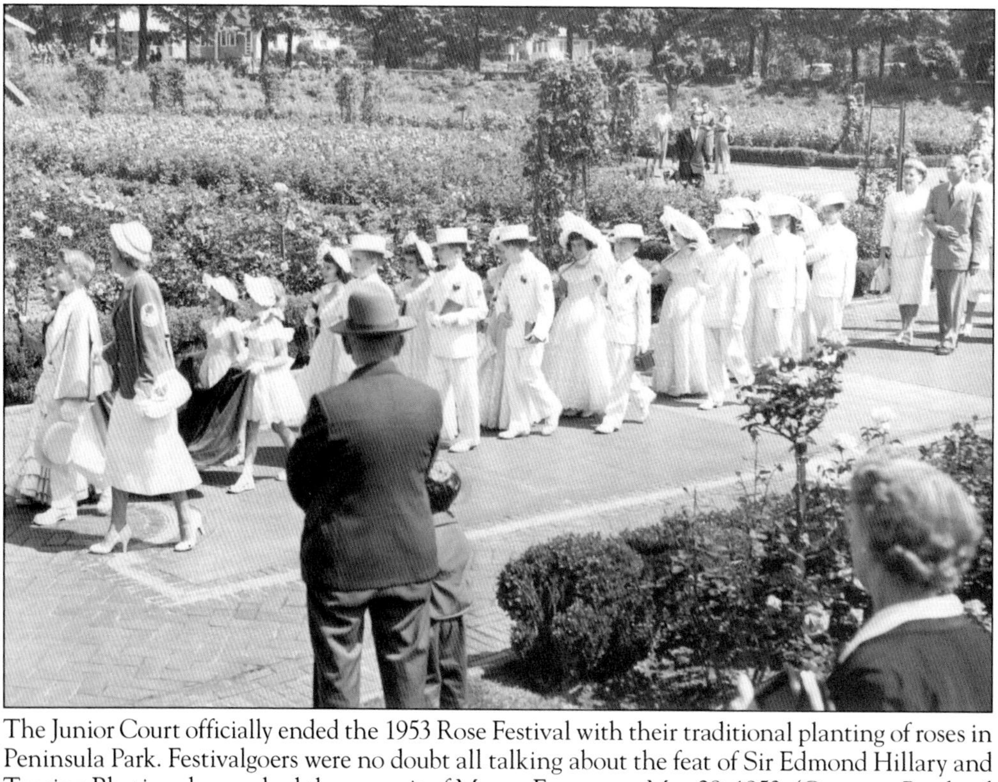

The Junior Court officially ended the 1953 Rose Festival with their traditional planting of roses in Peninsula Park. Festivalgoers were no doubt all talking about the feat of Sir Edmond Hillary and Tensing Bhutia, who reached the summit of Mount Everest on May 29, 1953. (Courtesy Portland Rose Festival Foundation.)

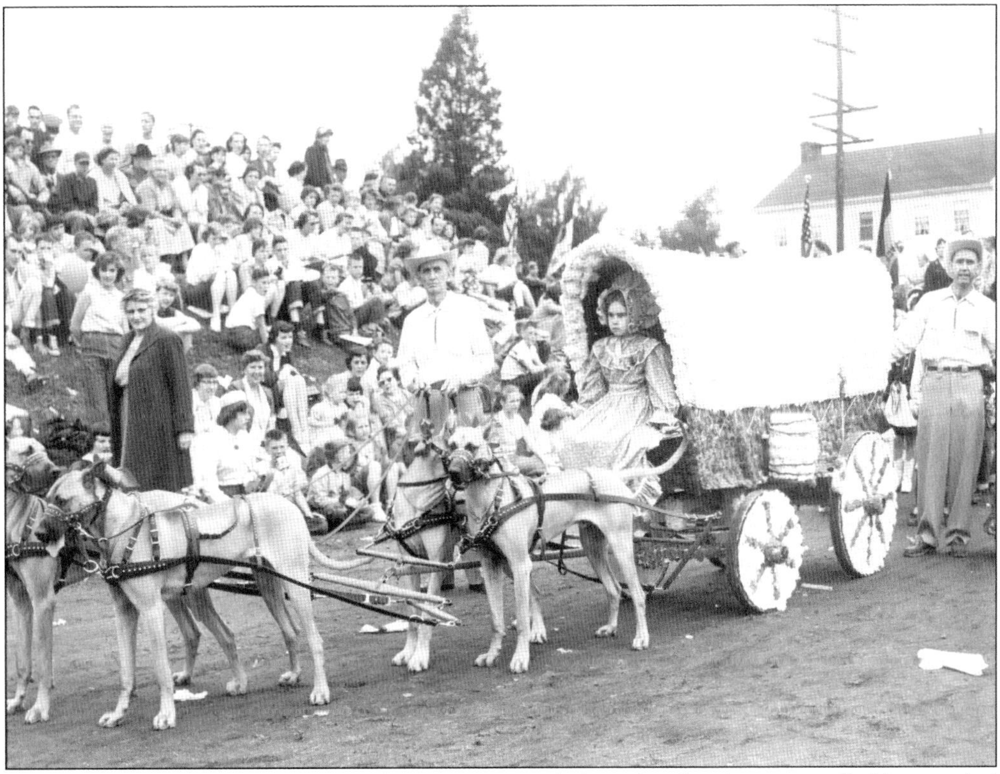

The Junior Parade is always full of clever entries, including this floral wagon pulled by muzzled dogs. The 1954 Junior Parade was held on Friday, June 11. For a healthy treat during the parade, Safeway was advertising watermelon for 5¢ a pound and cantaloupe for 9¢ a pound. (Courtesy Oregon Historical Society; OrgLot431,B6,F14.)

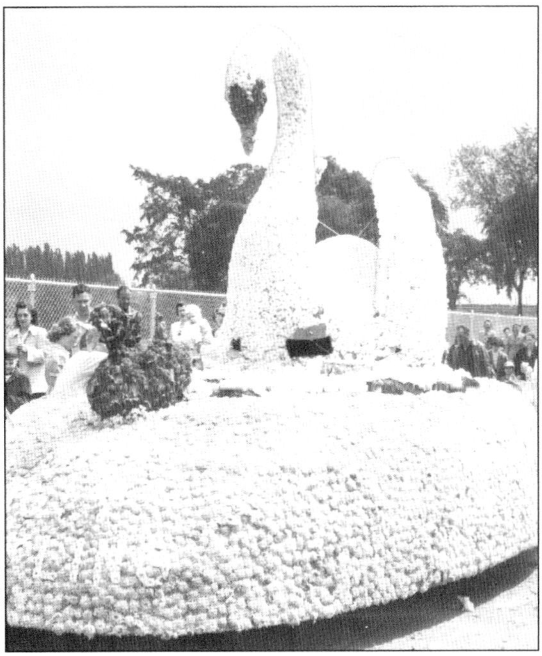

One of the beautiful entries in the Grand Floral Parade in 1954 was this graceful swan. Several noted celebrities visited the Rose Festival that year, including Grand Marshal Roy Rogers and his horse, Trigger. Ed Sullivan, Gordon MacRae, and singing cowboy Tex Ritter were on hand for the Starlight Serenade performances in Multnomah Stadium on Saturday, June 12. (Courtesy Portland Rose Festival Foundation.)

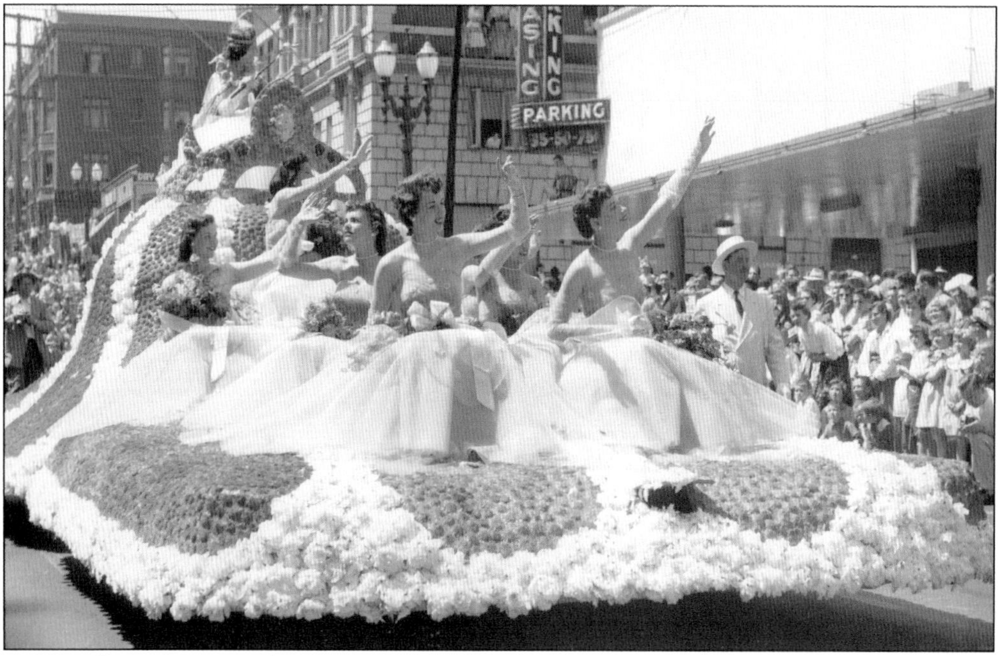

In 1955, due to a wet April and cold, dry May, Portland's roses were almost three weeks late, but the parade and its sparkling floats continued. Queen Nancy Wyly and her court enjoyed the sunny skies of the 1955 Grand Floral Parade, held on Saturday, June 11. The parade narrowly missed some of the hottest Rose Festival weather, which occurred just days earlier when the thermometer reached 96 and 97 on June 8 and 9. (Courtesy Portland Rose Festival Foundation.)

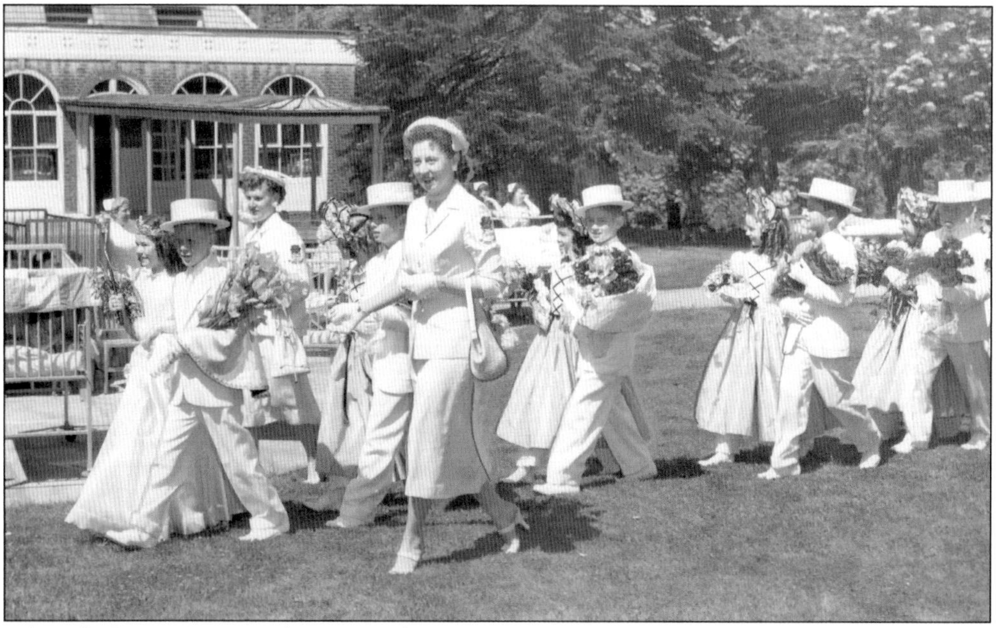

When the Junior Court made its annual visit to the Shriners Hospital for Children in 1955, sunny skies greeted the participants and the children watching. Charles Correll, better known as the Andy half of "Amos 'n' Andy" radio team, acted as master of ceremonies for the Rose Festival Starlight Serenade at Multnomah Stadium. (Courtesy Portland Rose Festival Foundation.)

Six

1956–1964
Lights, Camera, Action!

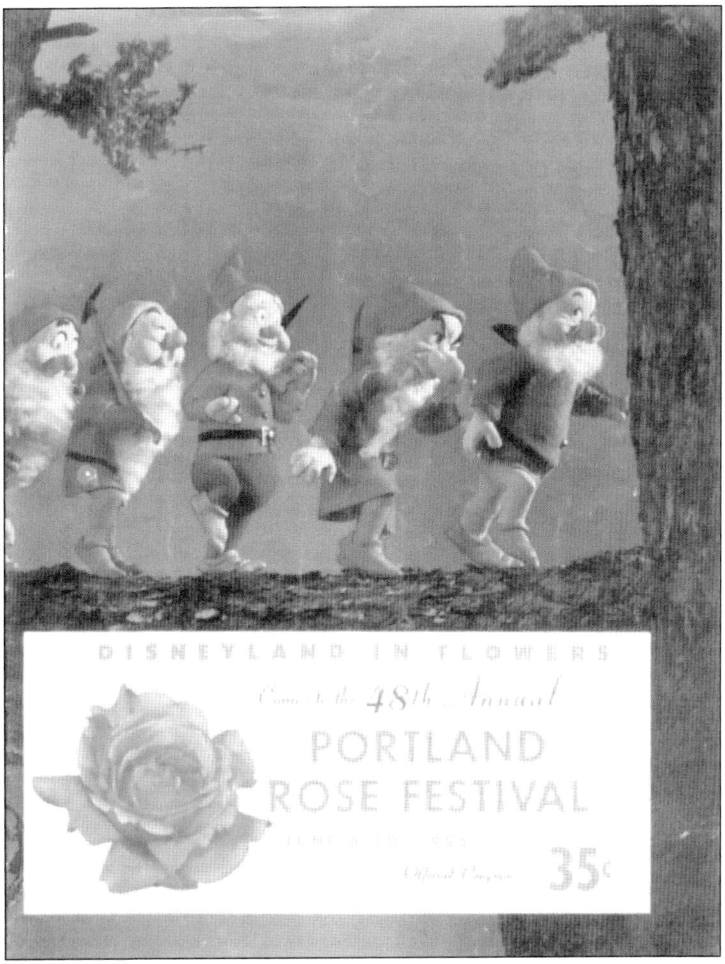

Disneyland opened in July 1955, and the 1956 Rose Festival theme was Disneyland in Flowers. Special programming included the Disneyland Circus and A *Night of Disneyland*, featuring Bob Amsberry and the Mouseketeers from the Mickey Mouse Club. Jimmie Dodd, the "Big Mouseketeer," was the honorary grand marshal of the Grand Floral Parade. For 35¢, festivalgoers could purchase the official program and have a spot to collect Dodd's autograph. (Courtesy Portland Rose Festival Foundation.)

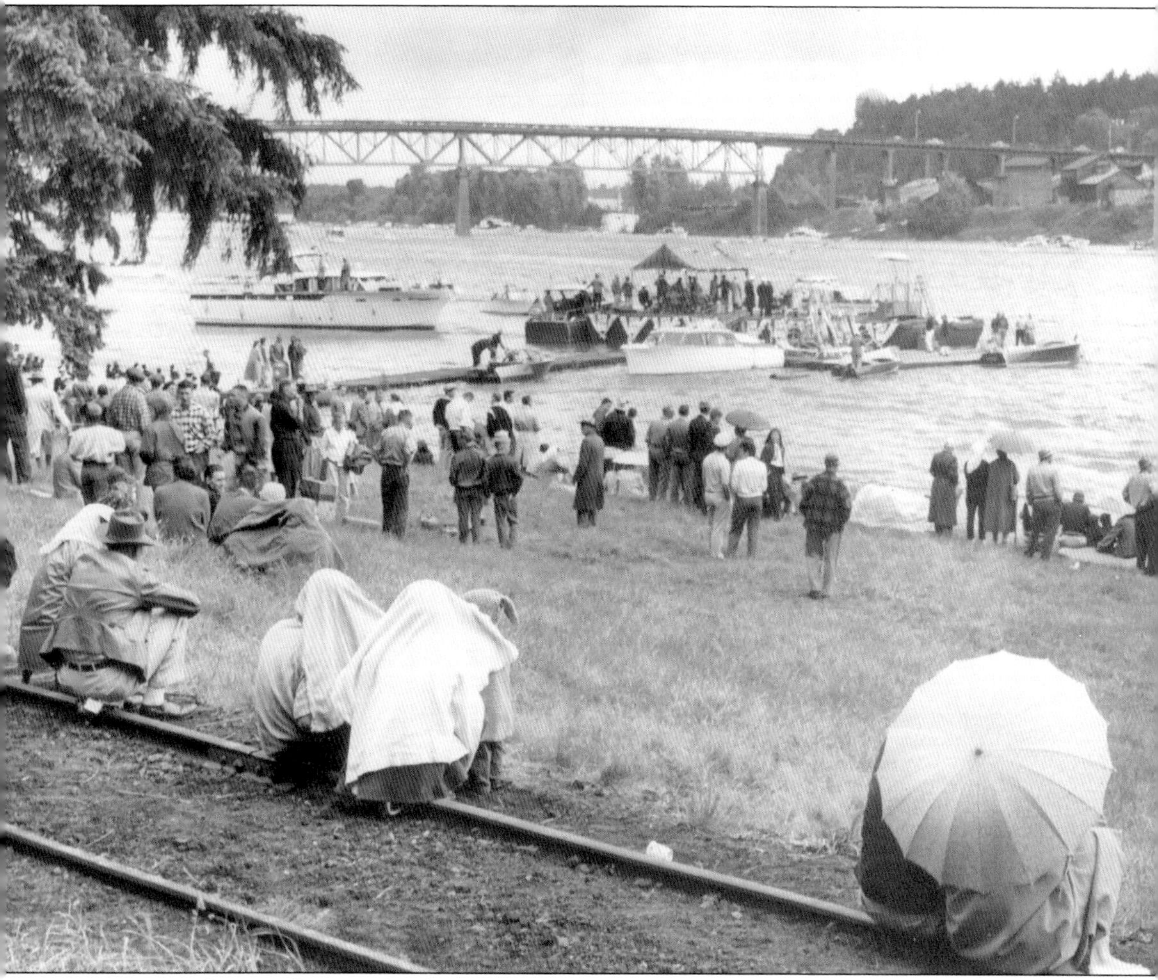

Rain and snow disrupted a few Rose Festival events in 1956. For the boat races on the Willamette River, people huddled under blankets and umbrellas. (Courtesy Oregon Historical Society; OrgLot431,B7F6.)

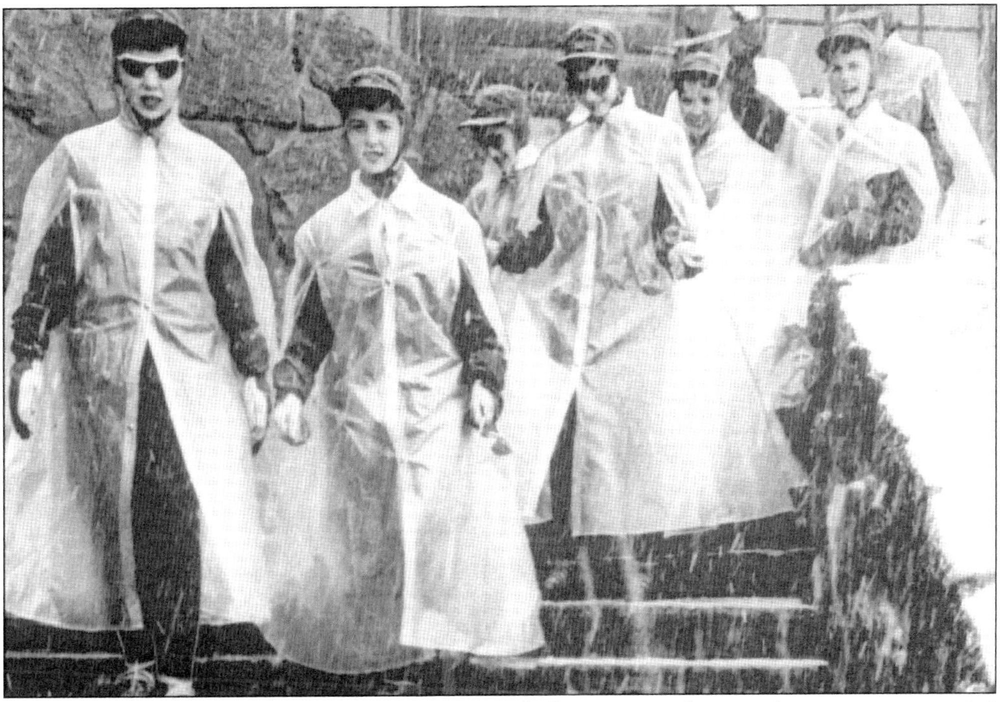

When the Rose Festival Court visited Mount Hood, plastic covers, hats, and mittens were needed as snow fell from noon on. (Courtesy Oregon Historical Society; OrgLot431,B7,F6.)

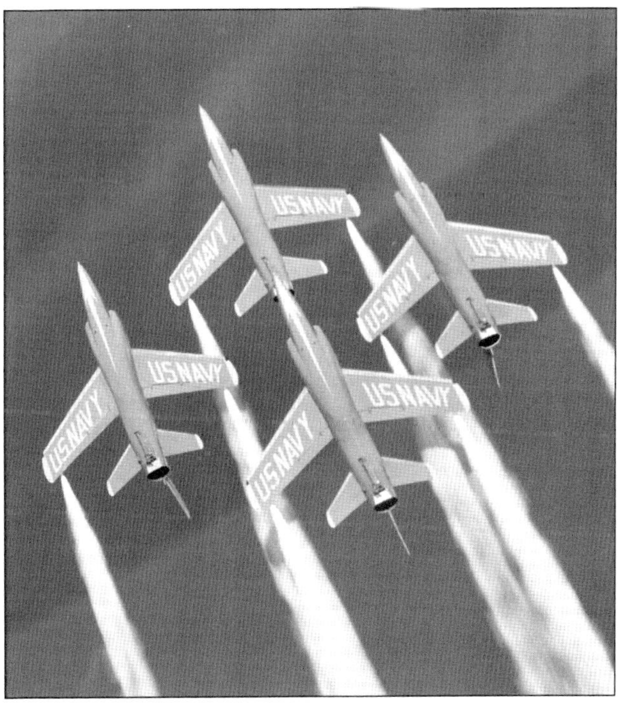

In 1957, the US Navy Blue Angels appeared as a special feature of the Marine Day activities. Marine Day featured waterskiing demonstrations, outboard races, and a floral-decorated parade of pleasure craft. Years later, the Blue Angels would return to the Rose Festival as the headliner for the first Rose Festival Airshow in 1988. (Courtesy of the US Navy.)

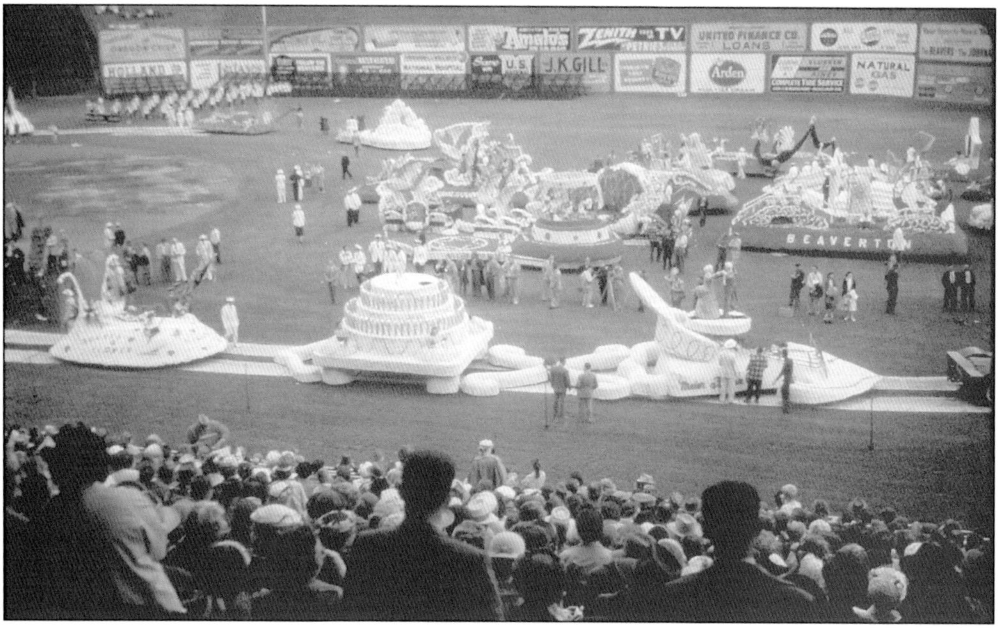

As had been the practice since the construction of Multnomah Stadium in 1926, floats gathered on the floor of the stadium prior to the 1957 Grand Floral Parade. This was one of the final years the stadium would be used to stage the parade, as the Veterans Memorial Coliseum was under construction and would become the home of the parade by 1961. A sudden wave of warm weather quickly ripened the local strawberry crop. The governor urged schools to take steps to give the students free time to pick the strawberries. As calls for pickers went unheeded, growers sought recruits from Portland's homeless. (Courtesy Portland Rose Festival Foundation.)

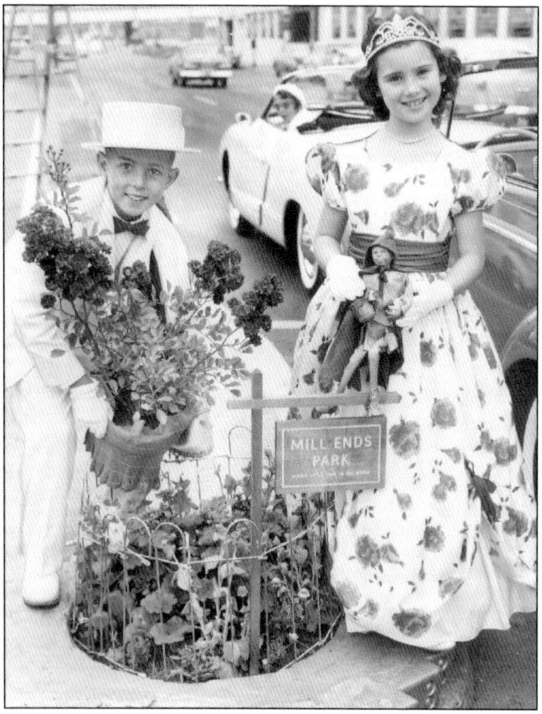

The Golden Anniversary of the Rose Festival occurred in 1958, and the eight-day event lasted from Sunday, June 8, through Sunday, June 15. Mill Ends Park, located at Naito Parkway and Southwest Taylor Street, was called the smallest park in the world. Junior Queen Pat Adams and Junior Prime Minister Pat Casey dedicated the rose planted there on June 8. They were greeted by a rare daylight appearance of Patrick O'Toole, head leprechaun of the park. (Courtesy Oregon Historical Society; OrHibb002374.)

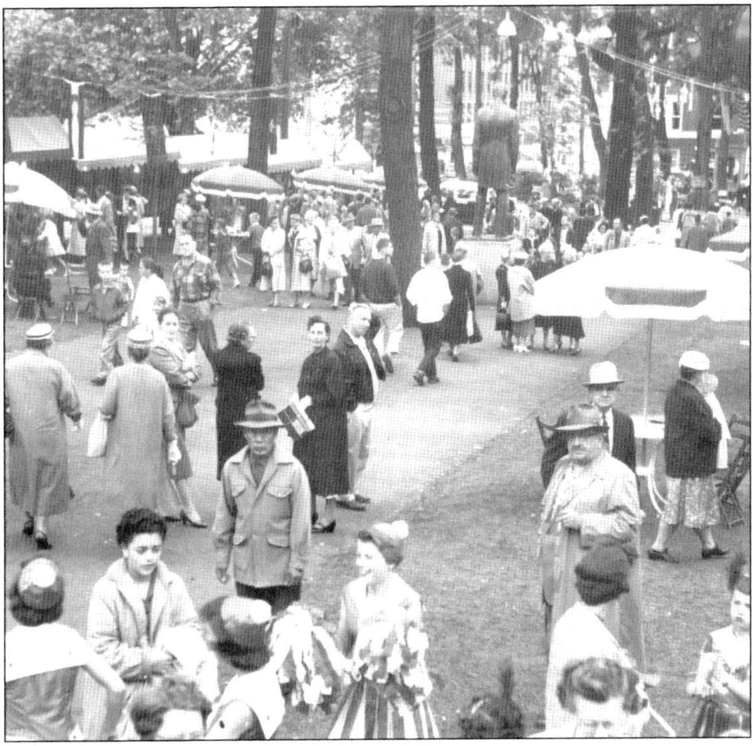

In 1958, the festival's Fun Center was held in the South Park blocks and occupied 13 park blocks south of Salmon Street. The nighttime parade, the Merrykhana Parade, was held on Wednesday, June 11. Fred Meyer stores offered rosebushes in full bloom for $1.49. (Courtesy Oregon Historical Society; OrHi67097.)

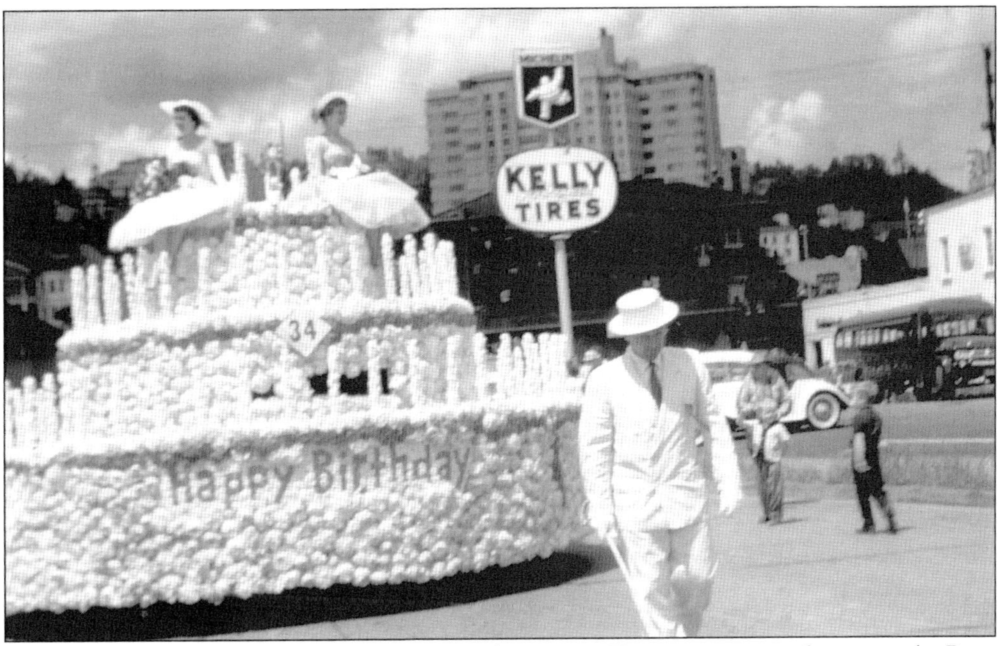

In February 1959, Oregon marked its centennial as a state. To commemorate the event, the Rose Festival theme was "Century in Flowers." Many floats in the Grand Floral Parade on Saturday, June 13 had a birthday or anniversary design, and volunteers worked toward the goal of pinning buttons on 100,000 people in Portland and surrounding communities. (Courtesy Portland Rose Festival Foundation.)

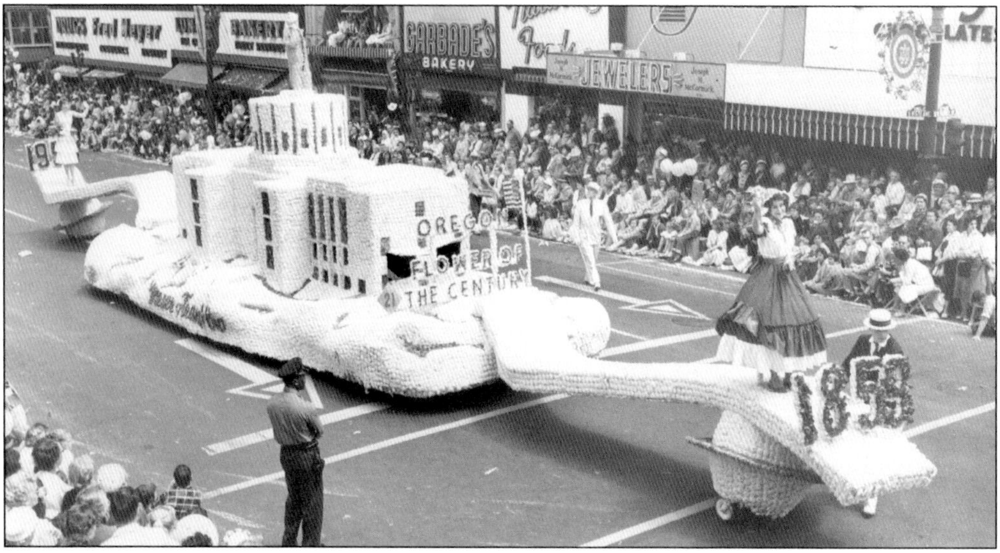

This gigantic, three-section Meier & Frank Company float won the Mayor's Trophy in 1959 in the Grand Floral Parade. There was a driver for each section of the 75-foot-long floral entry depicting the Oregon State Capitol. More than 70,000 Esther Read daisies adorned the structure. The statue of the pioneer on top was decorated in gold, like the original in Salem. Two Meier & Frank employees, Julie Hunter and Sandra Hogan, rode the award-winning float. (Courtesy Oregon Historical Society; OrHi67122.)

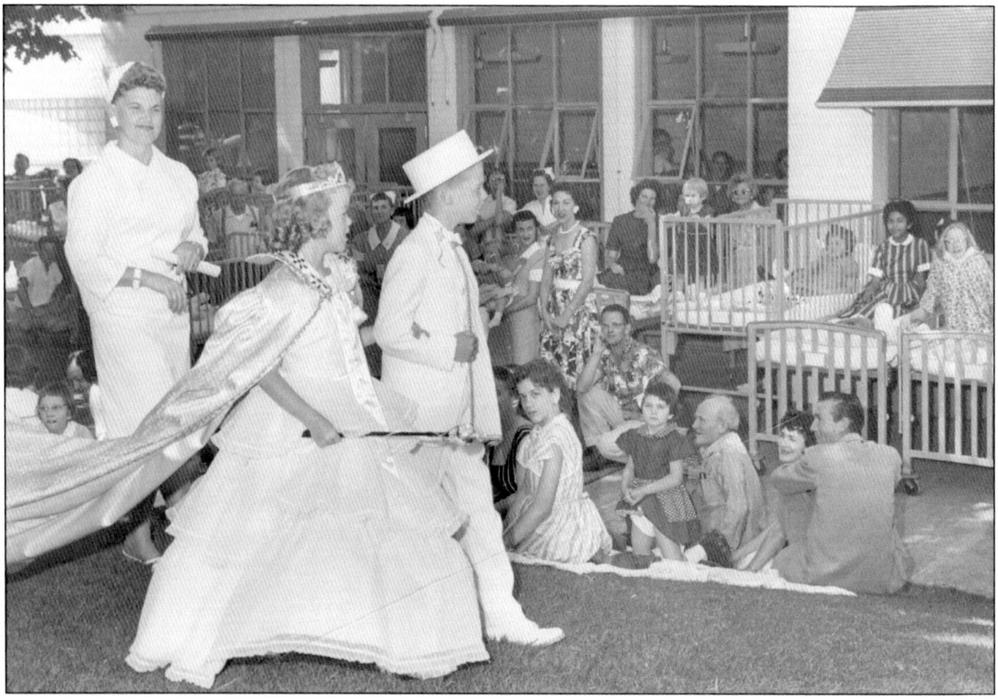

In 1960, for their annual visit to the Shriners Hospital for Children, Junior Queen Patricia Bentley and Junior Prime Minister Craig Evan marched past a group of youngsters on Sunday, June 5. Queen Patricia also knighted 14 Portlanders at the annual junior knighting ceremony. (Courtesy Oregon Historical Society; OrHi83701.)

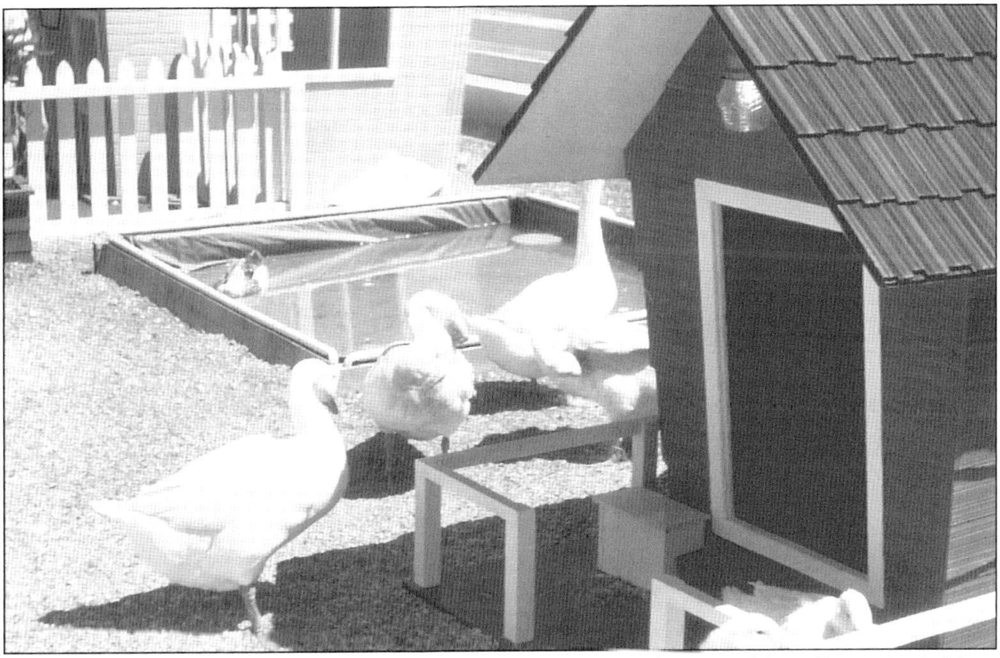

Alpenrose Dairy was always an attraction for youngsters during the annual Rose Festival. Children were allowed to mingle with small animals. For years, the Lil' Briches Rodeo was held at the dairy, so-named because the word "britches" would not fit on the belt buckle given to the winners. For the Grand Floral Parade, Richard Boone, better known as "Paladin," was grand marshal, and glamorous actress Jane Mansfield arrived in Portland for the Rose Festival activities. On the day before the Grand Floral Parade, record albums were selling for 66¢ at Meier & Frank Company's Friday Surprise. (Courtesy Portland Rose Festival Foundation.)

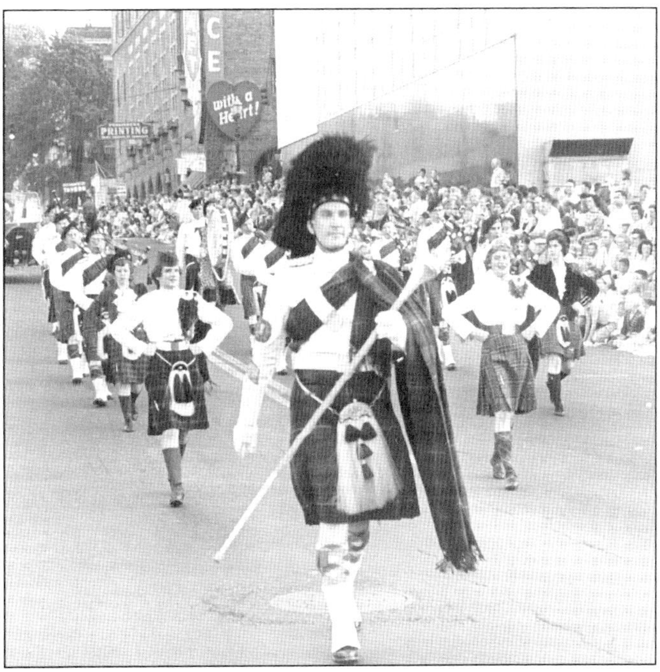

The 1961 Merrykhana Parade was moved a week early to accommodate an expanded Rose Festival schedule. The Clan Macleay Bagpipe Band, led by drum major Don Byrnes, marched along the two-mile route. No rain fell on this parade, but another festival event at the Lincoln High School stadium did get wet. Canadian sailors and Portland firemen competed for the International Championship in "Beer Barrel Polo" with their fire hoses. The Canadians doused the Portland team in a match that lasted three hours. (Courtesy Oregon Historical Society; OrHi54518.)

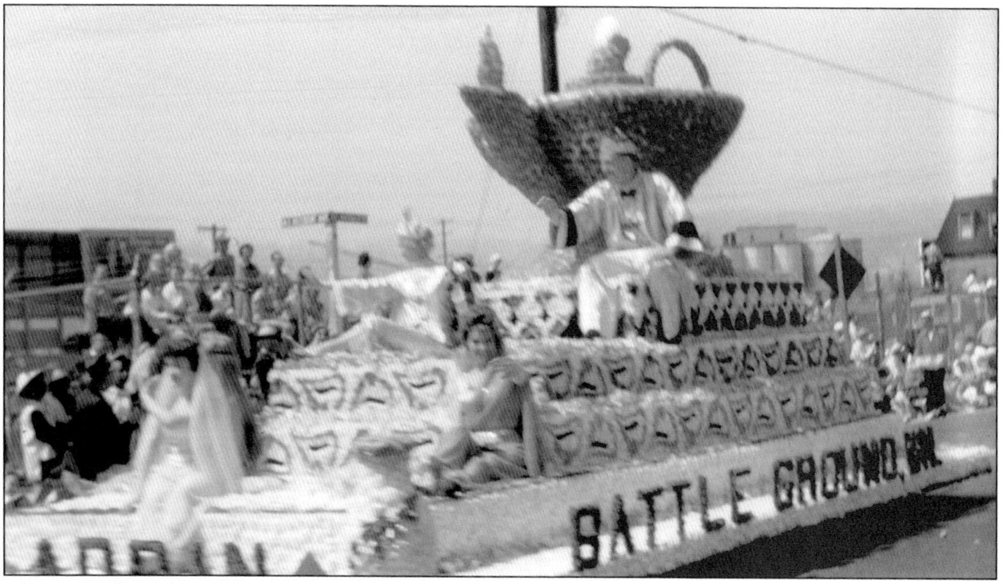

The city of Battle Ground, Washington, had a beautiful entry in the 1961 Grand Floral Parade, featuring "Aladdin and His Magic Lamp." Beginning their participation in 1955, Battle Ground continues to offer the longest-running, community-built entry in the parade to this day. (Courtesy Portland Rose Festival Foundation.)

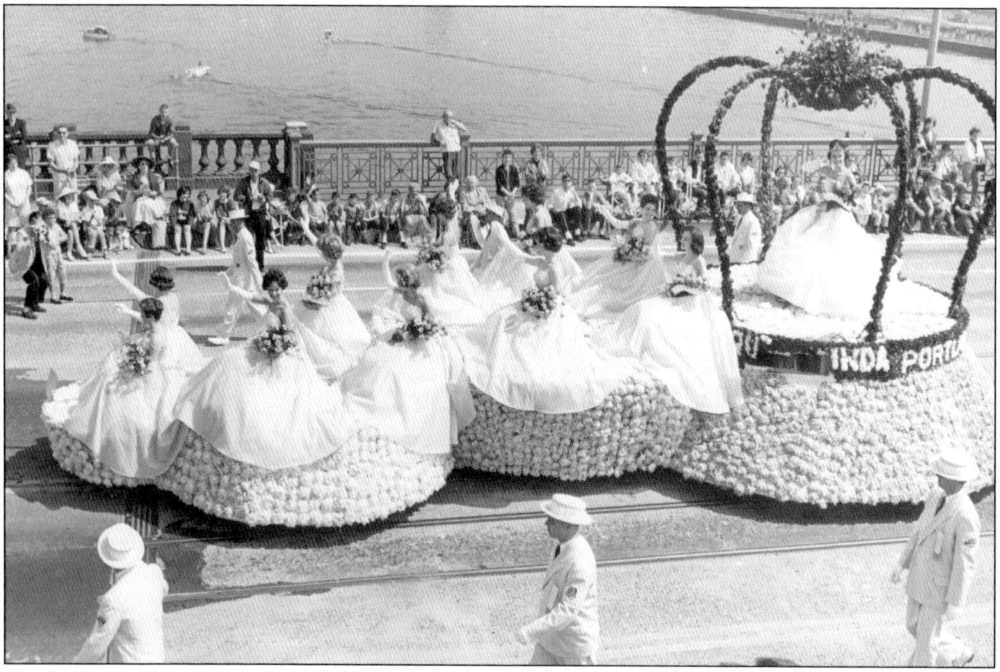
Linda Fuqua, the 1961 queen, and her court are pictured as their float, sponsored by the chamber of commerce, crossed the Burnside Bridge. Grand Marshal Lorne Green of television's *Bonanza* rode his palomino horse in the parade, following the tradition of many Western stars in the 1950s. The year 1961 marked the first that the parade passed through the Veterans Memorial Coliseum; the doors were built at either end of the arena for that very accommodation. (Courtesy Portland Rose Festival Foundation.)

The Farmers Insurance float in the 1962 Grand Floral Parade was staged in the Exhibition Hall of Veterans Memorial Coliseum. Riding the float was Joan Matthews of Leucadia, California, the niece of Carrie Lee Chamberlain, the first Rose Festival queen. Chamberlain was incorrectly identified as having served as the 1907 queen, when in reality she was "Queen Flora" in the 1908 Rose Festival. Barbara Miselli drove the daisy-covered float. (Courtesy Oregon Historical Society File1915.)

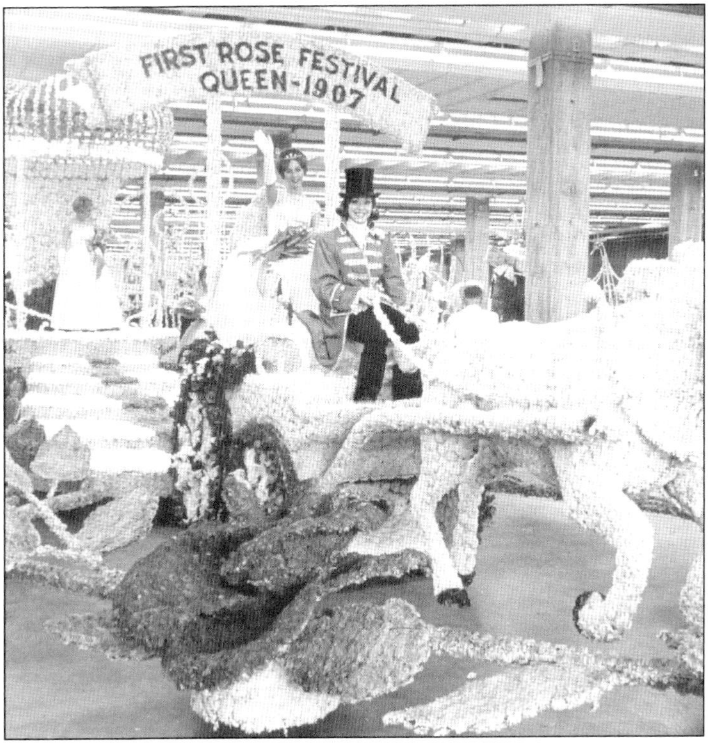

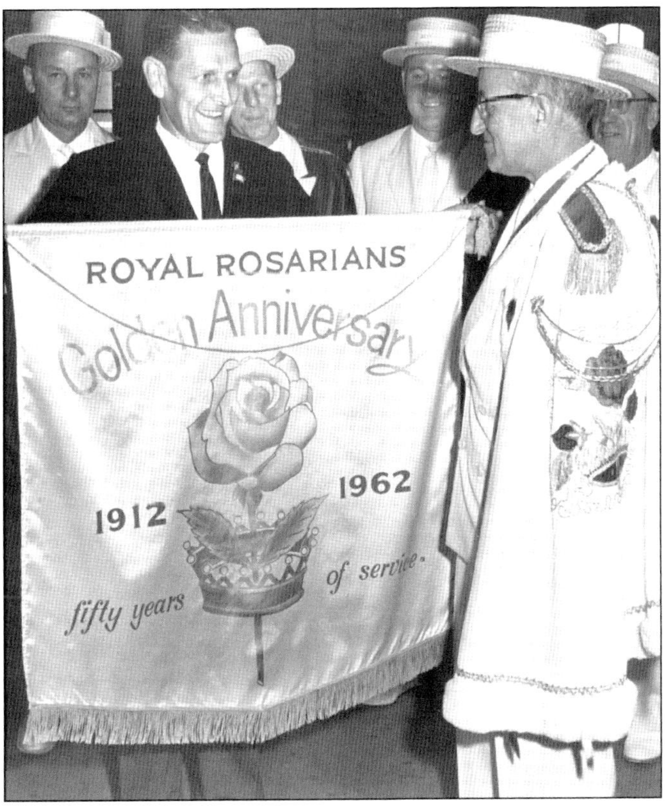

The Royal Rosarians celebrated their 50th Anniversary in 1962. Rose Festival president William R. Moore presented Prime Minister Ernest J. Burrows a new banner to commemorate the occasion. The banner was used by Rosarian marching units during the festival as well as during visits to other cities. (Courtesy of the *Oregonian*.)

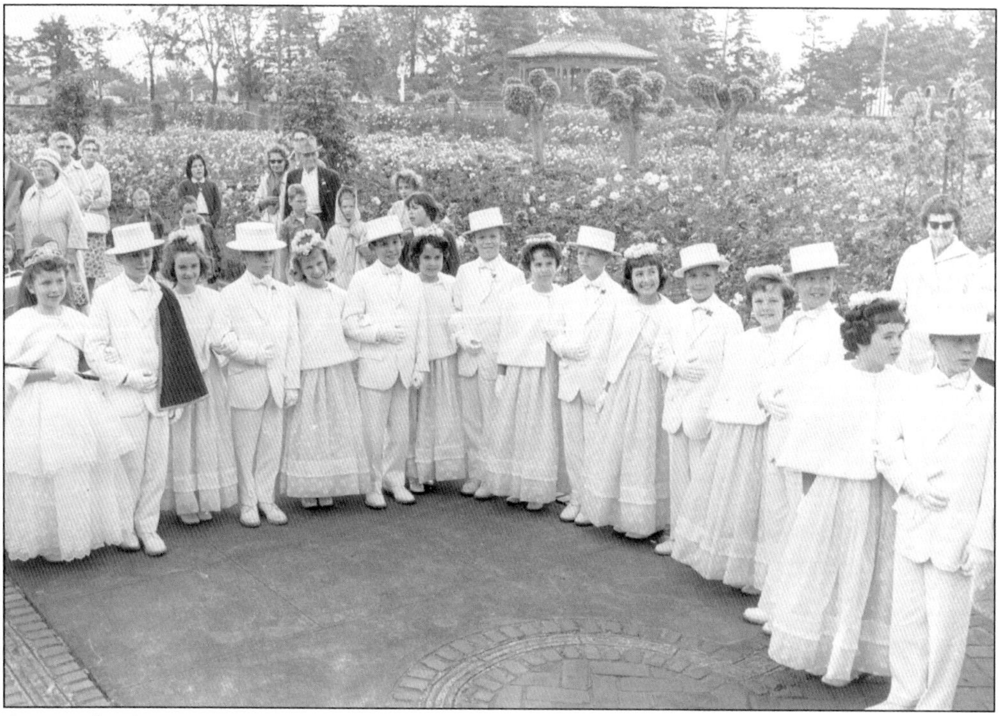

On Sunday, June 9, 1963, it was planting time for the Junior Court at Peninsula Park. From left to right are Queen Shannon and Junior Prime Minister William Childers. Other princesses and princes are Kathleen Ann Kissner, Scott Othus, Nancy Hellervik, John Brune, Daphne Holman, William David Todd, Patti Fontana, Prince Gordon James Patterson, Connie Sue Ross, Thomas John Miles, Michele Rolph, Shephen Weber, Shauna Newbrey, and James Edward Barton. (Courtesy Oregon Historical Society; OrHi83707.)

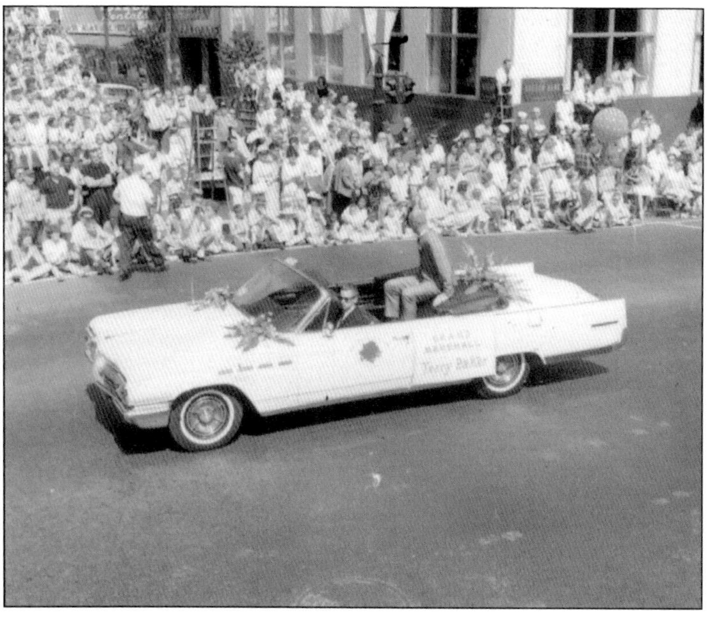

The grand marshal of the 1963 Grand Floral Parade was Terry Baker from Oregon State University, the only football player from Oregon to receive the Heisman Trophy. On Monday, June 17, the US Supreme Court ruled eight to one that the use of the Lord's Prayer and Bible reading in public schools was unconstitutional. (Courtesy Portland Rose Festival Foundation.)

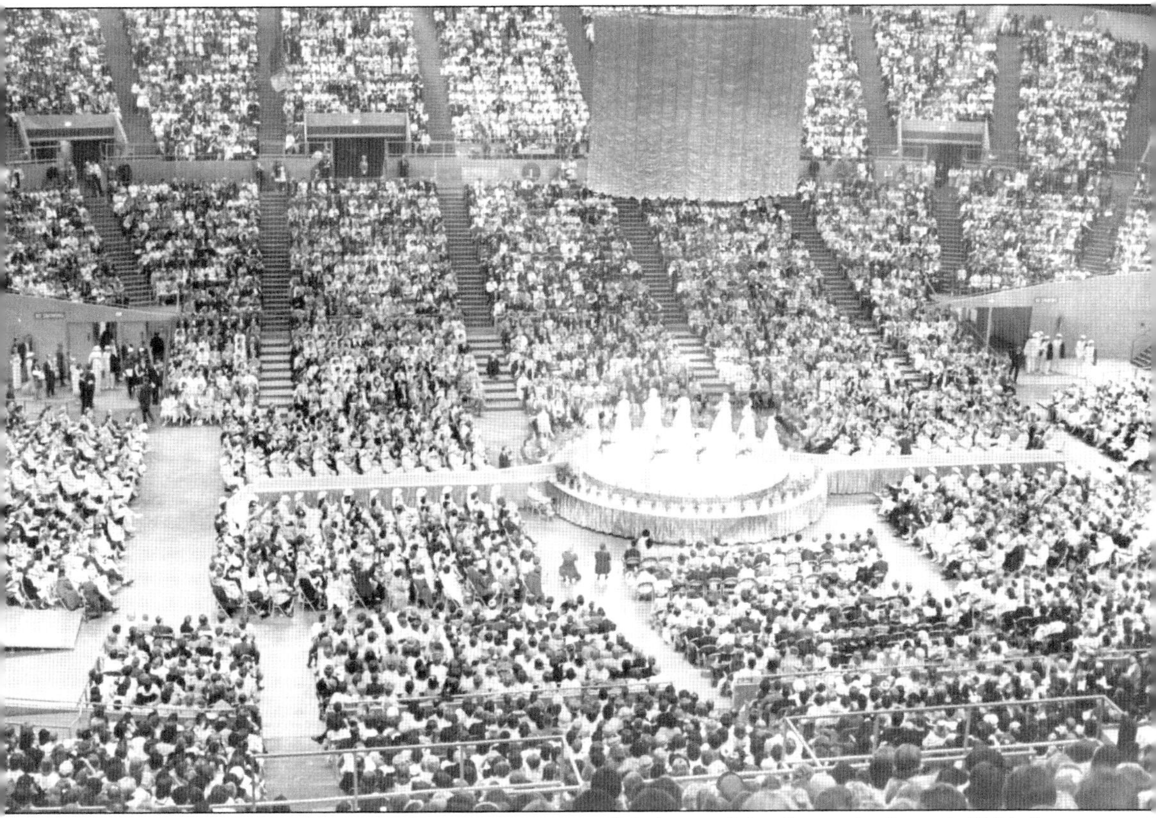

More than 12,000 people jammed Veterans Memorial Coliseum Monday night, June 8, 1964, for the queen's Coronation. After each princess had been given the spotlight individually for her five-minute speech, all members of the Royal Court returned to a revolving stage at the center of the arena. The stage was notoriously jerky, and court members often struggled to keep their balance. (Courtesy of the *Oregonian*.)

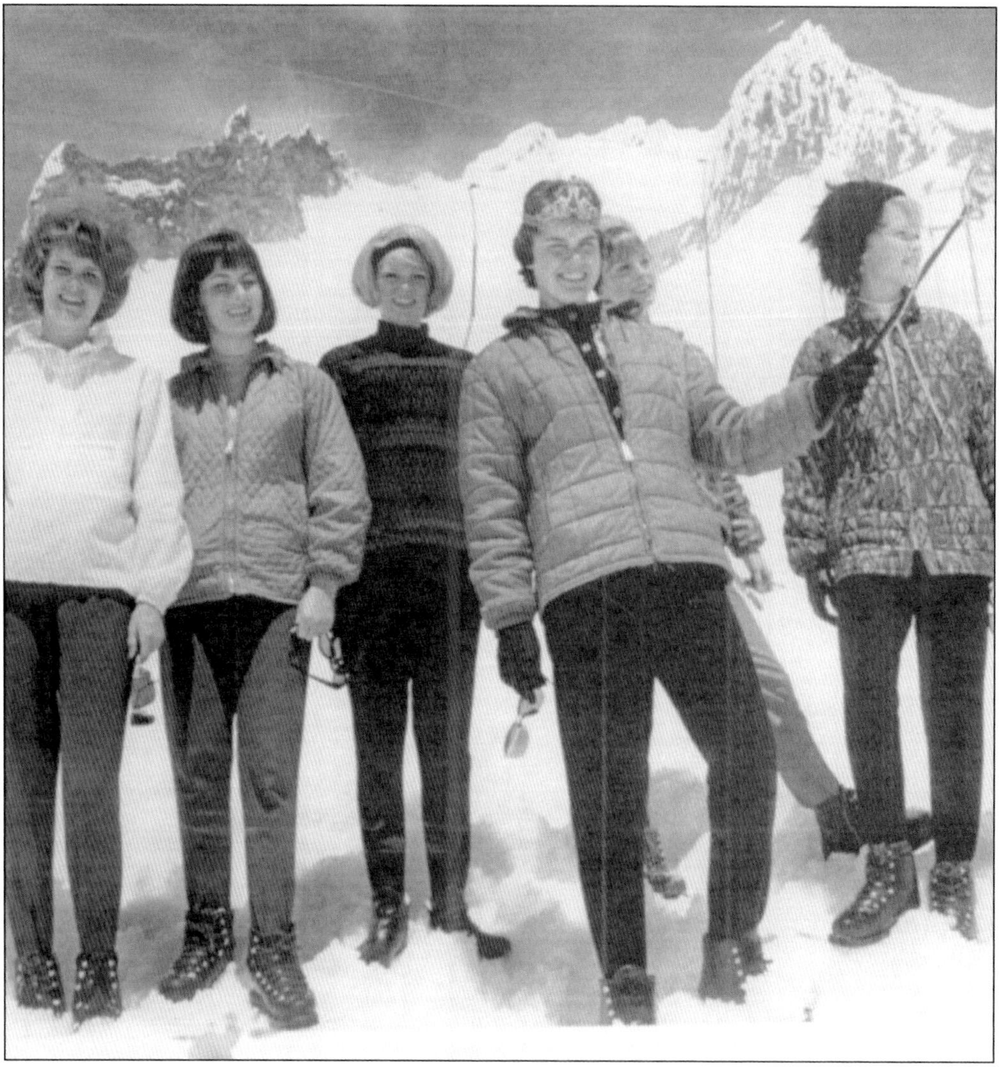

Queen Sharon Arneson and her court enjoyed the warm sun on Mount Hood for the annual Golden Rose Ski Classic in 1964. Singer and movie star Pat Boone arrived at the Portland International Airport on June 10 for shows in the Veterans Memorial Coliseum on Wednesday, Thursday, and Friday nights. Years later, Boone would return to the Rose Festival as the grand marshal of the Grand Floral Parade. (Courtesy Oregon Historical Society; OrgLot431,B11,F11.)

Seven

1965–1975

A Younger, Hipper Festival

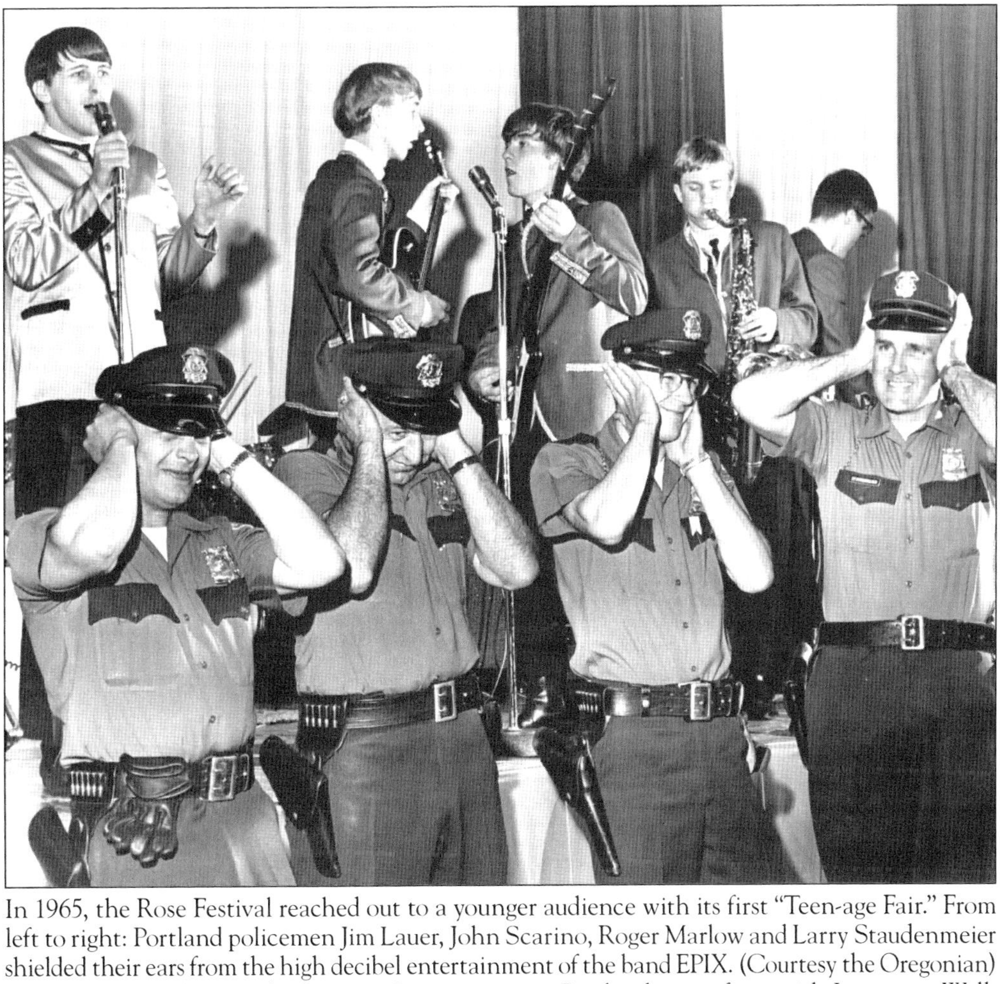

In 1965, the Rose Festival reached out to a younger audience with its first "Teen-age Fair." From left to right: Portland policemen Jim Lauer, John Scarino, Roger Marlow and Larry Staudenmeier shielded their ears from the high decibel entertainment of the band EPIX. (Courtesy the Oregonian) For the older audience, the Lennon Sisters came to Portland to perform with Lawrence Welk during the 1965 Rose Festival. (Courtesy of the *Oregonian*.)

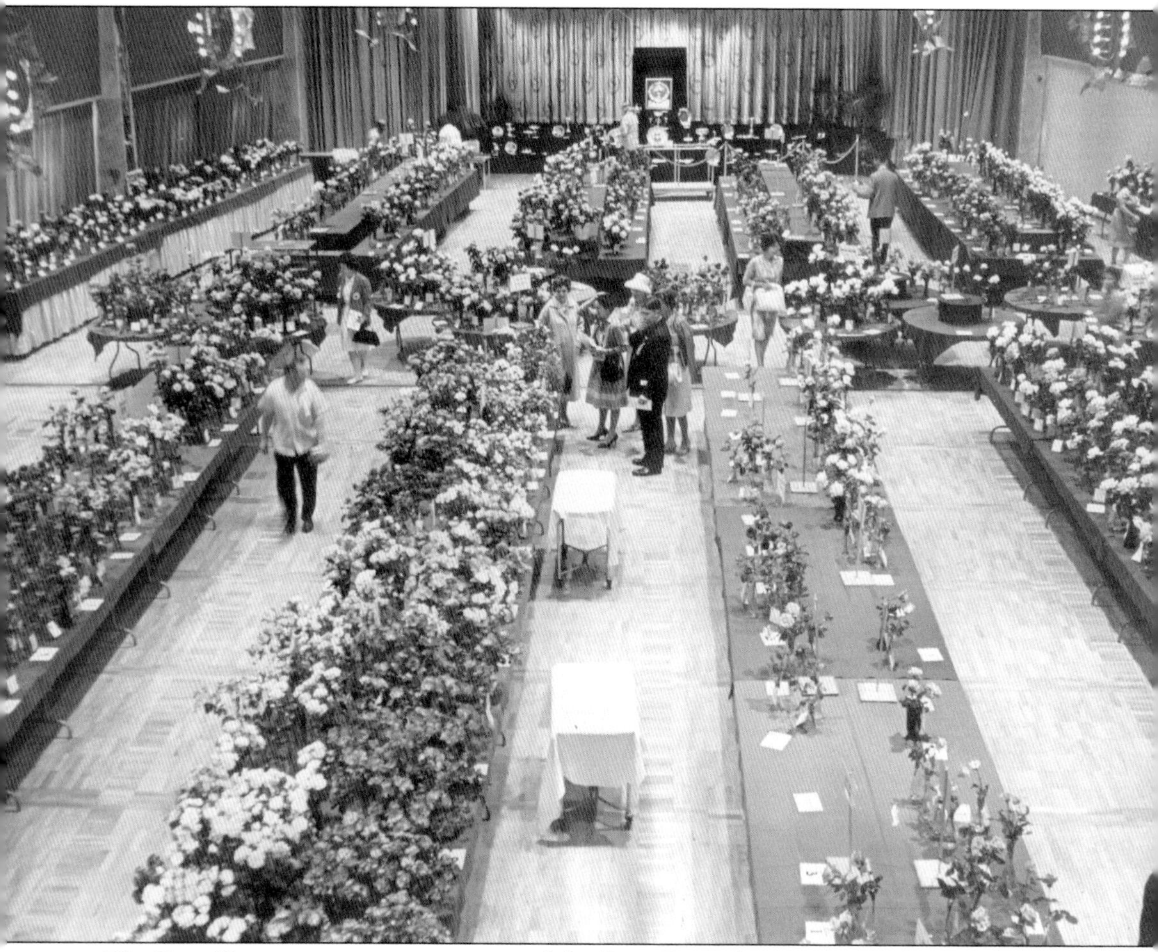

The Rose Show was an important part of the Rose Festival in 1966, as it had been from the beginning. The first Rose Show was held in 1889 in the backyard of Portland matron Georgiana Pittock; later, sites like the famous Forestry Building and Oaks Park hosted the event. Today's Rose Show is held at the Lloyd Center on the ice rink. In 1966, people from all over the world came to Portland for the American Rose Society's annual convention. Portland's Rose Show is the nation's oldest. (Courtesy Portland Rose Festival Foundation.)

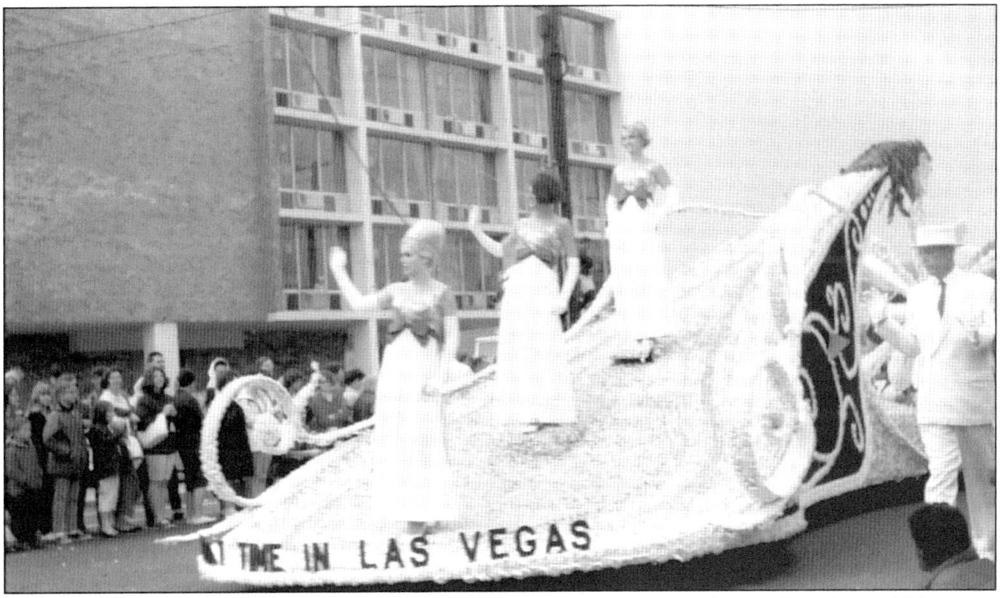

As a testament to its increasing popularity, cities as far away as Las Vegas, Nevada, and Victoria, British Columbia, entered floats in the Grand Floral Parade. One year, the schools from the small town of Long Creek in Eastern Oregon placed an entry in the parade. (Courtesy Portland Rose Festival Foundation.)

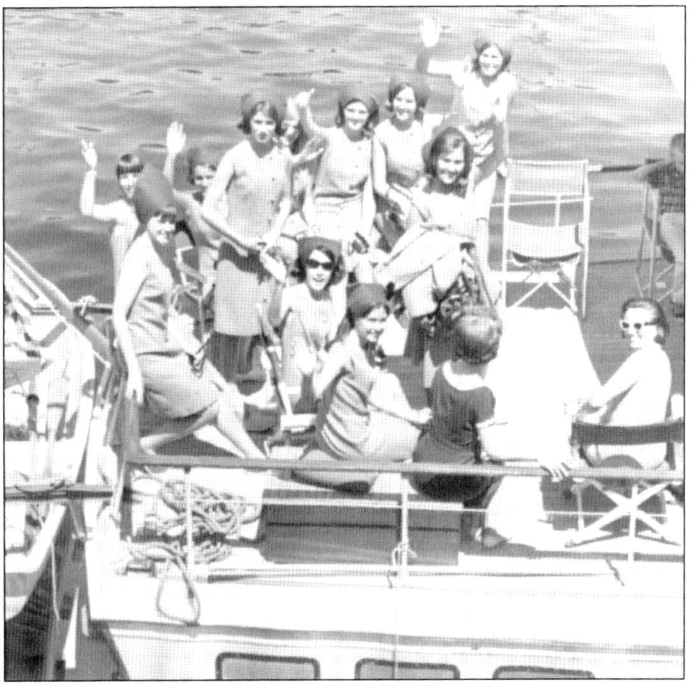

In 1966, the United States had launched itself well into space exploration as *Surveyor I* landed on the moon. At home, the Vietnam War was on the minds of Americans, and President Johnson's approval rating was 46 percent. Rose Festival ratings, however, continued high, and the Royal Court members enjoyed themselves on the Willamette River for Marine Day. (Courtesy Oregon Historical Society; OrgLot431,B12,F5.)

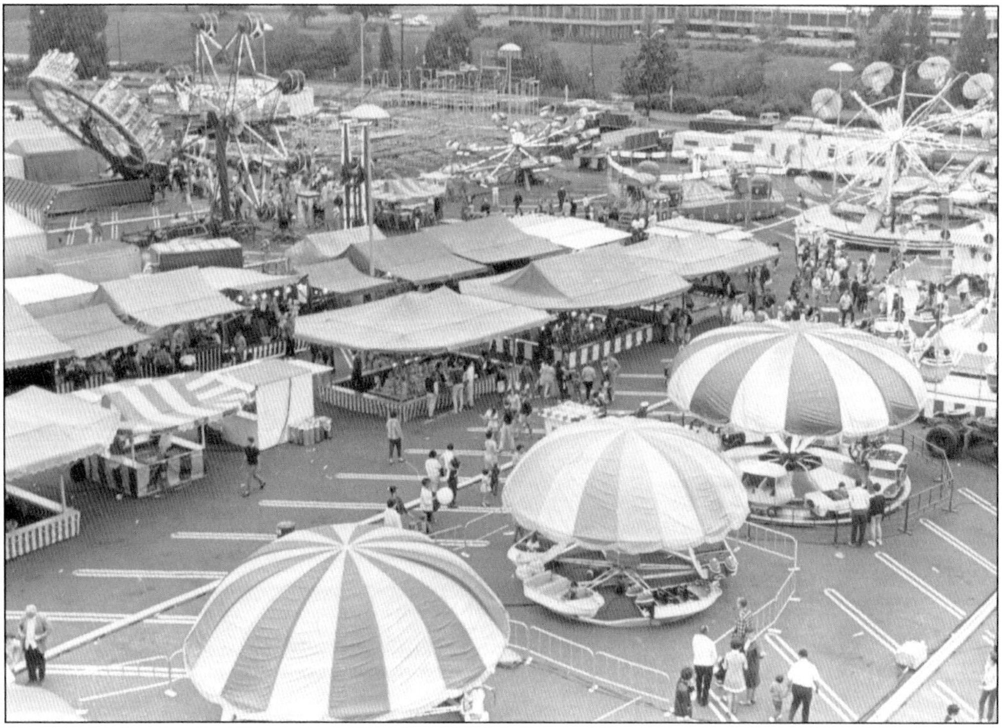

Over the years, the Rose Festival Fun Center occupied various places. It became an integral part of the celebration, and in 1967, was located in Holladay Park near the Lloyd Center in northeast Portland. It featured many attractions for citizens of all ages, offering fair food, rides for the young, and exhibits for grown-ups. It sometimes suffered through days of cold, wet rain, but also days of warm sunshine. Such was the case on Friday, June 2, when it opened with a high temperature of 72 degrees under sunny skies. (Courtesy Oregon Historical Society; OrHi67080; the *Oregonian*.)

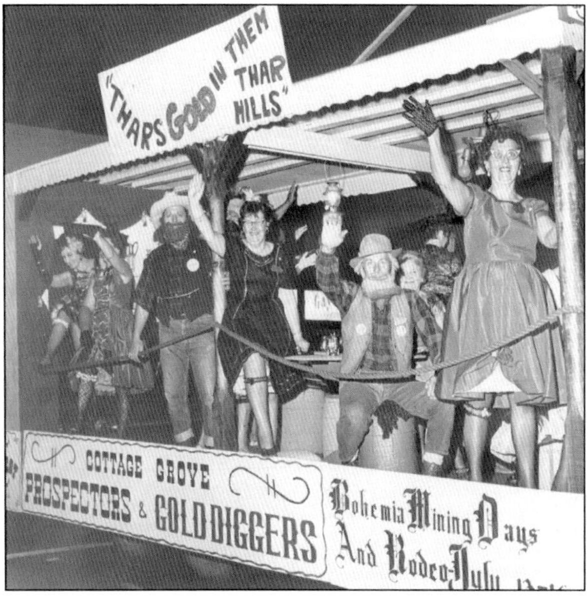

The Merrykhana Parade had become such a widespread favorite at the Rose Festival that it drew entries from various points in Oregon. In 1967, the city of Cottage Grove promoted its own celebration, Bohemia Mining Days. Bob Hope arrived in Portland to perform, and television's Mr. Spock, Leonard Nimoy of Star Trek fame, was grand marshal of the Grand Floral Parade—sporting human-shaped ears! Around the world, Israel and Egypt were involved in conflict, and Sen. Mark Hatfield of Oregon told a convention of Baptists in Florida that the United States should get out of Vietnam. (Courtesy Oregon Historical Society; OrgLot431,B12,F16.)

In 1968, the Rose Festival opened the Fun Center on its earliest date, May 31, at Holladay Park near Lloyd Center. It was a cloudy, drizzly day, but nothing compared to what was to fall from the heavens on the Merrykhana Parade the next day on June 1. The Portland Rainmakers, a hijinks organization that added fun and frolic to the pageant and the Portland area, had selected their Miss Raindrop, Judy Bozeman (center). Also pictured are Leslie Morgan and Bobyn Cantrel. They certainly needed umbrellas, as close to an inch of rain doused the festivities that day. (Courtesy Oregon Historical Society; OrgLot431,B13,F4.)

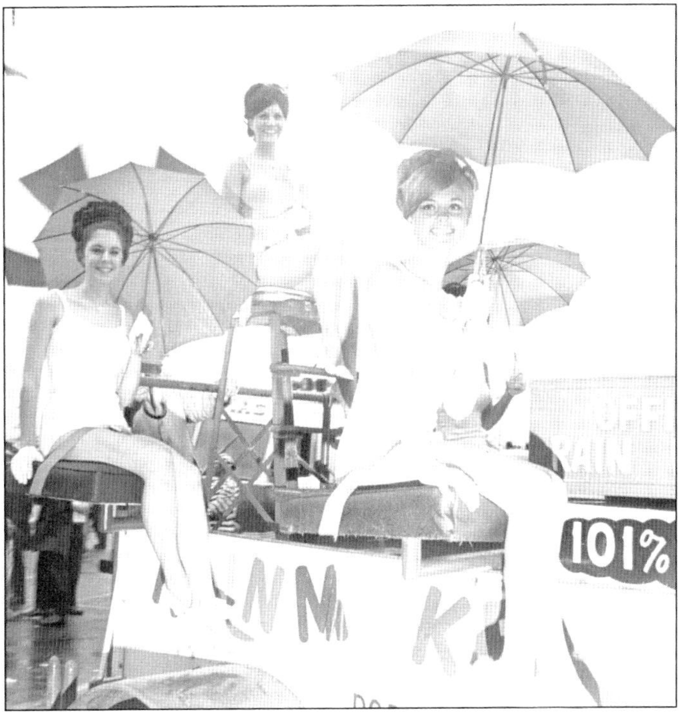

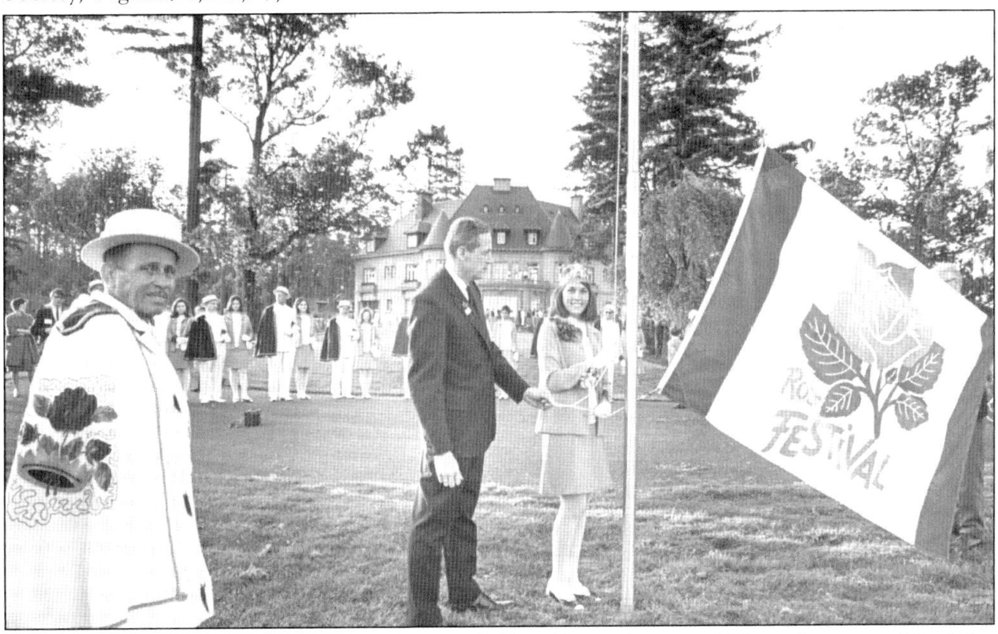

Afterward, the weather began cooperating with Rose Festival events. When the court visited the Pittock Mansion, it was only cloudy. Queen Margaret Huelskamp raised the Rosaria flag, assisted by City Commissioner Frank Ivancie and Rosarian prime minister Arnold Yeomans, left. The festival was sobered by the assassination of presidential candidate Sen. Robert F. Kennedy, who had just left Oregon for Los Angeles. Paradegoers with Veterans Memorial Coliseum seats shared a moment of silence before the Grand Floral Parade on June 8, the day of Kennedy's funeral. (Courtesy Portland Rose Festival Foundation.)

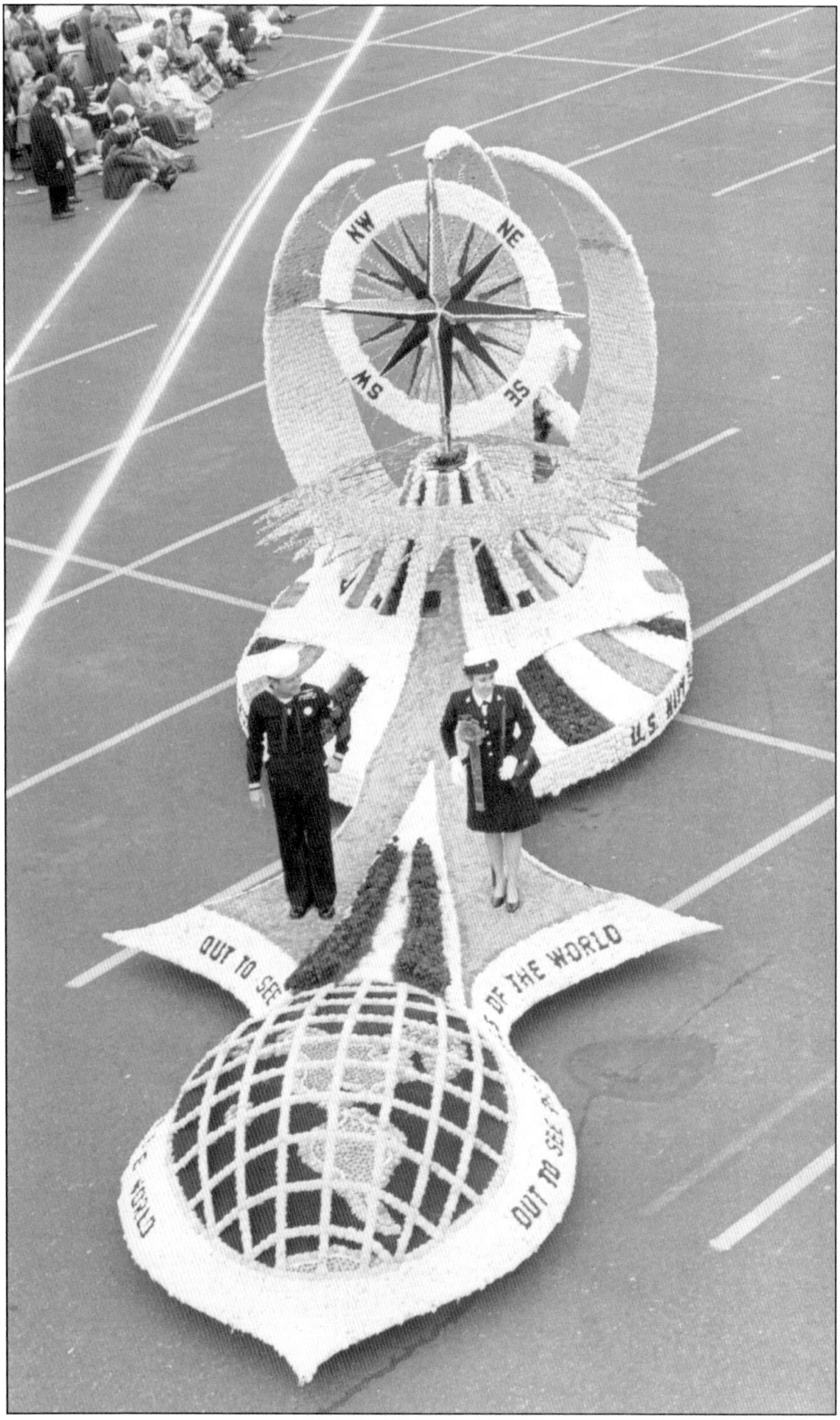

In the 1968 Grand Floral Parade, a 32-pointed wind rose was the highlight of the US Navy Recruiting Station's float. It depicted a navigational device found on marine charts all over the world and was selected by the judges for the Royal Rosarian trophy. (Courtesy Oregon Historical Society; OHSFile1915.)

When the Junior Court visited the Portland Oregon Zoo on Saturday, June 7, 1969, it was a sunny 77 degrees. From left to right: Queen Dana Easley and Princesses Shelia Weaver, Rhonda Ryan, Kellie Smith, Deserah Waterman, Suzanne Kirkland, Cathryn Smith, and Tamera Parker. Their tour that day also included a visit to the Shriners Hospital for Children and a knighting ceremony. (Courtesy Oregon Historical Society; OrHi67129.)

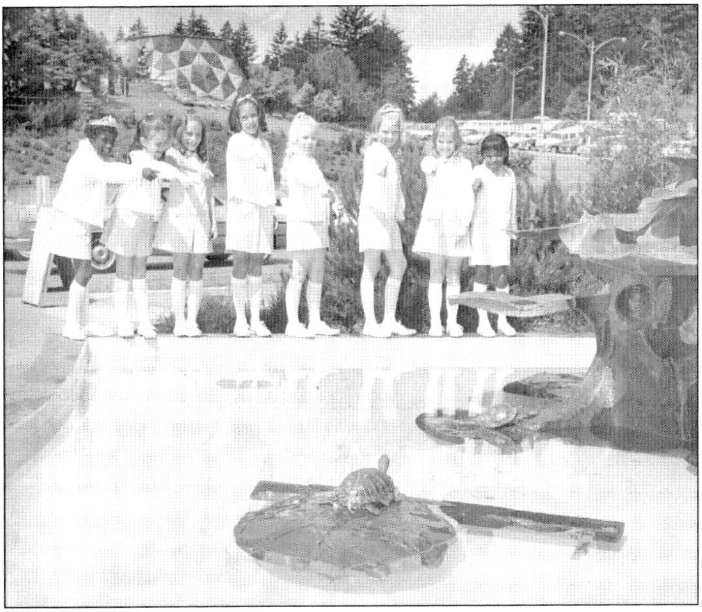

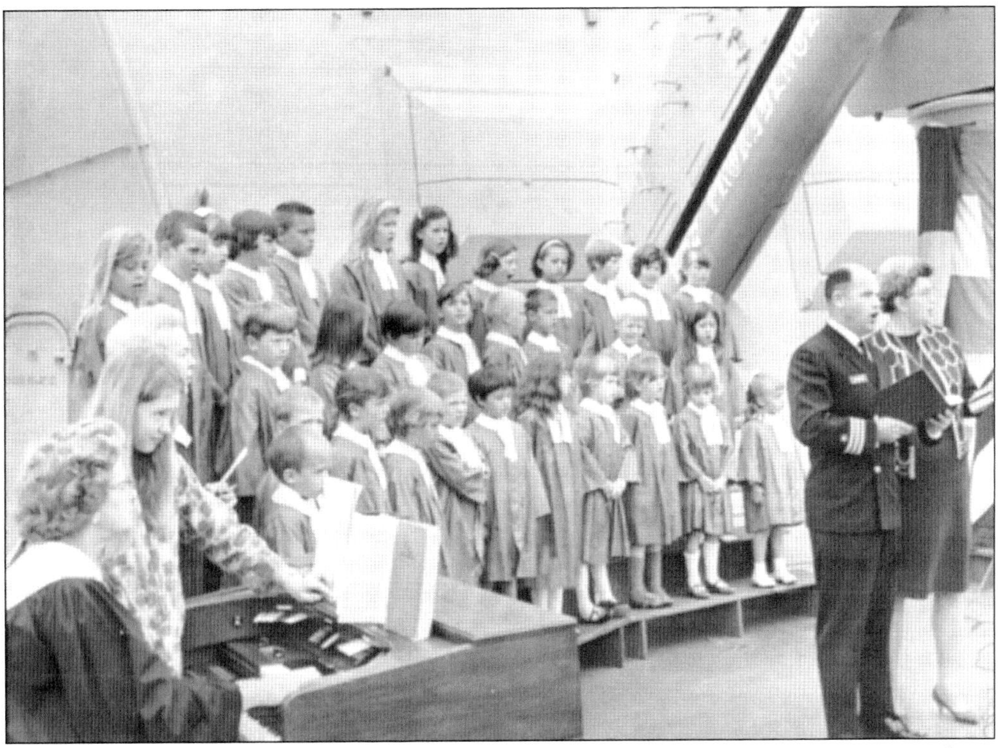

On Sunday, June 15, 1969, the Peace Lutheran Church Junior Choir visited the USS *Providence* in town as part of the Rose Festival Fleet. Oregon State coach Dee Andros was selected as "King of Fun" for the Merrykhana Parade, which was turning into a water fight between participants and viewers. (Courtesy Oregon Historical Society.)

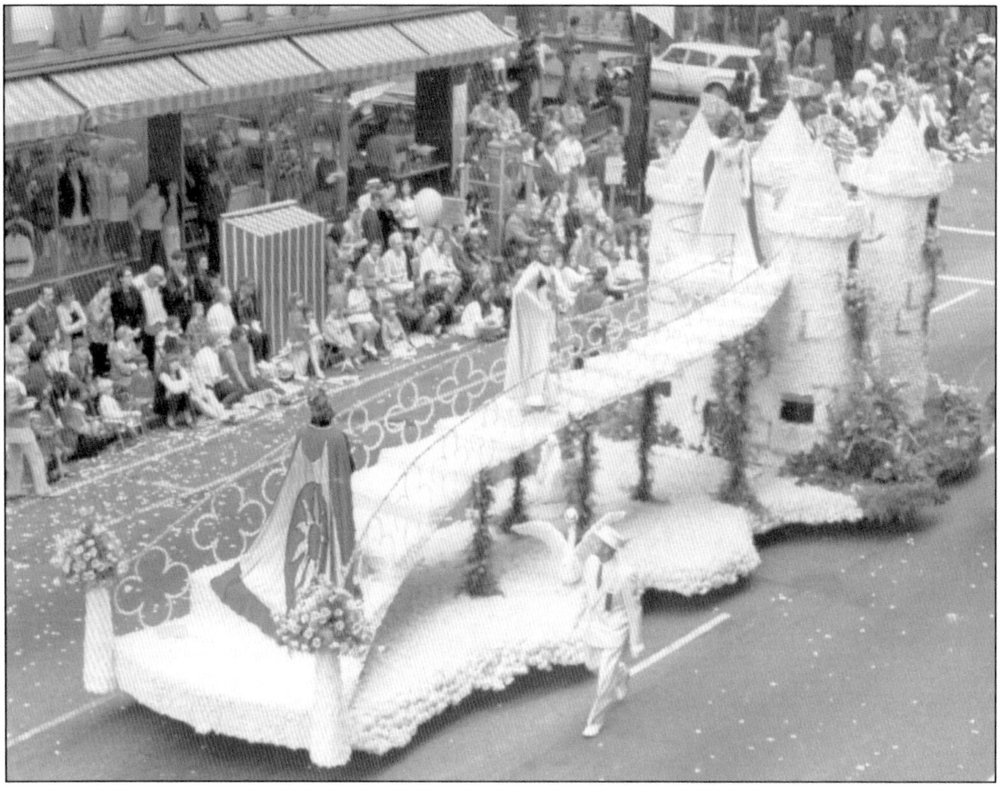

In early June 1970, Portland was in the middle of a rare heat wave. On Sunday, June 1, the thermometer reached 94 and rose to a sizzling 98 the next day. However, after cooling into the 70s for a couple of days, it reached 91 for the opening of the Rose Festival Fun Center on Friday, June 5. One of the most spectacular floats in the Grand Floral Parade on Saturday, June 13 was the one entered by the First National Bank. (Courtesy Portland Rose Festival Foundation.)

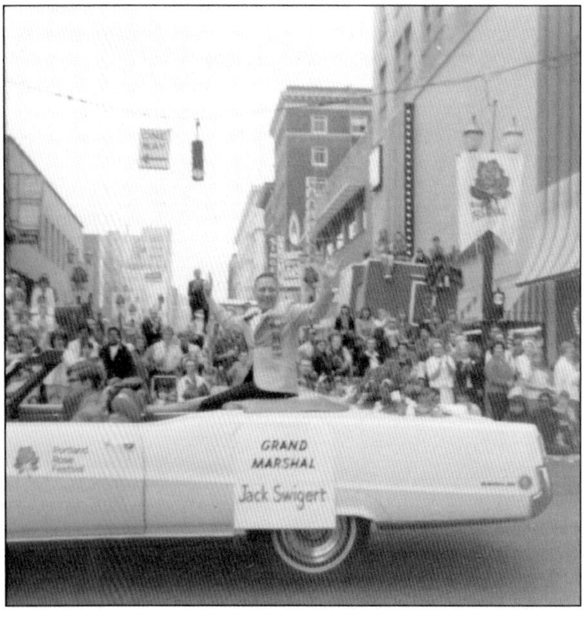

Astronaut Jack Swigert of the Apollo 13 campaign was grand marshal of the 1970 Grand Floral Parade. To promote the festival, Rose Festival officials wanted to hang signs from the Broadway and Hawthorne bridges, but county commissioners denied their request. The sale of US Savings Stamps, so popular during World War II, fell to $19 million in 1969, down from a high of $558 million in 1942. The program ended June 30 of 1970. (Courtesy Portland Rose Festival Foundation.)

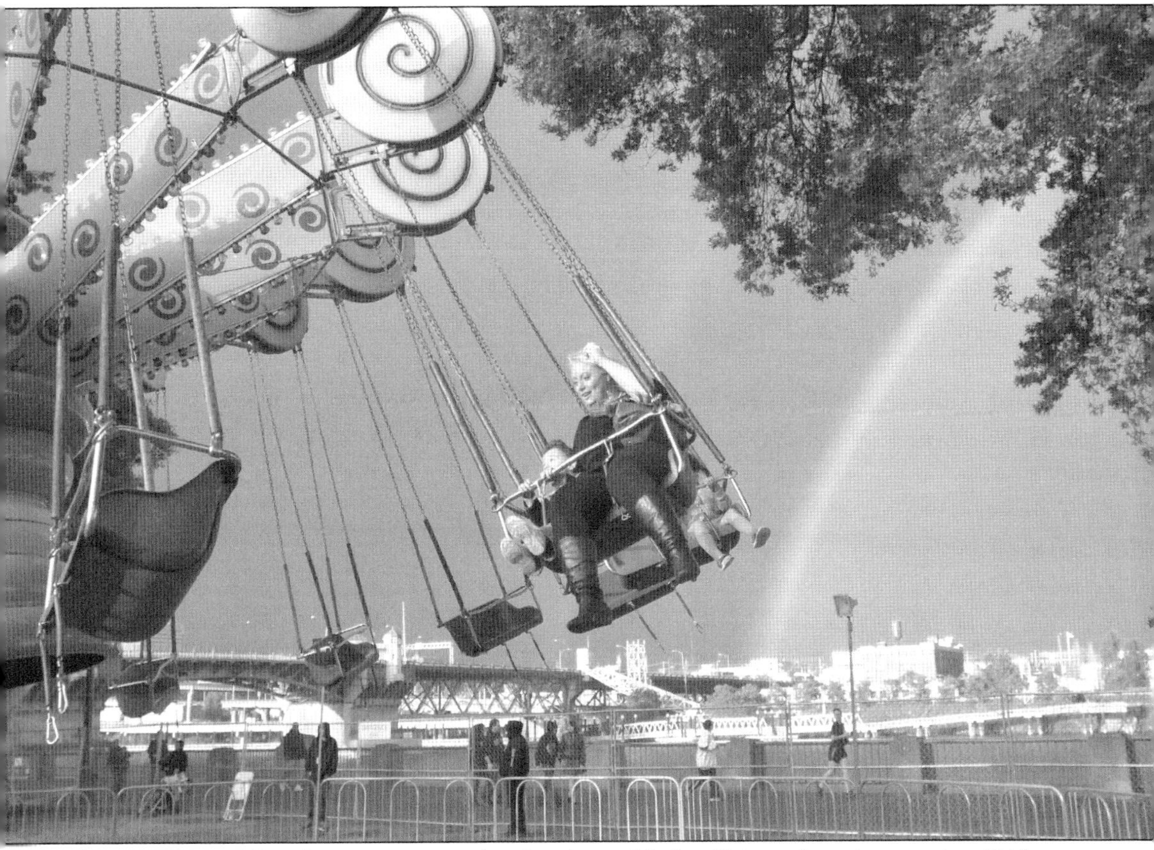

The Rose Festival Fun Center was moved to Southwest Harbor Drive, where it opened on Friday, June 4, 1971. Today's event, Rose Festival CityFair, is located in Tom McCall Waterfront Park, the city park that now covers the old Harbor Drive. On Thursday, June 10, seventy-five members of the Rose Festival Peace Committee marched across the Broadway Bridge to protest having war vessels as part of the Rose Festival. Protests during the festival became more common, including women's groups picketing the queen's Coronation. (Courtesy Portland Rose Festival Foundation.)

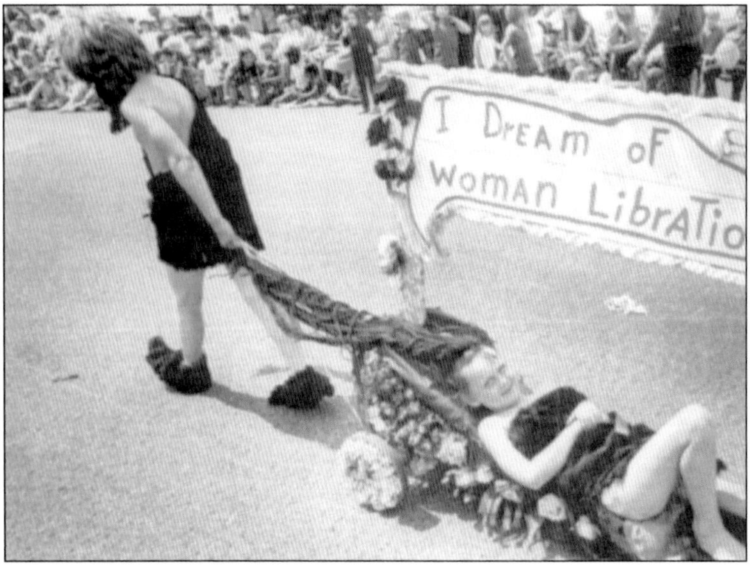

The 1971 Junior Parade enjoyed sunny skies, and even here, the mood of the country was evident. (Courtesy Oregon Historical Society; OrgLot431,B14,F9.)

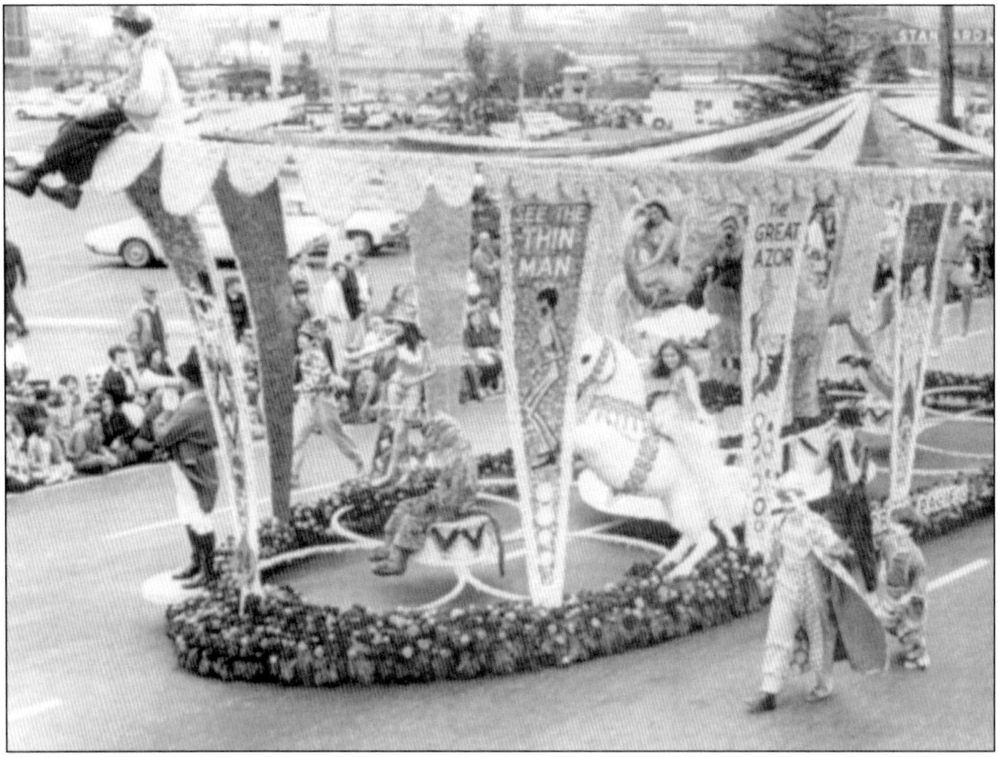

A rain-free Grand Floral Parade made its way east on Broadway near the Veterans Memorial Coliseum on Saturday, June 12. The 4.2-mile route is much the same today. In Salem, Oregon's legislature passed the controversial Bottle Bill, announcing Oregon as one of the first environmentally conscious states in the United States. (Courtesy Oregon Historical Society; OrgLot431,B14,F8.)

The 1972 Merrykhana Parade would be the last. Clear skies blessed the event, but the streets were wet from the water fights between spectators and participants. The after-action police report called it "the wildest, wettest, drunkenest brawl ever seen on the streets of Portland." The headline in the *Oregonian* on June 8 read: "Parade, Hah! It Was Only A Water Fight." The parade was canceled for the next three years before being reinvented in 1976 as the slightly more sedate Bicentennial Starlight Parade. (Courtesy Oregon Historical Society.)

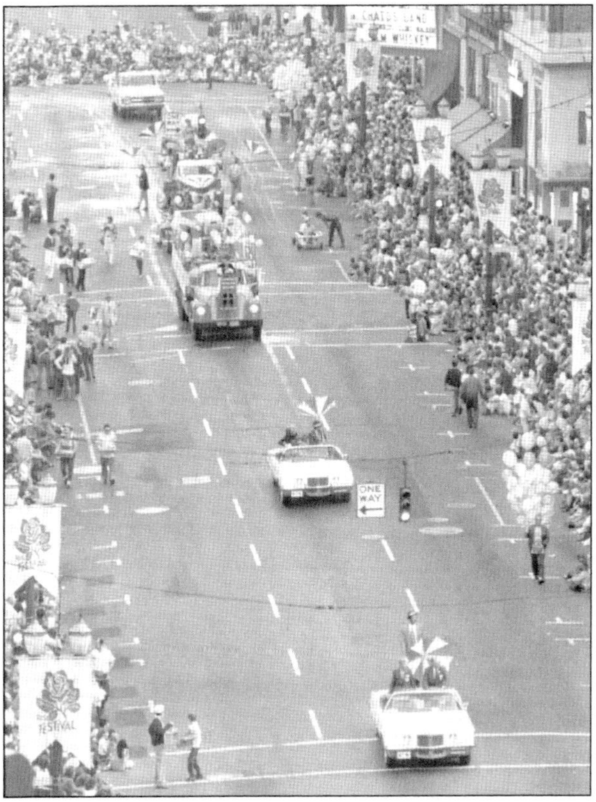

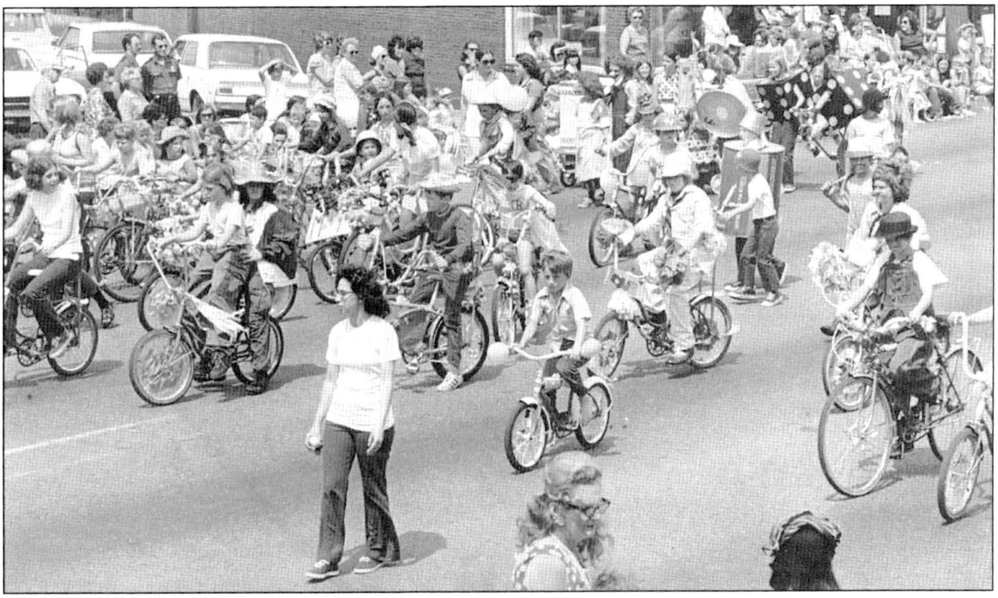

The 1972 Junior Parade was moved to Thursday (from Friday) complete with a plethora of bicycles. In Salem, the constitutionality of Oregon's "dry sands" beach law (prohibiting the use of alcohol on Oregon beaches) was upheld by a panel of three federal judges. And US representative George P. Miller of California advocated extensive research into solar power to alleviate the world's energy crisis. (Courtesy Portland Rose Festival Foundation.)

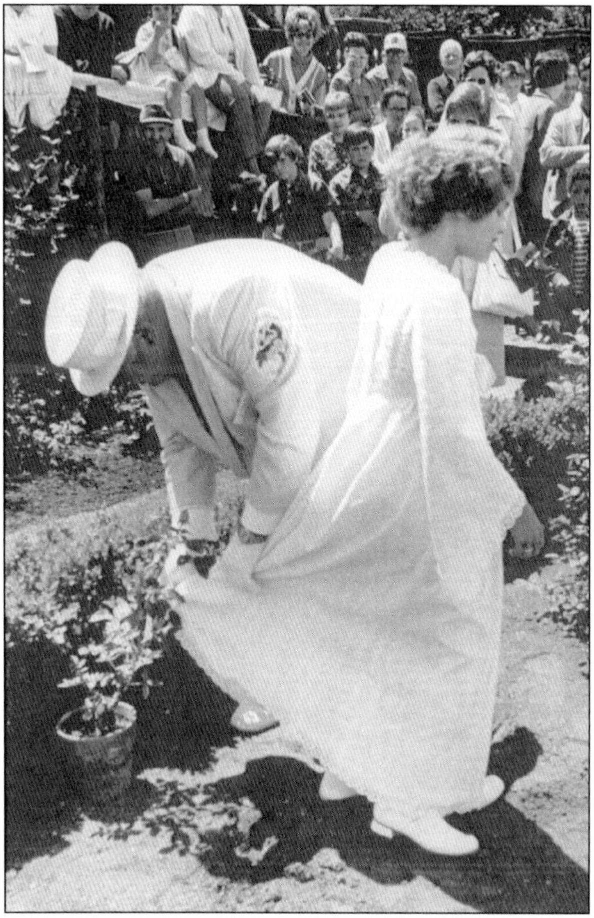

The Rose Festival junior queen got hung-up during the annual rose planting and honorary knighting ceremony in Peninsula Park in 1973. She was quickly aided by Rosarian Cebert Bryan. (Courtesy Oregon Historical Society; OrgLot431,B15,F3; the *Oregonian*.)

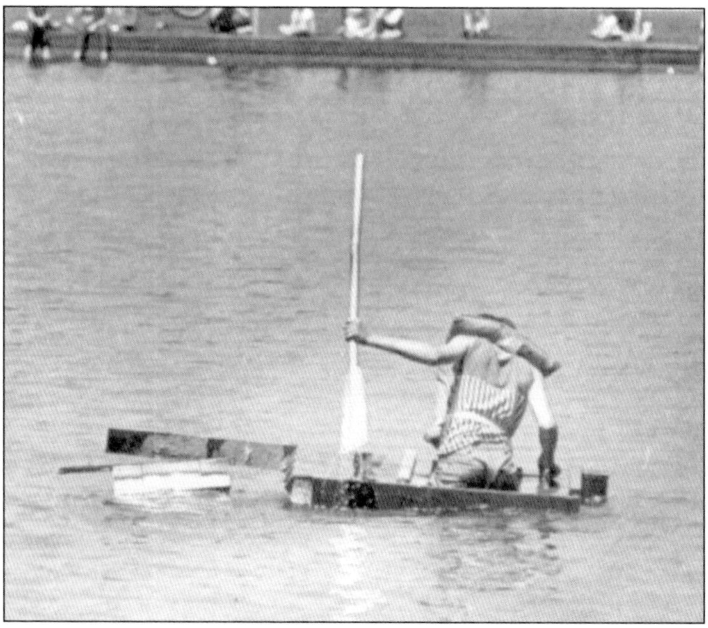

At Westmoreland Park, participants in the annual Milk Carton Boat Races risked getting wet as they piloted their homemade vessels made primarily from empty milk cartons across the casting pond. Nobody minded, as the temperature that day, June 5, was a warm 88 degrees. (Courtesy Oregon Historical Society; OrgLot431,B15,F5; the *Oregonian*.)

The weather in early June 1974 was cool and cloudy. On Friday, June 7, the Festival Center opened with a high temperature of 67 degrees and a trace of rain. However, the weather quickly changed, and Portland entered a heat wave (or as close to one as Pacific Northwest cities can ever get) as temperatures rose well into the mid-80s. At the Milk Carton Boat Races in Westmoreland Park on Tuesday, June 11, it was reported that 200 gallons of vanilla ice cream, four gallons of chocolate topping, three gallons of whipped cream, and five pounds of chocolate sprinkles were consumed. Hillman Lueddemann Jr., became the first second-generation president of the Rose Festival as his father had served as president in 1934, signing the Rose Festival's first Articles of Incorporation. (Courtesy Oregon Historical Society; OrHi93452.)

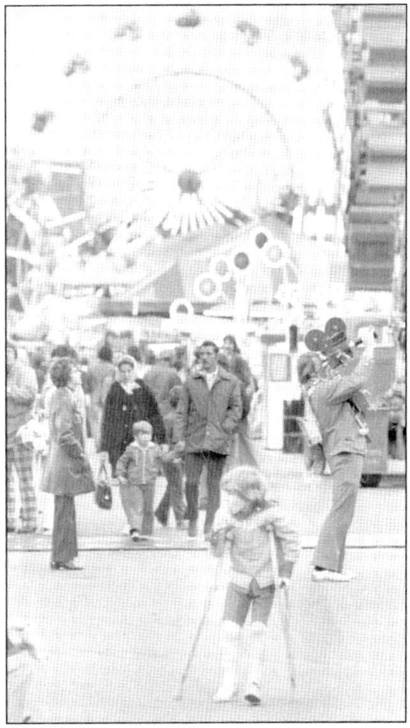

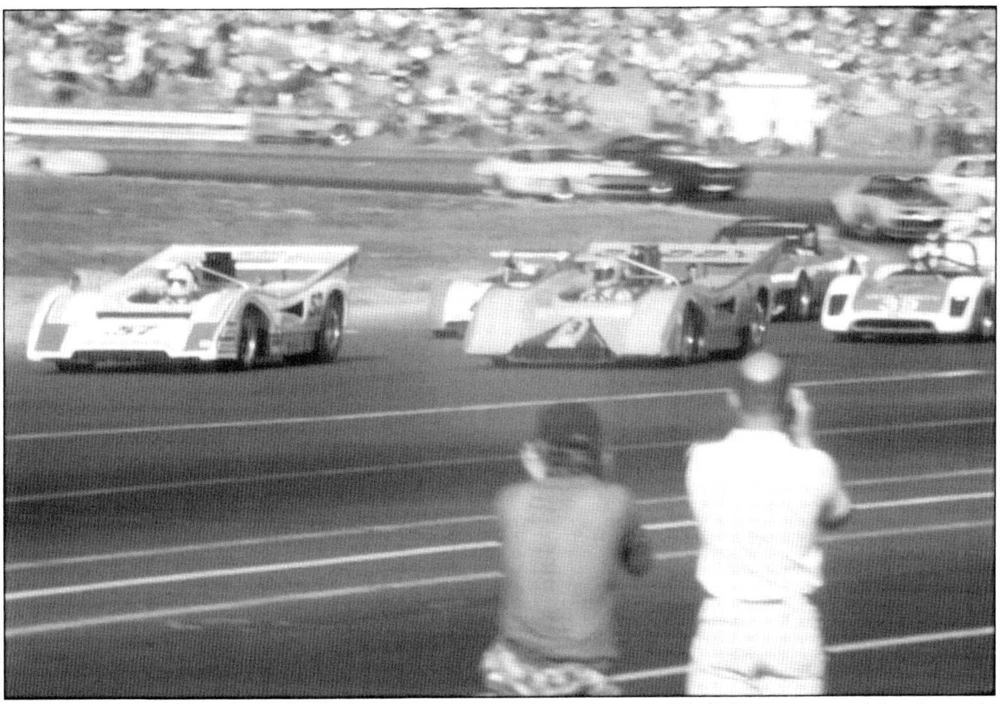

Auto races have been popular at the Rose Festival since Barney Oldfield set a record for the mile in Portland in June 1907. The Rose Cup Races, amateur races sponsored by the Sports Car Club of America, joined the festival lineup in 1961. In 1974, they enjoyed a large, appreciative audience. (Courtesy Portland Rose Festival Foundation.)

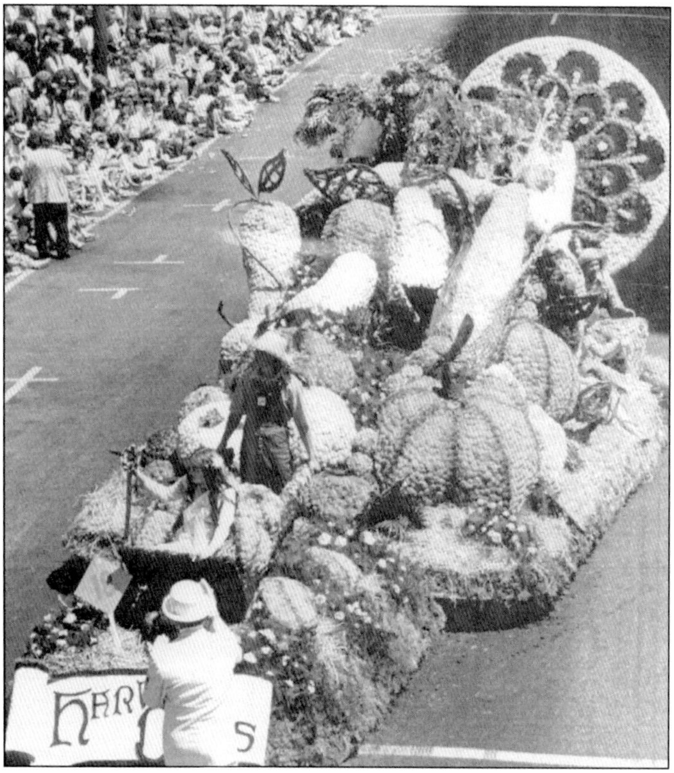

Weather-wise, 1975 was a repeat of 1974 for Rose Festival events. The first part of June saw temperatures into the low 90s. Most events experienced high temperatures in the 70s and 80s. For the Grand Floral Parade, the afternoon high reached 84 degrees; spectators waved fans, while some waved flags. Burl Ives was grand marshal of the Grand Floral Parade. The famous folk singer also appeared in concert at the Civic Auditorium and sang at the Veterans Hospital Wheelchair Parade on Wednesday. (Left, courtesy Portland Rose Festival Foundation; below, courtesy Oregon Historical Society; the *Oregonian*.)

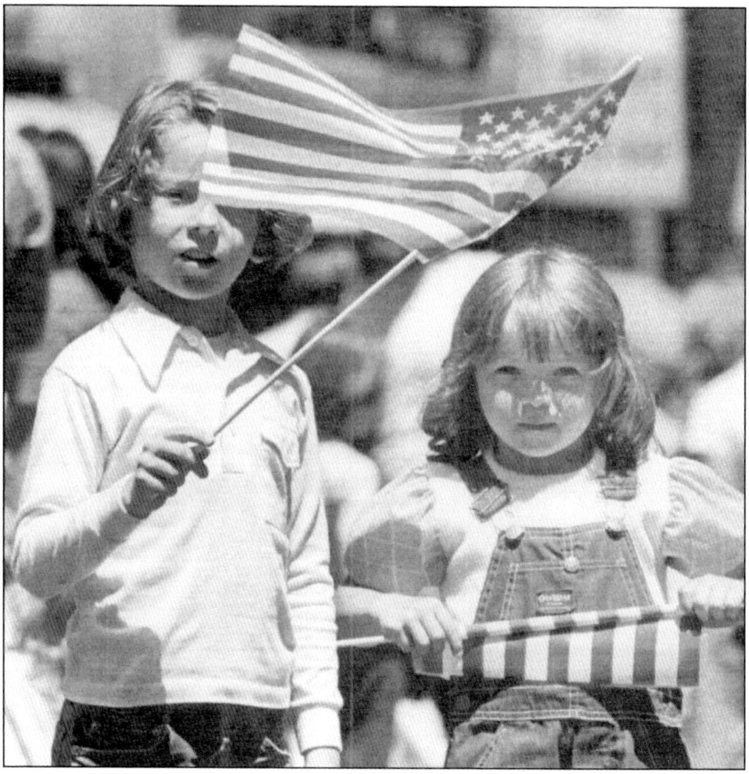

Eight

1976–1983
Multicolored Garden

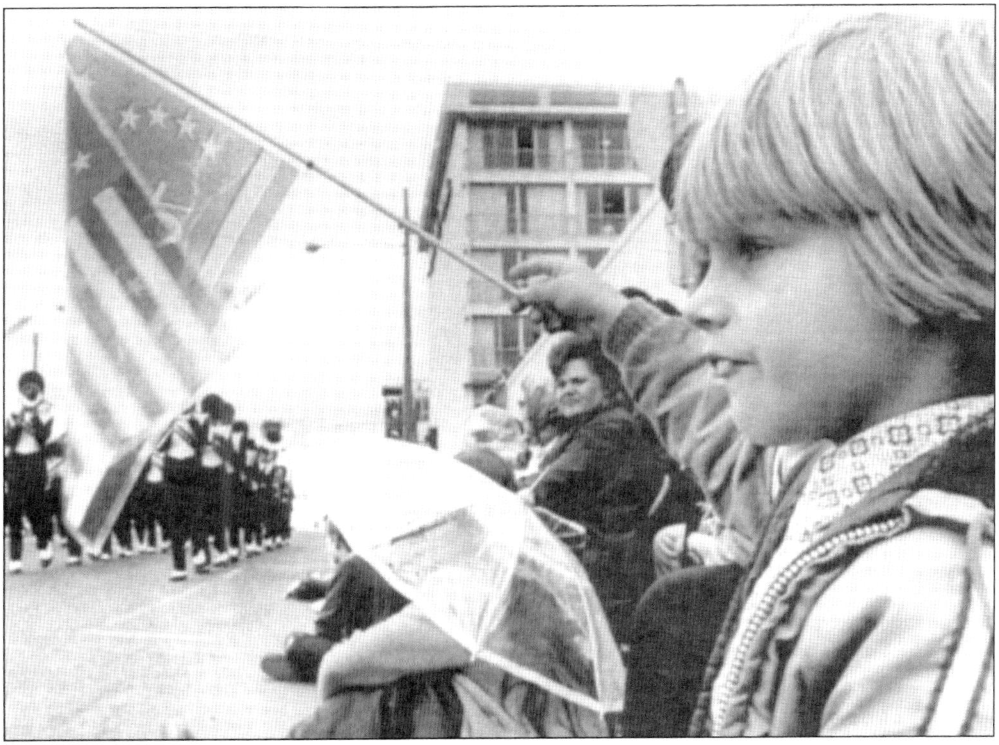

The Starlight Parade, honoring the bicentennial of the United States, was introduced in 1976, replacing the waterlogged Merrykhana Parade with a colorful salute to the red, white, and blue. Ole Jupiter Pluvius slightly dampened that event as well as the Junior Parade. Plastic covering was needed as a light rain fell intermittently during the parade. Two federal geologists, Dwight Crandall and Donald Mullineaux, predicted that Mount St. Helens in Southwest Washington could blow its top "today, tomorrow or anytime between now and the year 2000." (Courtesy Oregon Historical Society; OrgLot431,B15,F18.)

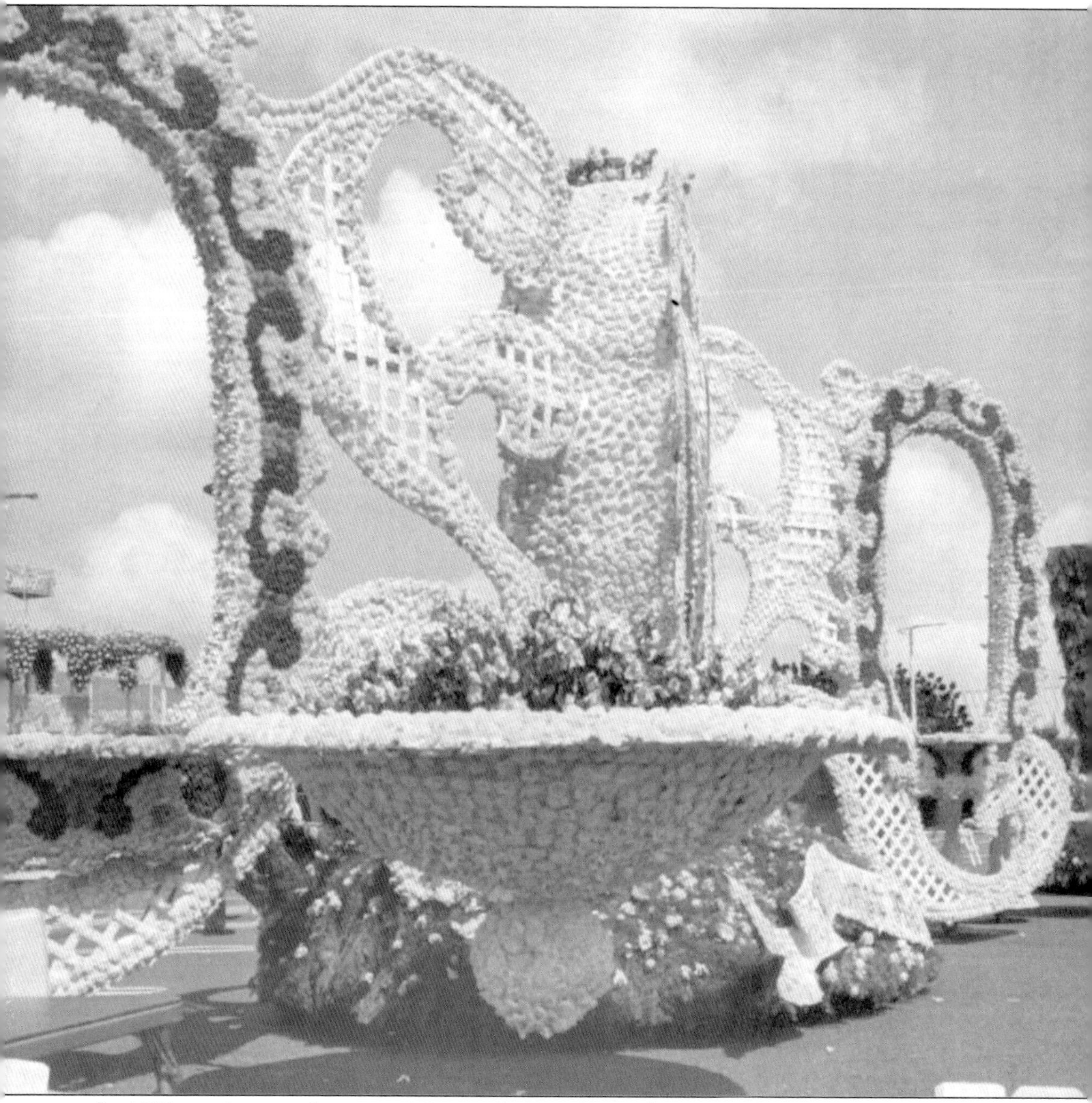

In 1977, another parade occurred during the Rose Festival, one not planned by festival officials. It was held Monday, June 6, for the Portland Trail Blazers professional basketball team. On Sunday, they defeated the Philadelphia 76ers for the NBA championship, 109 to 107. The Grand Floral Parade was held under cloudy skies with the sun breaking through at times. But it was not the weather of June that had Rose Festival officials concerned. It was the lack of rain during the winter of 1976 to 1977 that left little snowpack in the mountains. This resulted in very low water levels in both the Columbia and Willamette Rivers, which made travel treacherous for naval vessels coming to Portland for Rose Festival. (Courtesy Portland Rose Festival Foundation.)

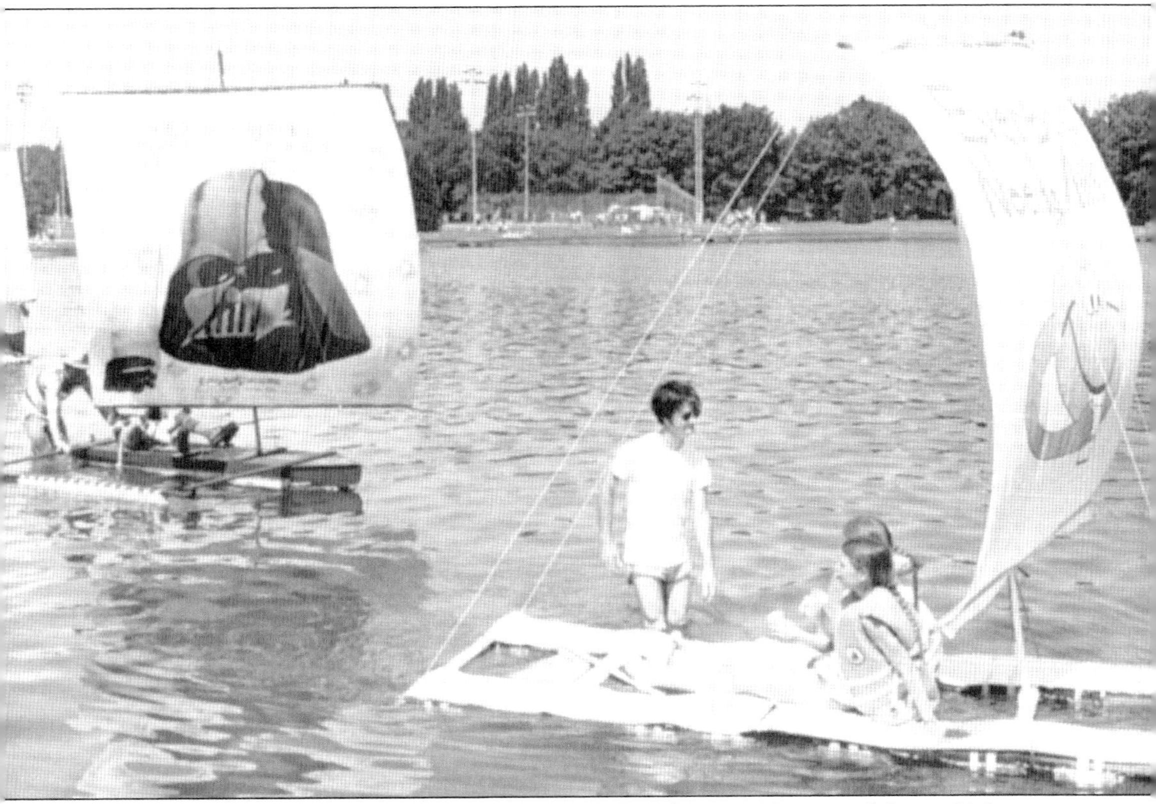

Over the years, the Milk Carton Boat Races got fancier and more sophisticated. It was 90 degrees on Sunday, June 4, 1978. A slight east wind filled the colorful sails of some of the participants. (Courtesy Oregon Historical Photograph Archives; the *Oregonian*.)

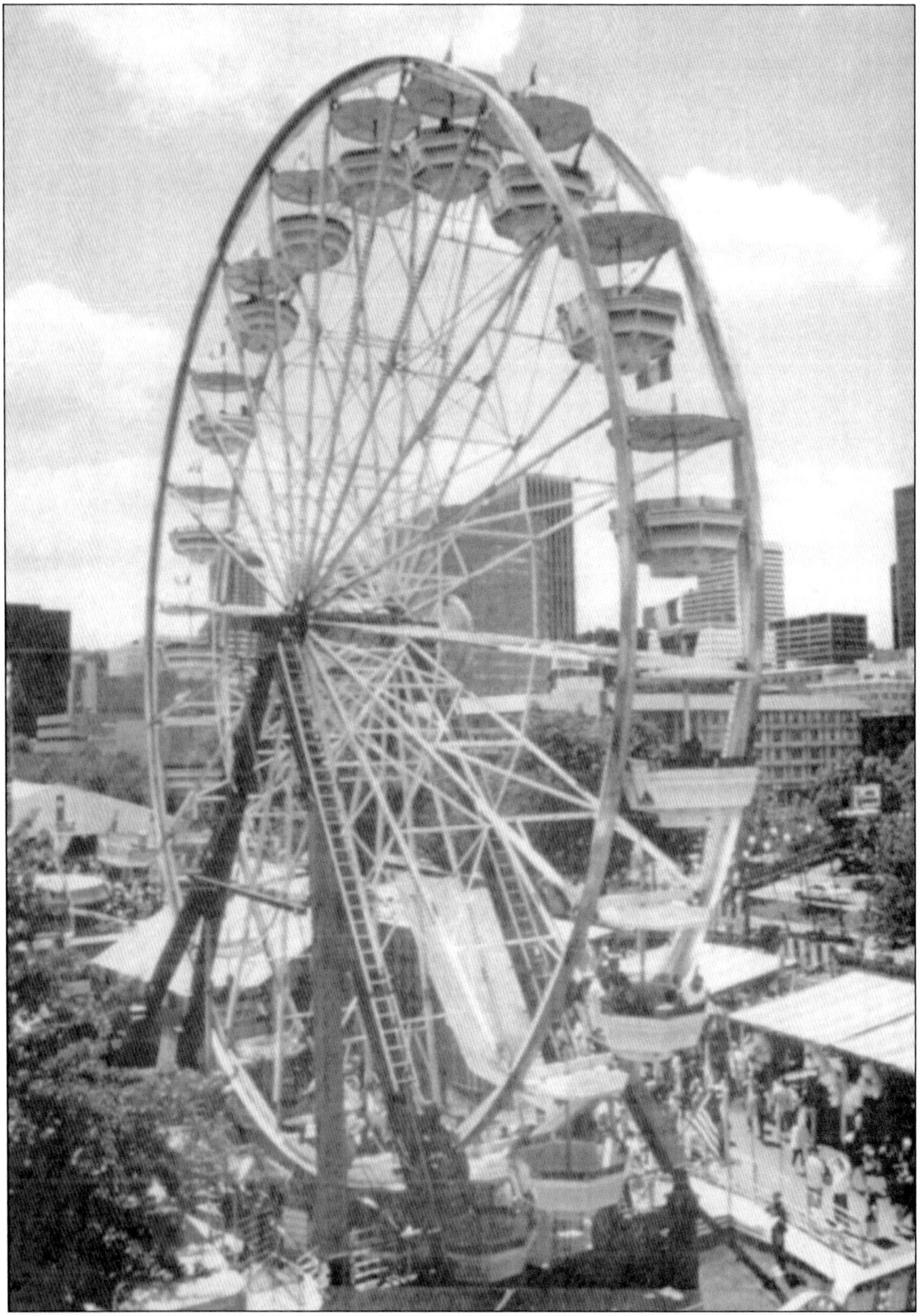

Over the years, the Festival Fun Center occupied several locations. Originally in the South Park Blocks, it moved to the Holladay Park area east of the Willamette River and then to Waterfront Park. It often has the distinction of holding the key to Rose Festival financial success, drawing large crowds of young people and grown-ups. (Courtesy Portland Rose Festival Foundation.)

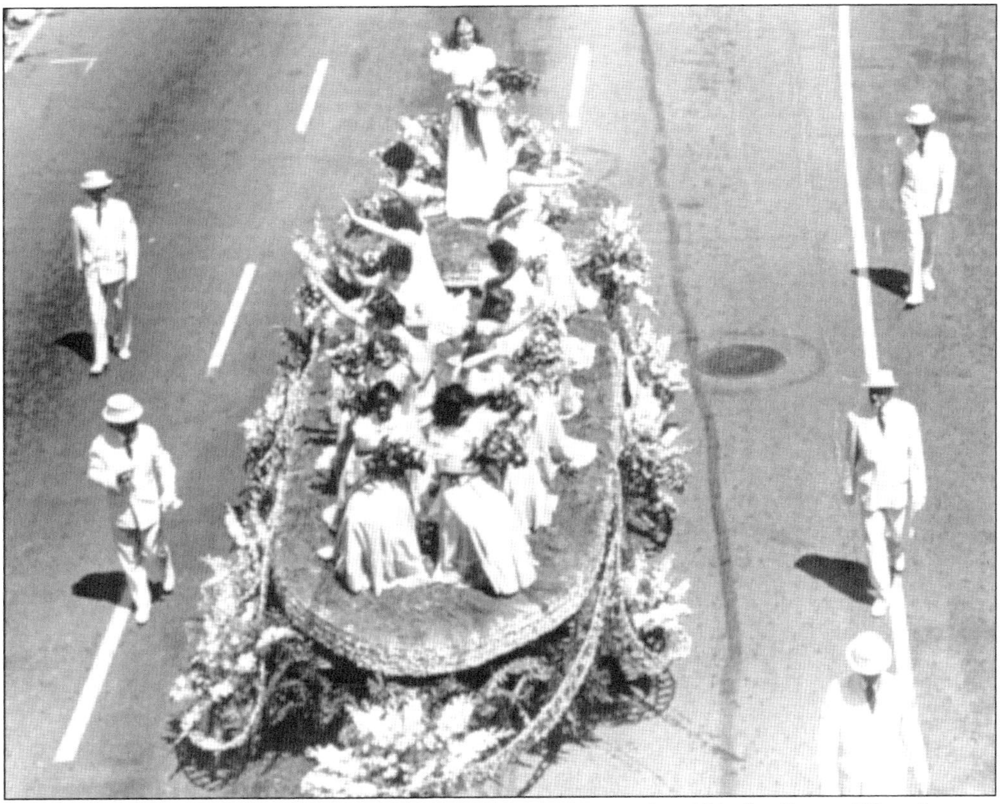

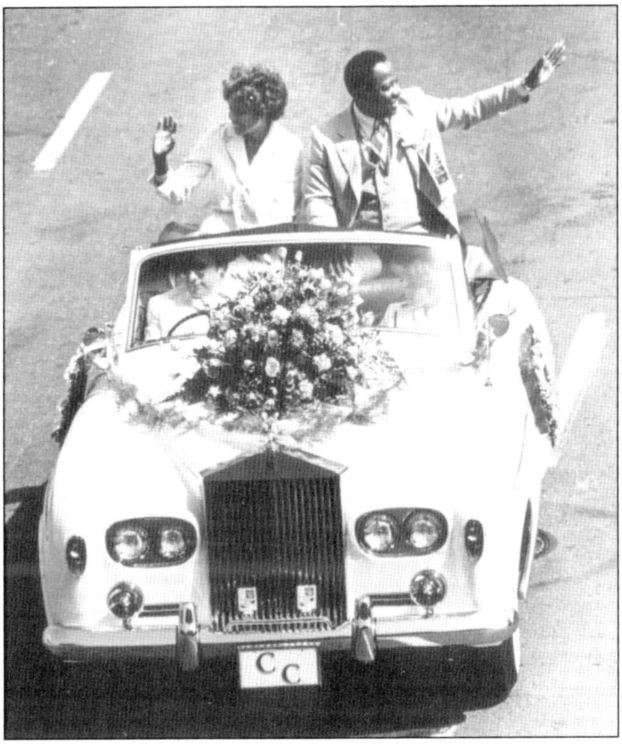

In 1979, the Festival Fun Center opened to sunny skies and a high temperature of 92 degrees. Ice cream and cold beverages were in demand. The theme of the Grand Floral Parade was "World Records on Parade." Queen Rochelle Anderson and her princesses were flanked by Royal Rosarians as their float made its way down the street. Rochelle's sister Rhonda served as the Rose Festival queen in 1969. The grand marshal of the parade was Hank Aaron, reigning Major League Baseball home run leader. In ceremonies in Washington Park, he was officially knighted on Friday, June 8. At some gas stations in Portland, gas reached 99.9¢ per gallon. (Above, courtesy Oregon Historical Society, OrHi67169; left, courtesy Oregon Historical Society, OrHi67151.)

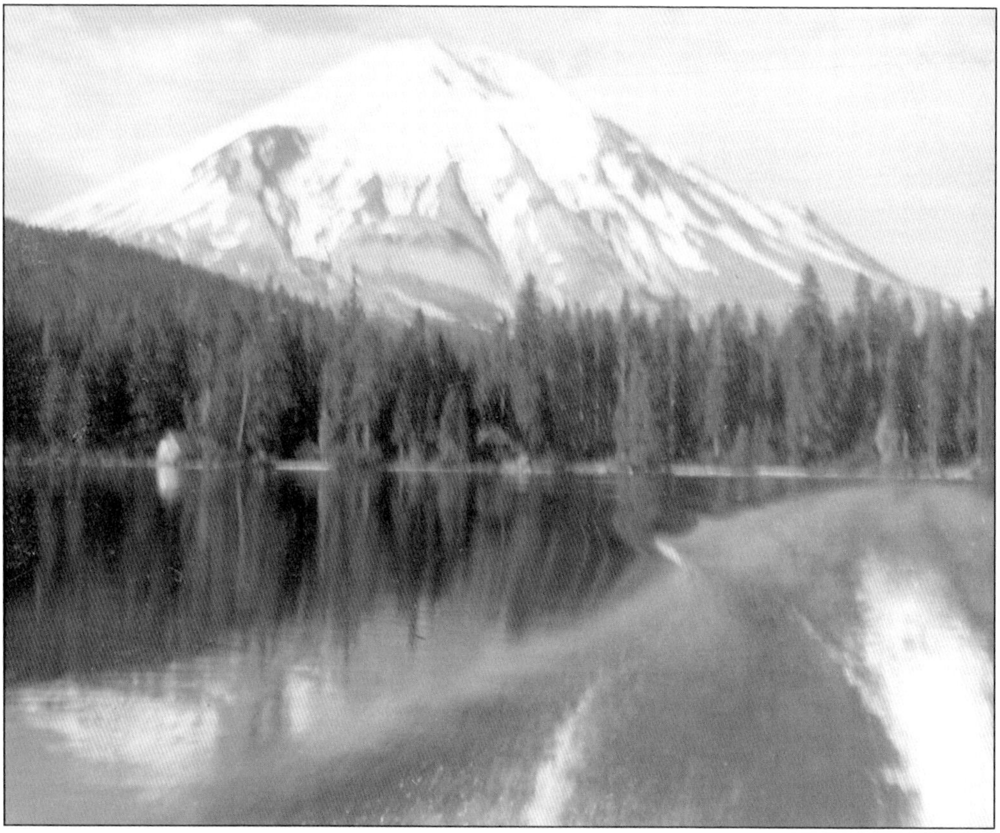

On May 18, 1980, the beautiful Mount St. Helens in Southwest Washington erupted. The original eruption sent ash clouds over all of Eastern Washington and farther east into Idaho, Montana, and the Midwest. Logs and debris from the eruption flowed down the Toutle River, into the Cowlitz River, and then into the Columbia River, raising concerns whether the Rose Festival Fleet would be able to navigate the river. Dredges, working 24 hours a day, eventually cleared the mud and debris. (Both, courtesy the author.)

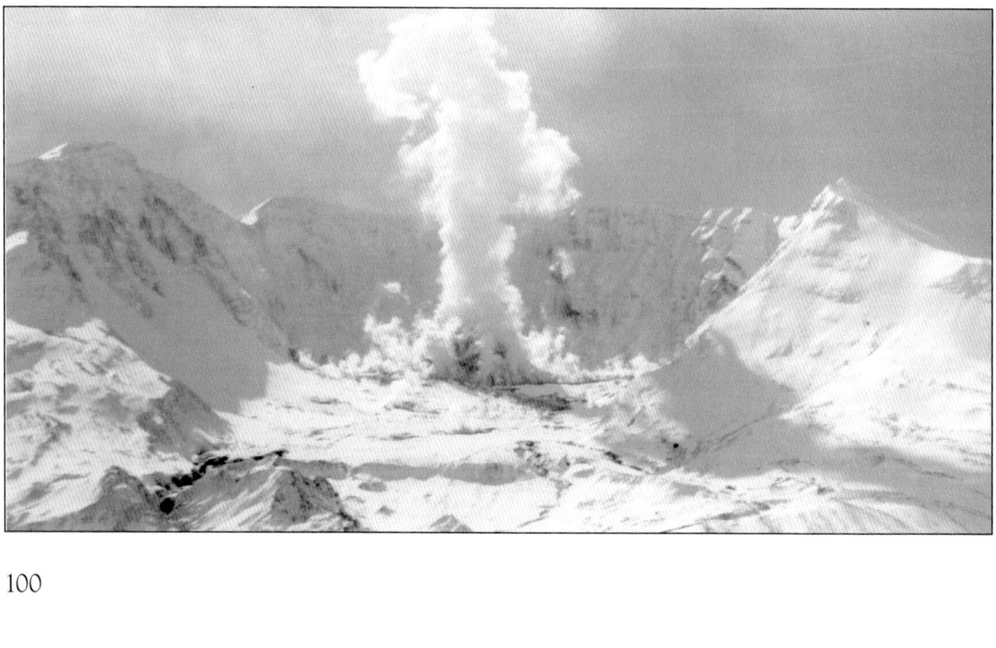

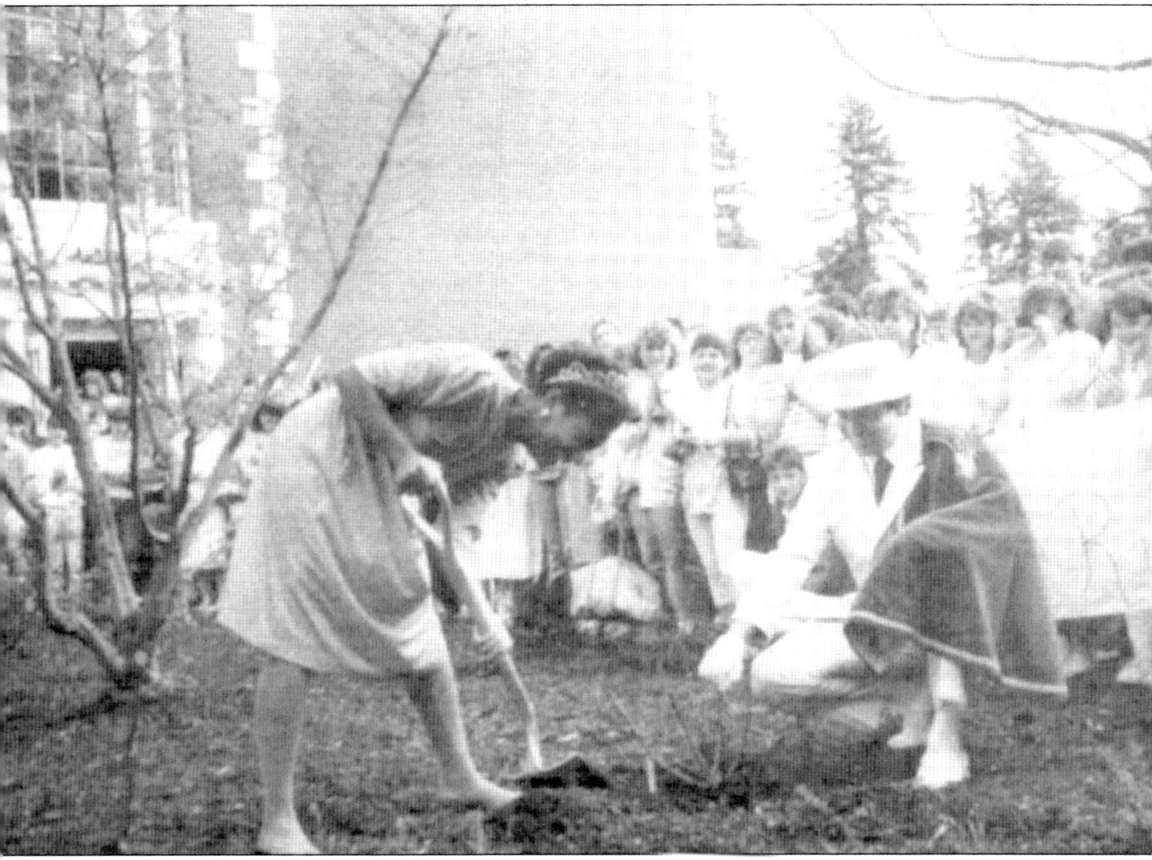

Once more, questions were raised about whether the Rose Festival should be held. It went on, including events like this traditional Rose Planting Ceremony to honor Rose Festival's first African American queen, Robin Marks. Marks would go on to be the Fiesta Bowl queen while attending college in Arizona. Smaller eruptions continued, and one occurred just days before the Grand Floral Parade, sending a cloud of ash toward the Portland area under northeast winds. On Friday, the knighting ceremony was moved from Washington Park to the basement of the Marriott Hotel because of the threat of both rain and falling ash. Attendance at the parade itself was estimated at just over half of the prior year, and many viewers showed up along the route wearing masks. City crews had worked throughout the night to clear the worst of the wet ash from the streets. (Courtesy Oregon Historical Society; OrgLot850,B8,F6.)

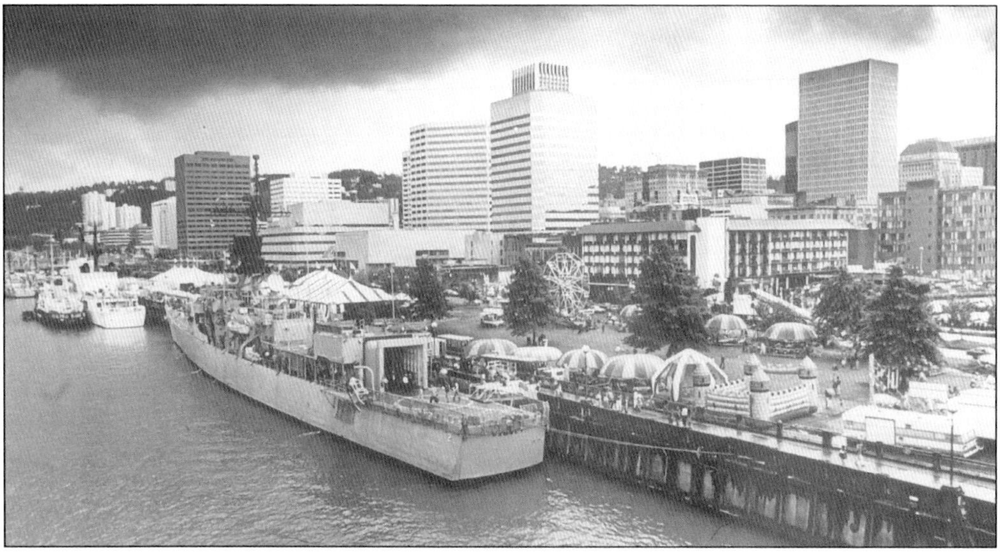

The 1981 festival offered a different twist. The Royal Rosarians sponsored a church service to "call God's blessing on the Portland Rose Festival." It was believed to be the first such event since World War II. The service, in cooperation with Portland-area Lutheran churches, began at 1:30 p.m. on Saturday, May 30, at Peace Lutheran Church on North Portland Boulevard. The 170-voice Portland Lutheran Choral Association provided the music. June 1981 was as wet as a Portland June can get. Rainfall totaled 3.73 inches for the month, and measurable rain fell on 19 days out of the month. Dark clouds hovered over the festival. (Courtesy Oregon Historical Society; OrHi67177.)

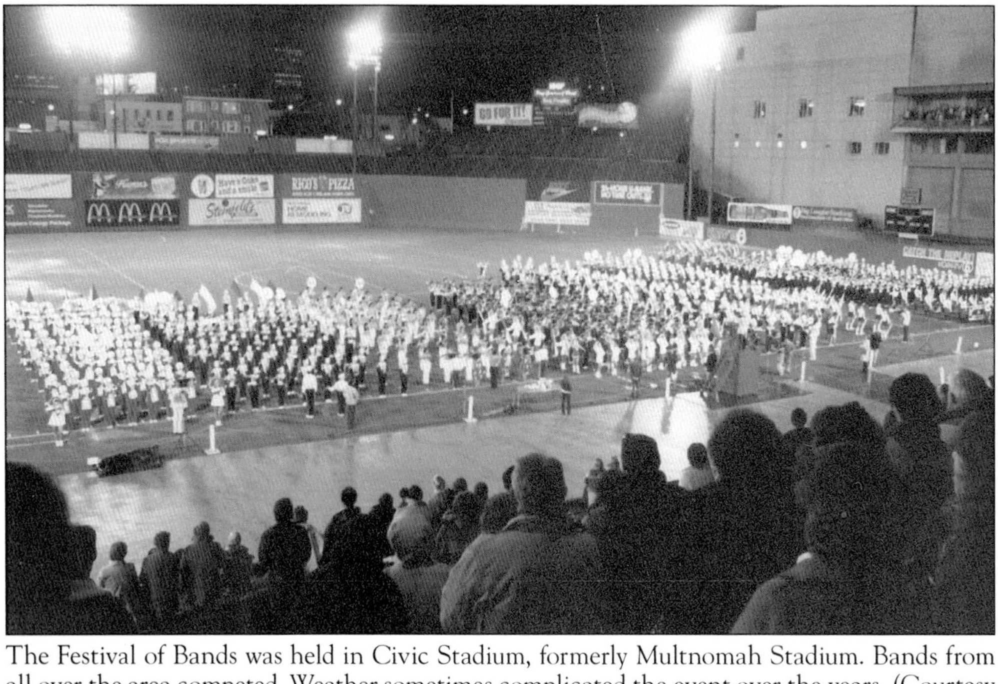

The Festival of Bands was held in Civic Stadium, formerly Multnomah Stadium. Bands from all over the area competed. Weather sometimes complicated the event over the years. (Courtesy Oregon Historical Society; OrgLot850,B8,F3.)

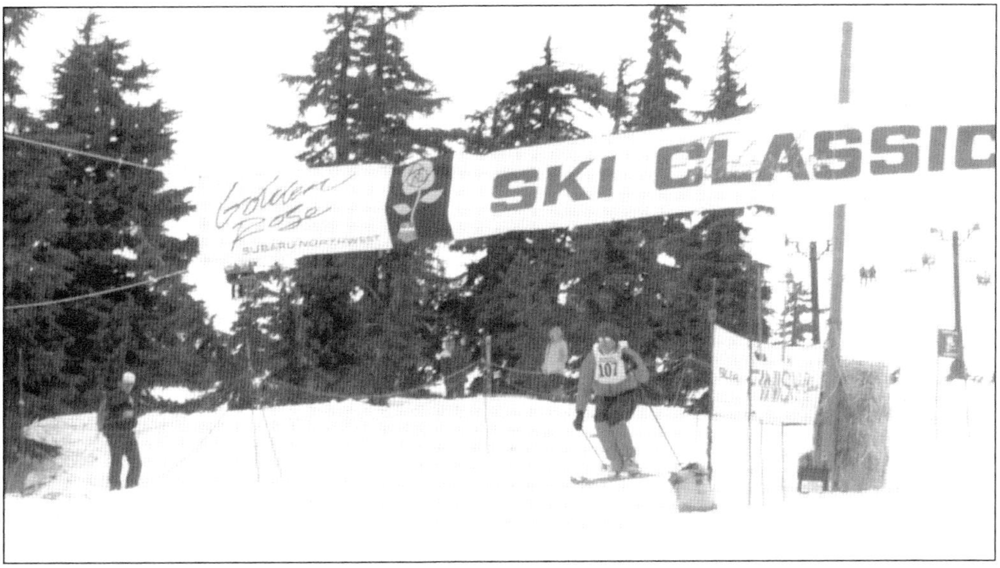

Perhaps a noted television weather forecaster could change things for the 1982 Rose Festival. Willard Scott from NBC's *Today Show* was selected to serve as grand marshal of the Grand Floral Parade. He did not have much luck for the start of the Fun Center, which opened on Friday, June 4. One-third inch of rain fell that day, and it was a chilly 61 degrees. (Oregon Historical Society; OrgLot850, B10, F14.)

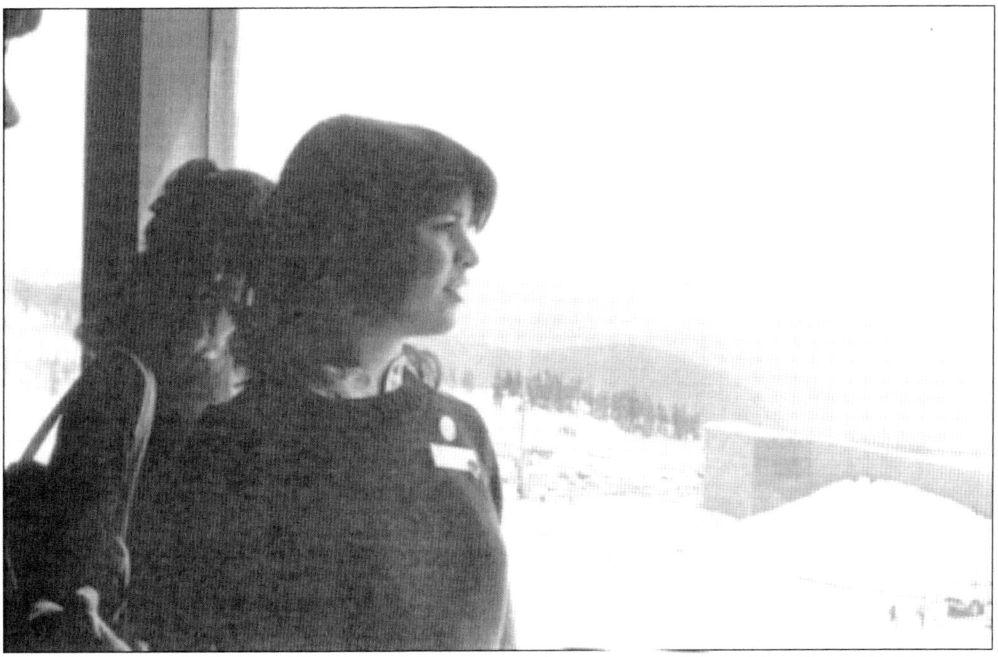

When the Rose Festival Court visited Mount Hood for the annual Golden Rose Ski Races on Saturday, June 5, visibility ranged from good to lousy. The Junior Parade escaped the rain on Wednesday, but the Grand Floral Parade on Saturday, June 12, did not. A half-inch of rain fell on Portland that day. The rain might have been blamed on Scott, but a more likely cause was the author George Miller's return to Portland as meteorologist in charge of the National Weather Service Forecast Office. (Oregon Historical Society; OrgLot850, B8, F12.)

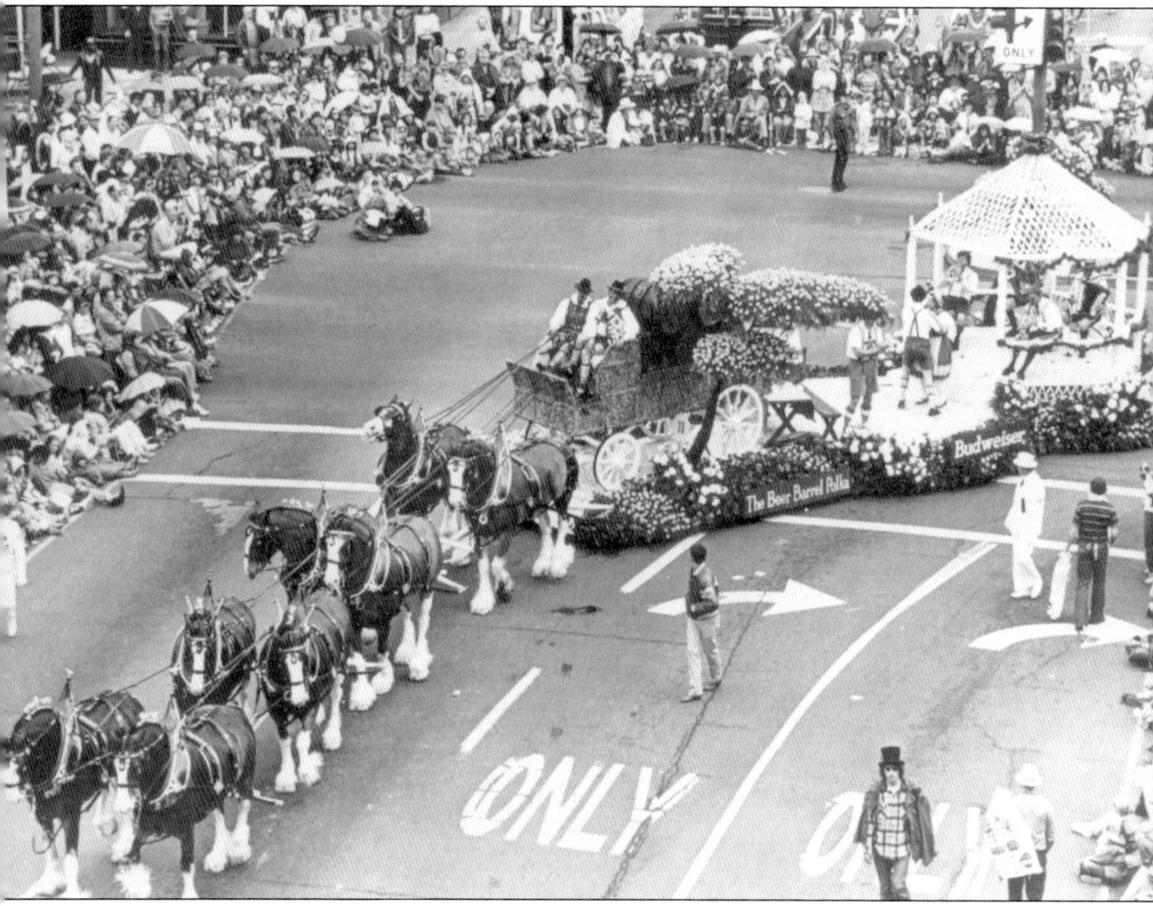

The famous Clydesdales have been a welcome entry in the Portland Rose Festival for many years. These gentle giants march rain or shine. In 1982, questions were raised about the location of the Fun Center at Waterfront Park. In an unscientific survey, a majority of 126 responses indicated the event should be relocated. Thirty years later, the Fun Center—now known as Rose Festival CityFair—still occupies its home in Waterfront Park. Respondents also indicated that the Rose Festival Court should be expanded to high schools outside Portland, which finally happened in 2009. (Courtesy Oregon Historical Society; OrHi67153.)

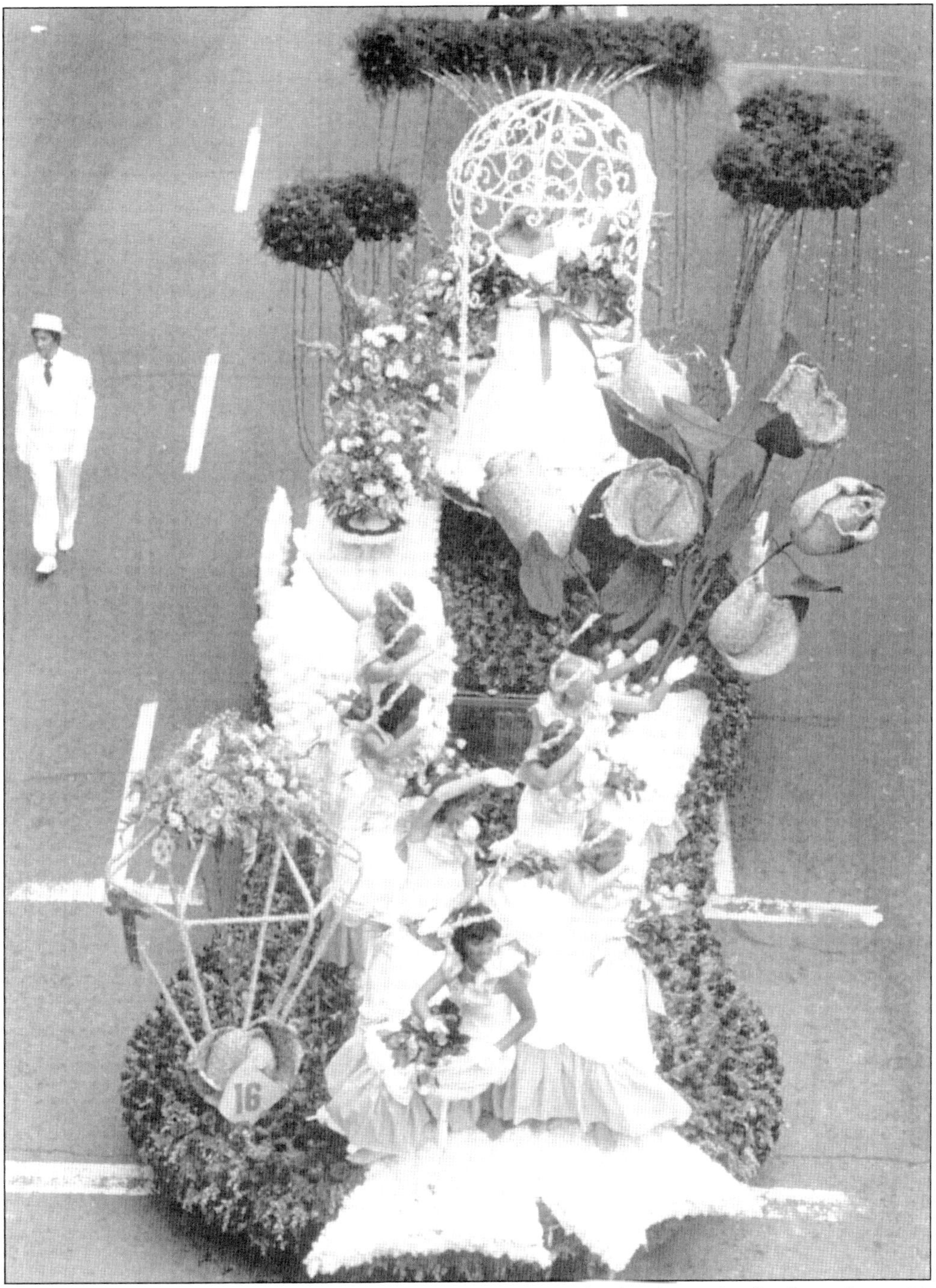

The year 1983 marked the Silver Jubilee of the Rose Festival. The theme for the festival was, "A Backward Glance . . . A Future Dream." Rose Festival officials had experienced three years of net losses due to factors outside their control, including the weather and the eruption of Mount St. Helens. They were looking ahead to much rosier conditions in 1983. It was cloudy for the Grand Floral Parade, but despite the threat of rain, attendance was high. (Courtesy Portland Rose Festival Foundation.)

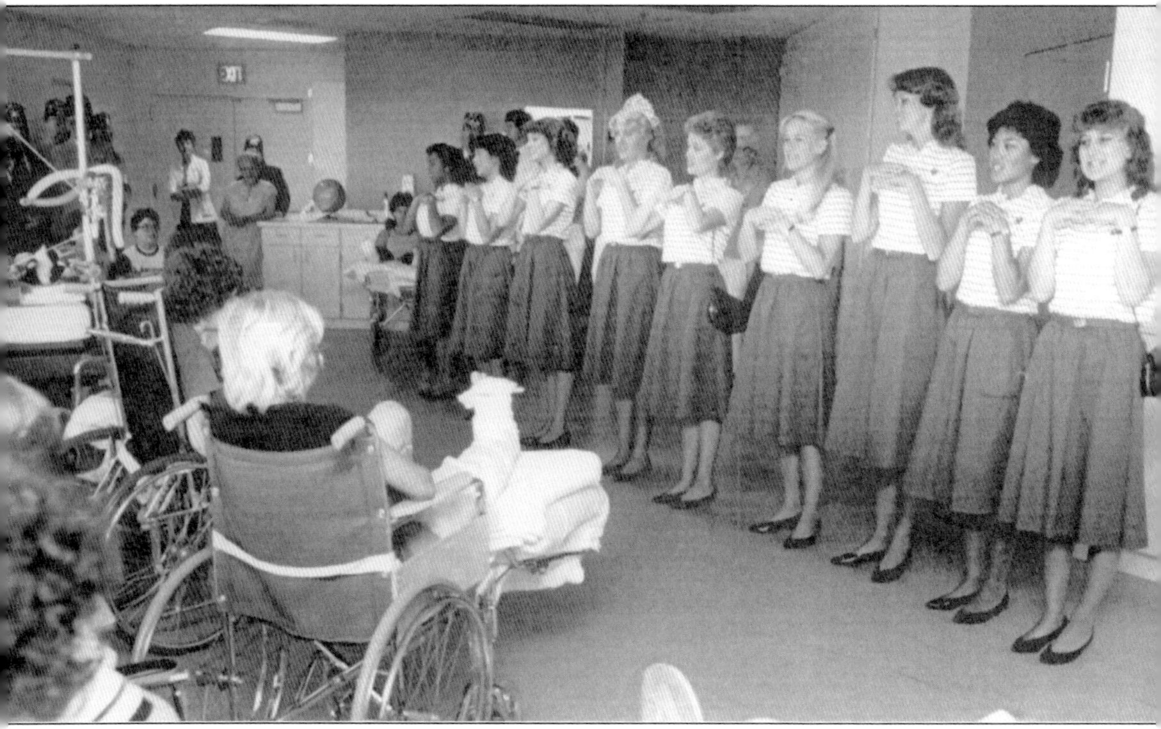

In 1983, the Rose Festival Court, led by Queen Kira Rembold (wearing crown), made its annual visit to the Shriners Hospital for Children. The Fun Center opened on Friday, June 3, under mostly sunny skies. It was a balmy evening for the Starlight Parade on Saturday. The Junior Parade enjoyed an 80-degree day. Clouds and a little light rain returned for the Grand Floral Parade, but it did not dampen the attendance. One citizen at the parade remarked, "I think the rain bothers the parade committee more than it does the public." (Courtesy Portland Rose Festival Foundation.)

Nine

1984–2000

Zoom, Zoom, Zoom!

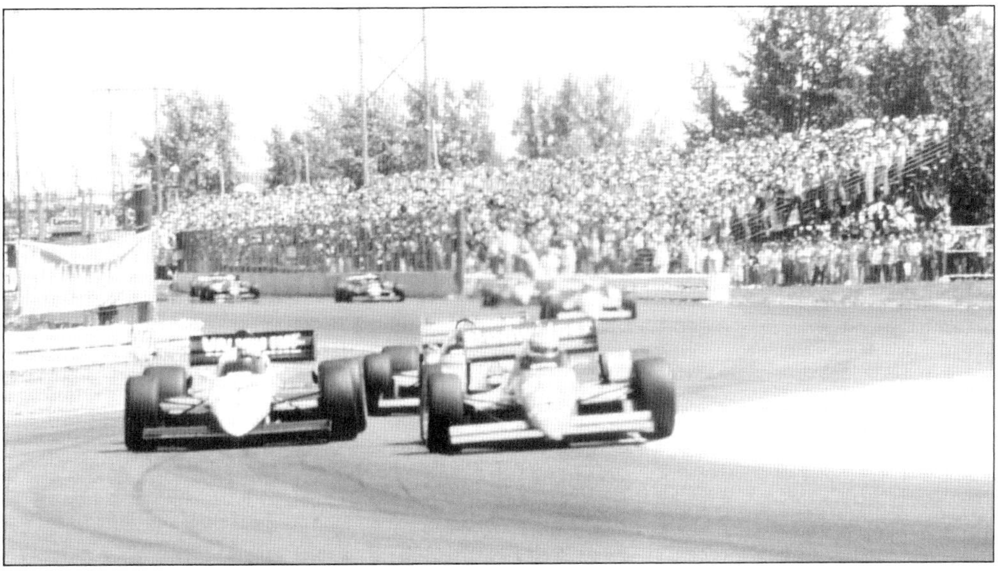

The year 1984 was a milestone for the Rose Festival. Years of negotiations paid off when the first Indy-car race came to town, the GI Joe's 200, produced by the organization Championship Auto Racing Teams. This mega-event was to pump millions of dollars into the Portland economy and was an important financial engine (pun intended) for the Rose Festival for many years, just as soon as a seven-figure loan from the City of Portland was paid off. The loan was for track improvements to Portland International Raceway, which had to be significantly upgraded to host the world-class auto race. The race would remain a major Rose Festival event through 2007, by then known as the Champ Car Grand Prix. Over the course of the event's history, racing giants like Al Unser Jr. and Mario Andretti regularly came to Portland with their respective race teams. Although 1984 was the fourth year in a row that some rain dampened the Grand Floral Parade, mostly sunny weather prevailed for the races. (Courtesy Portland Rose Festival Foundation.)

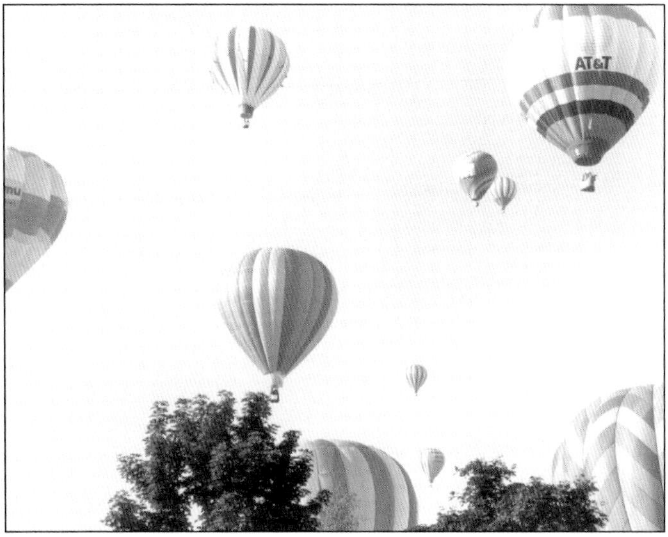

The inaugural Hot Air Balloon Classic was also held in 1984. The event was often staged in Delta Park in North Portland. A "night glow" activity was a popular feature of this event, with balloons tethered to the ground and lit from within by their burners. One year, the night glow was held at Waterfront Park and another year it was staged inside Civic Stadium. The City of Tigard now holds the Tigard Festival of Balloons. (Courtesy Oregon Historical Society; OrgLot850, B9, F8.)

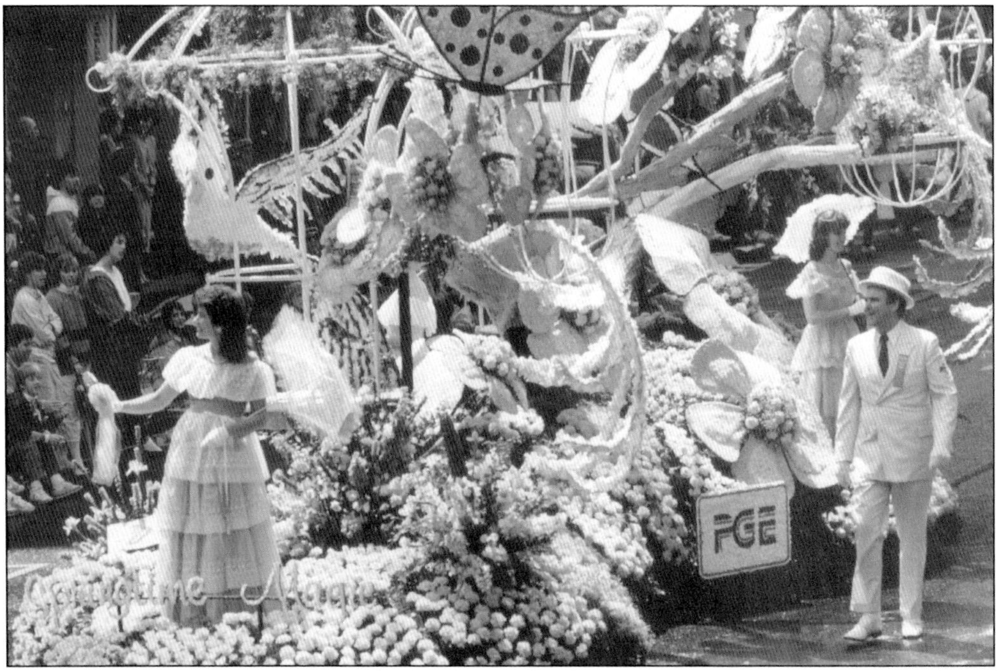

In 1985, congratulations were in order for the Portland Rose Festival. It made the top 25 list of North America's "super events" with a number 22 rating. That placed it ahead of such notable events as the World Series, Cheyenne Frontier Days, and the Calgary Stampede. The festival definitely had come a long way since that first event in 1907. The PGE float was one of the more spectacular entries. Portland General Electric is the longest-running sponsor of the Portland Rose Festival, participating with floats in the first Grand Floral Parades. (Courtesy Oregon Historical Society; OrgLot850, B9, F8.)

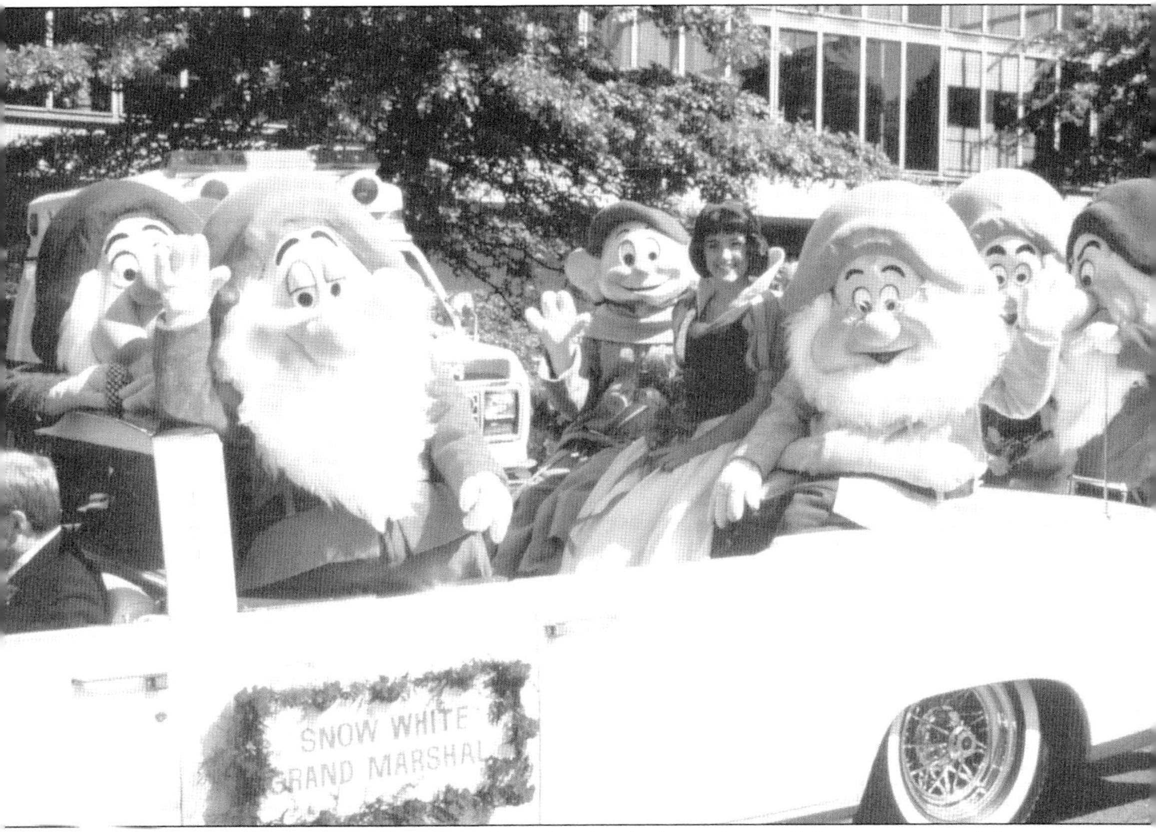

In 1987, the Fun Center opened on May 29 under cloudy skies. Rain fell that evening and during most of the day on Saturday, June 30, but quit just in time for the Starlight Parade. The Starlight grand marshal was Libby Riddles, the first woman to win the Iditarod Trail Sled Race. After the Starlight Parade, Ole Jupiter Pluvius left town, and the temperature climbed to 91 degrees for the Junior Parade, nearly suffocating the grand marshal in the thick costume of comic strip cat Garfield. Snow White and the Seven Dwarfs were grand marshals of the 1987 Grand Floral Parade. They hold the record for the most hotel rooms ever used by a grand marshal, as there were two people for every dwarf costume, plus Snow White herself—totaling 15 hotel rooms. The weather had cooled down by parade day, but onlookers on the route still enjoyed 75-degree temperatures. (Courtesy Portland Rose Festival Foundation.)

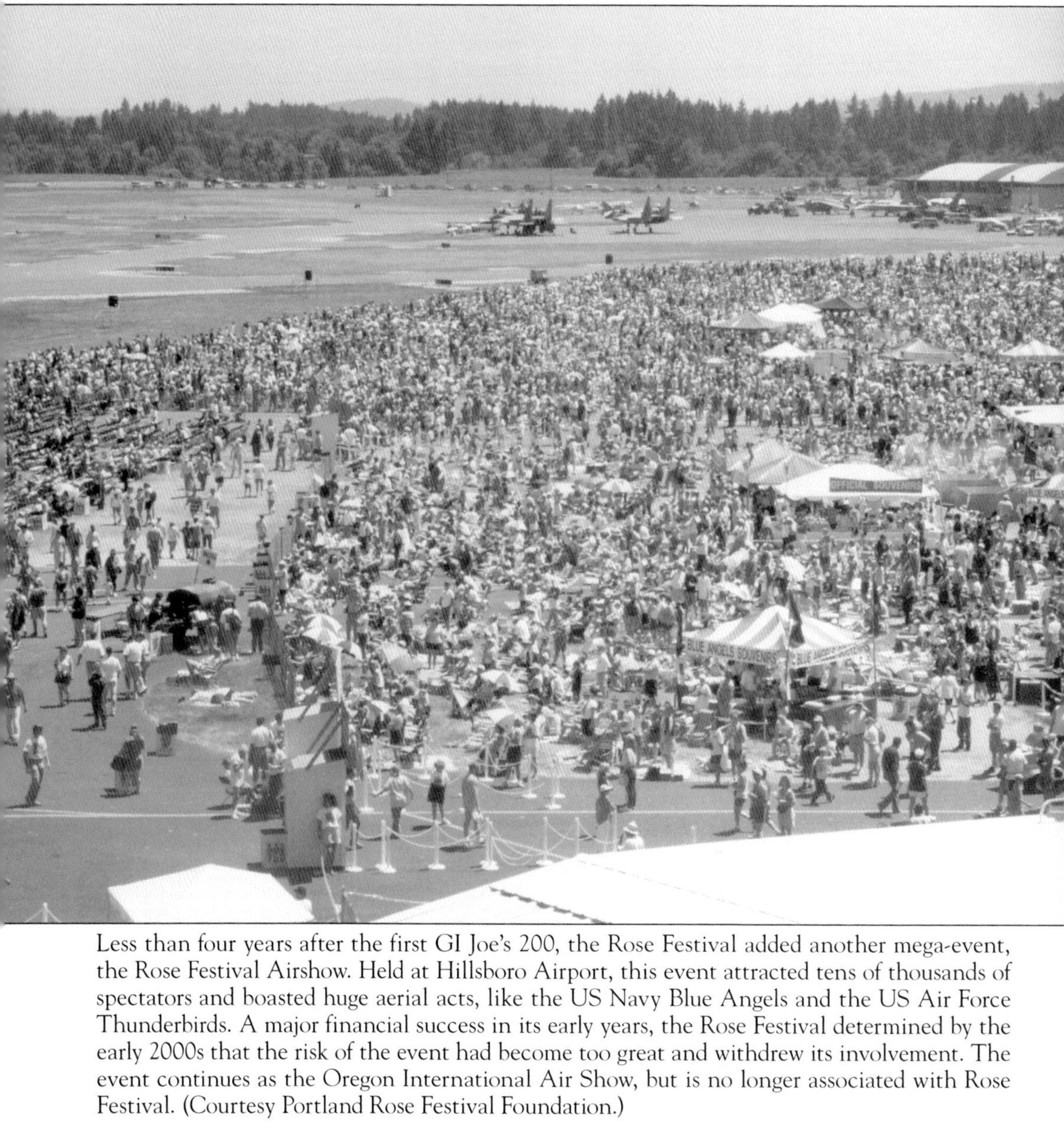

Less than four years after the first GI Joe's 200, the Rose Festival added another mega-event, the Rose Festival Airshow. Held at Hillsboro Airport, this event attracted tens of thousands of spectators and boasted huge aerial acts, like the US Navy Blue Angels and the US Air Force Thunderbirds. A major financial success in its early years, the Rose Festival determined by the early 2000s that the risk of the event had become too great and withdrew its involvement. The event continues as the Oregon International Air Show, but is no longer associated with Rose Festival. (Courtesy Portland Rose Festival Foundation.)

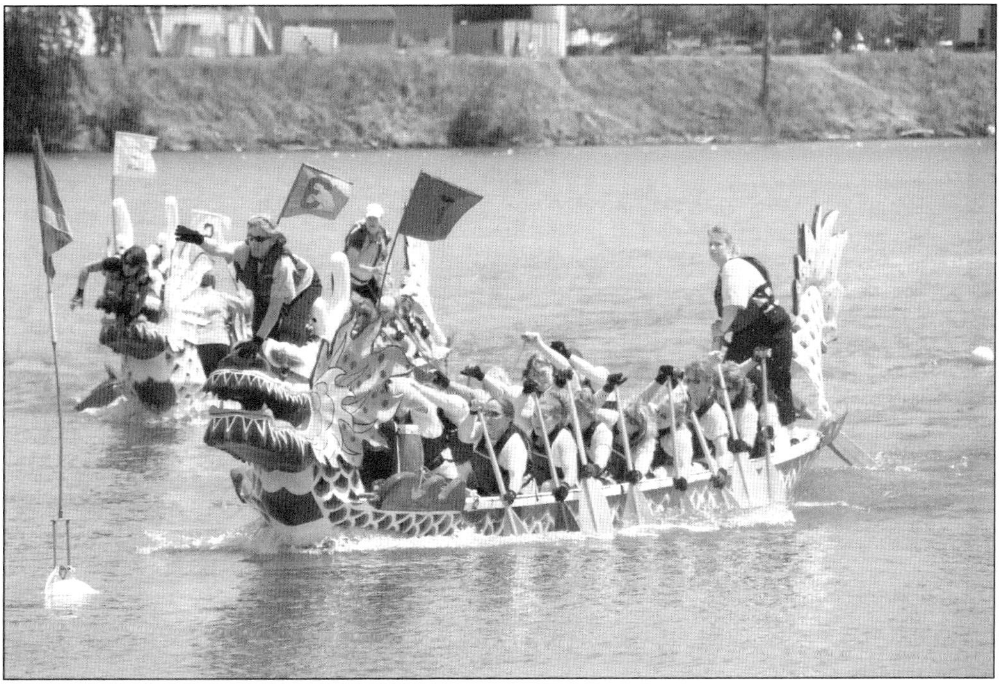

The Rose Festival Dragon Boat Race was added to the lineup in the late 1980s, quickly becoming one of the festival's most popular and colorful events. The event is produced by the Portland-Kaohsiung Sister City Association, which also participates with a float in the Grand Floral Parade. The Dragon Boat Race is held annually on the Willamette River, utilizing boats gifted to Portland by the city of Kaohsiung. Many of Portland's sister cities have been Rose Festival participants since the inception of the program in 1959, especially Sapporo, Japan, Portland's first official sister city. These international organizations are a mainstay of the international section in the Grand Floral Parade. (Both, courtesy Portland Rose Festival Foundation.)

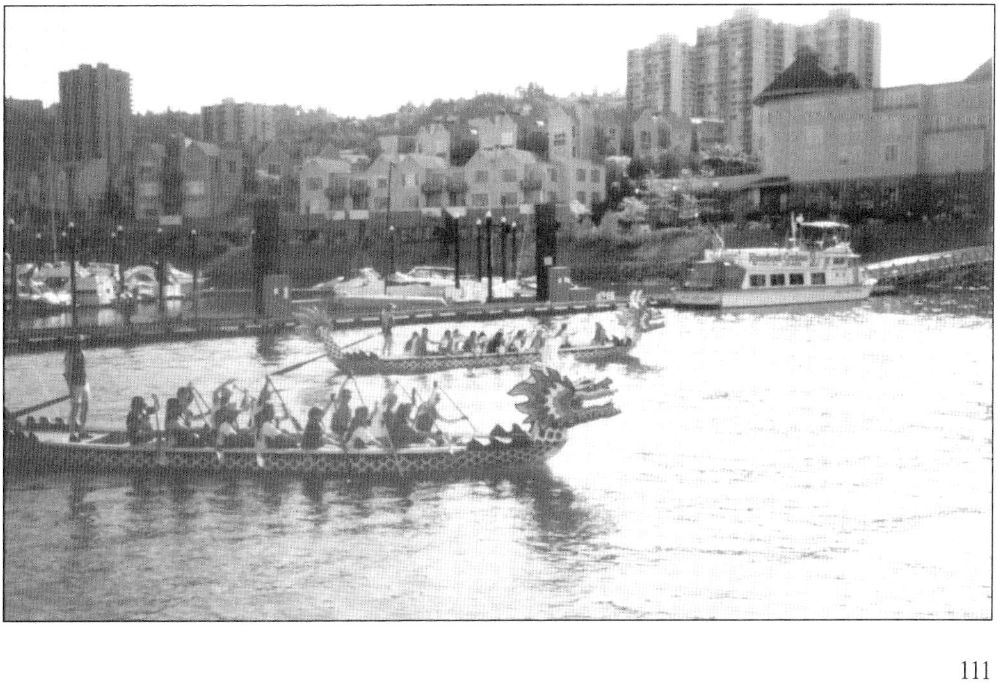

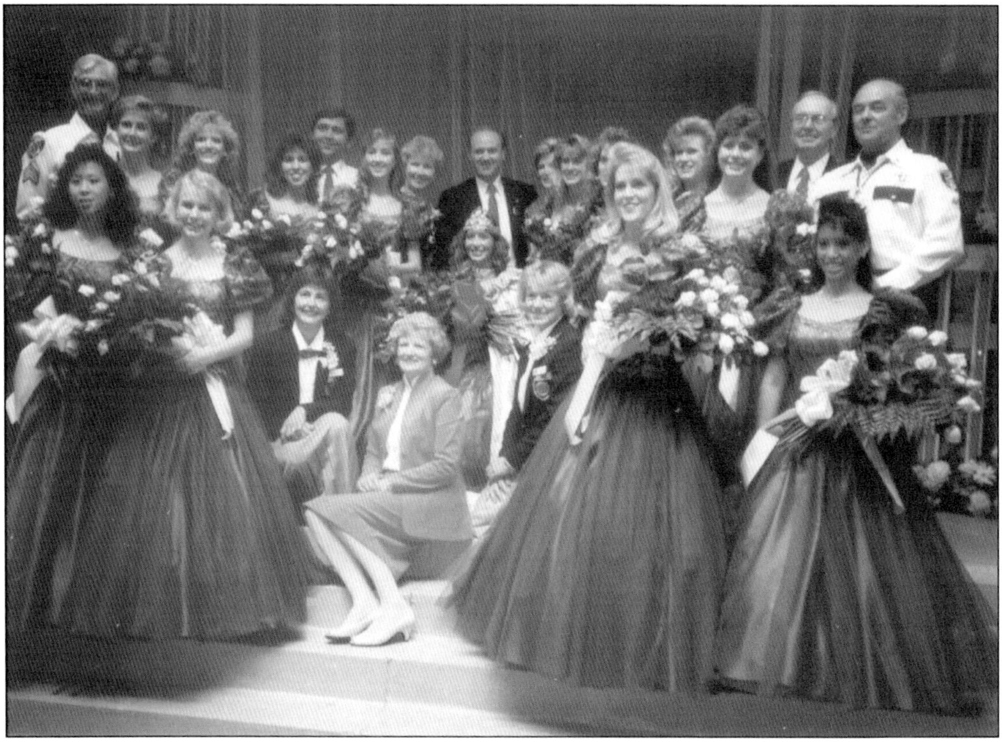

Over the years, the queen's Coronation was held in many different venues, including Laurelhurst Park, Multnomah Stadium, and the Veterans Memorial Coliseum. During the late 1980s and 1990s, the queen's Coronation alternated between Keller Auditorium and the Arlene Schnitzer Concert Hall, where it was unaffected by the weather. An elaborate stage production, the event was telecast live on television until 2005. Kelly Manning (center), the 1988 queen, is pictured with court chairman Myron Child, surrounded by her princesses and chaperones and other news and sound people. (Both, courtesy Portland Rose Festival Foundation.)

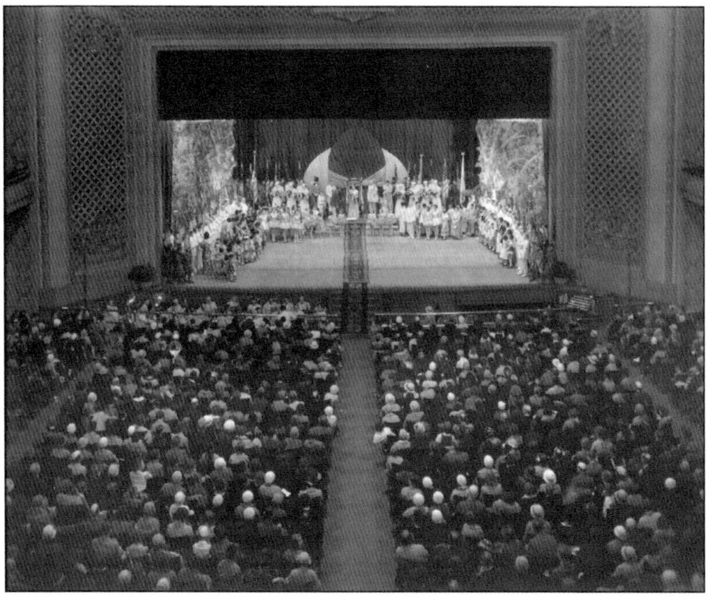

In the early 1990s, public grumbling about the Rose Festival Court precipitated the Portland School Board asking for a significant study of the program. The 1994 Rose Festival queen, Joy Lawrence (pictured with KOIN-TV anchor Eric Schmidt), went a long way toward quieting the noise, since Lawrence had served as the place kicker for the Lincoln High School football team. (Courtesy Portland Rose Festival Foundation.)

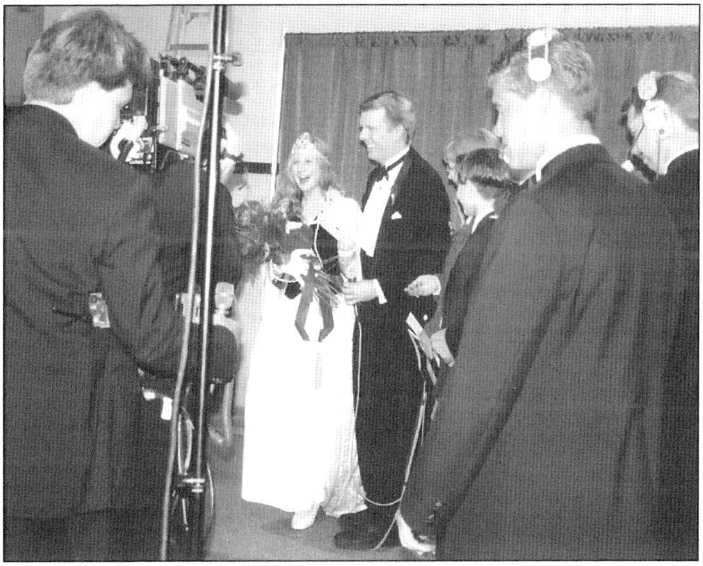

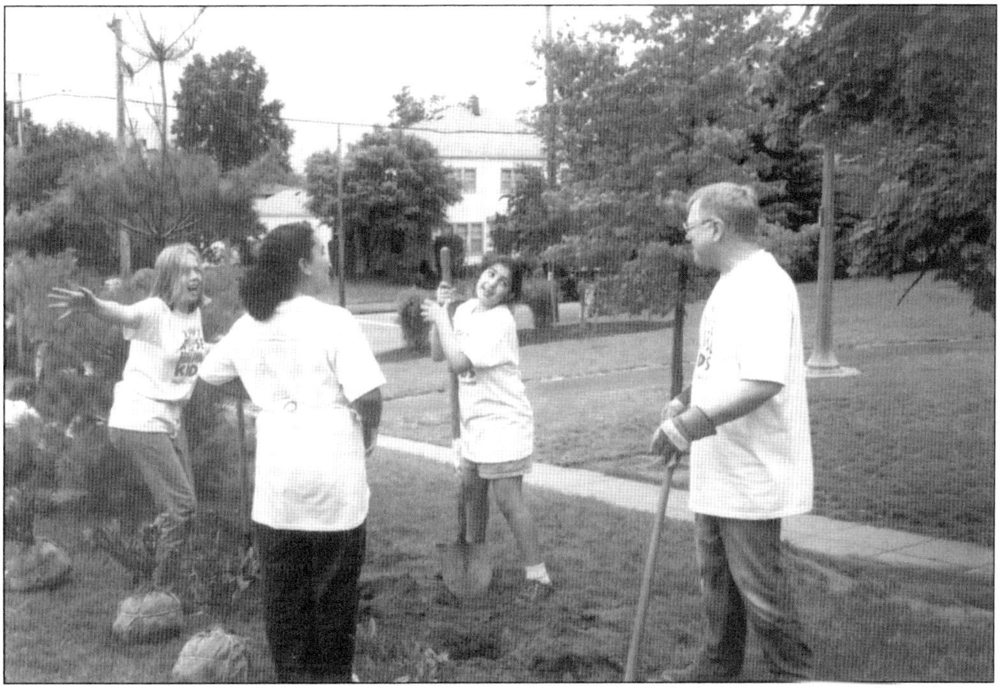

A community-based task force in the mid-1990s recommended the elimination of the Junior Court, which was replaced the following year with a program called Rose Festival Kids, a public service opportunity for grade-school and middle-school children. Rose Festival Kids remained a part of the festival through 2005. Rose Festival director Wayne Huddleston (right) was one of dozens of board members who worked with the kids on specific service projects. (Courtesy Portland Rose Festival Foundation.)

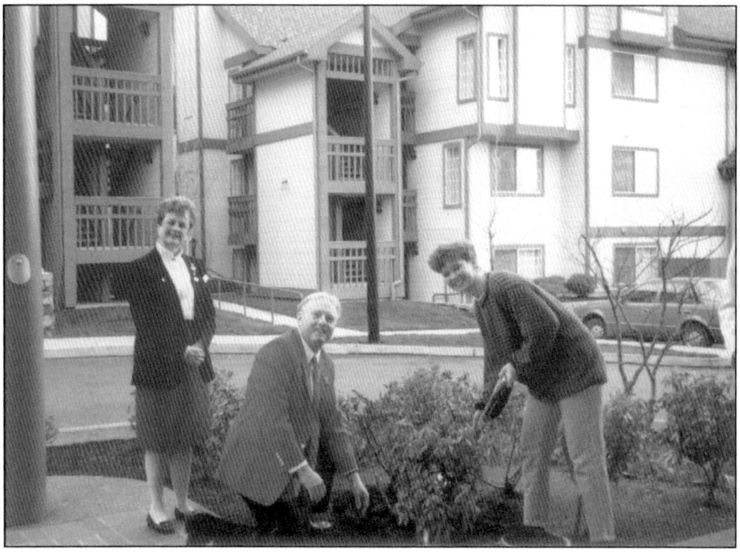

In 1993, Gerri Tisdel (left) became the first female president of the Rose Festival. Her election was greeted with great public interest and media attention. Here, she participates in a traditional Rose Planting Ceremony overseen by Portland Rose Society president Mike Rich. (Courtesy Portland Rose Festival Foundation.)

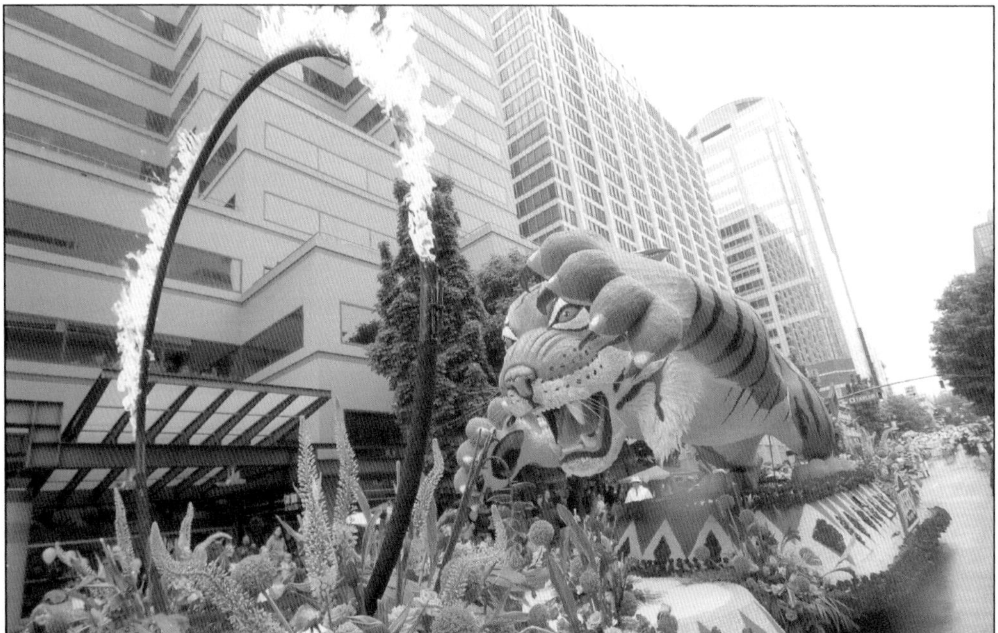

In 1995, Reser's Fine Foods sponsored a spectacular circus-themed float that it later put in the Pasadena Tournament of Roses Parade, where it was featured on the front page of the *L.A. Times*. The float was so popular that Reser's repeated the same design for the Rose Festival's Centennial Grand Floral Parade in 2007. Al Reser's enthusiasm for the parade was recognized after his death in 2010 when the parade's sweepstakes award was named after him. (Courtesy Portland Rose Festival Foundation.)

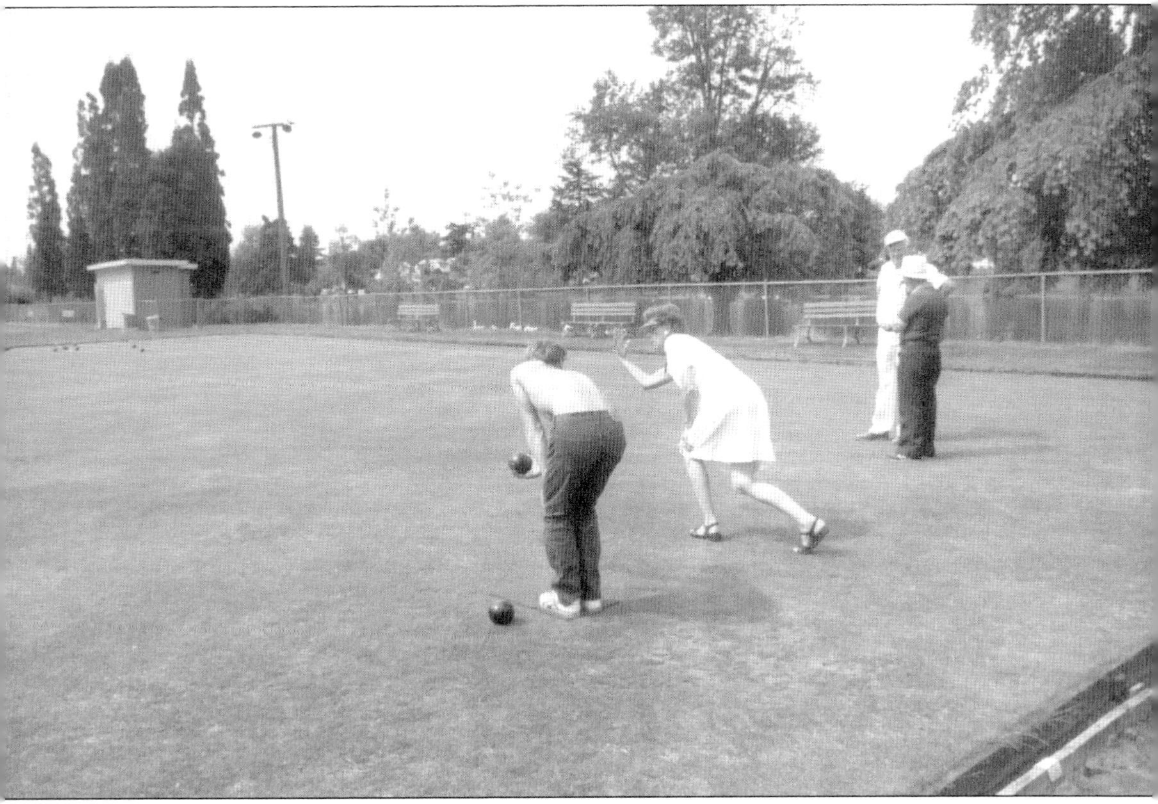

For decades, the Rose Festival has sanctioned events produced by other entities as part of its schedule. These events come and go, with some rising to the status of highlight events of the Rose Festival, as the Dragon Boat Race has. For years, lawn bowling was part of the schedule, and one year, the Rose Festival hosted the world championship. Other activities like curling, tennis, bowling, bicycle racing, and even egg-decorating have been sanctioned events. With the addition of these activities, the Rose Festival calendar often stretches to more than 50 events over seven or eight weeks. (Courtesy Oregon Historical Society; OrgLot850,B10,F15.)

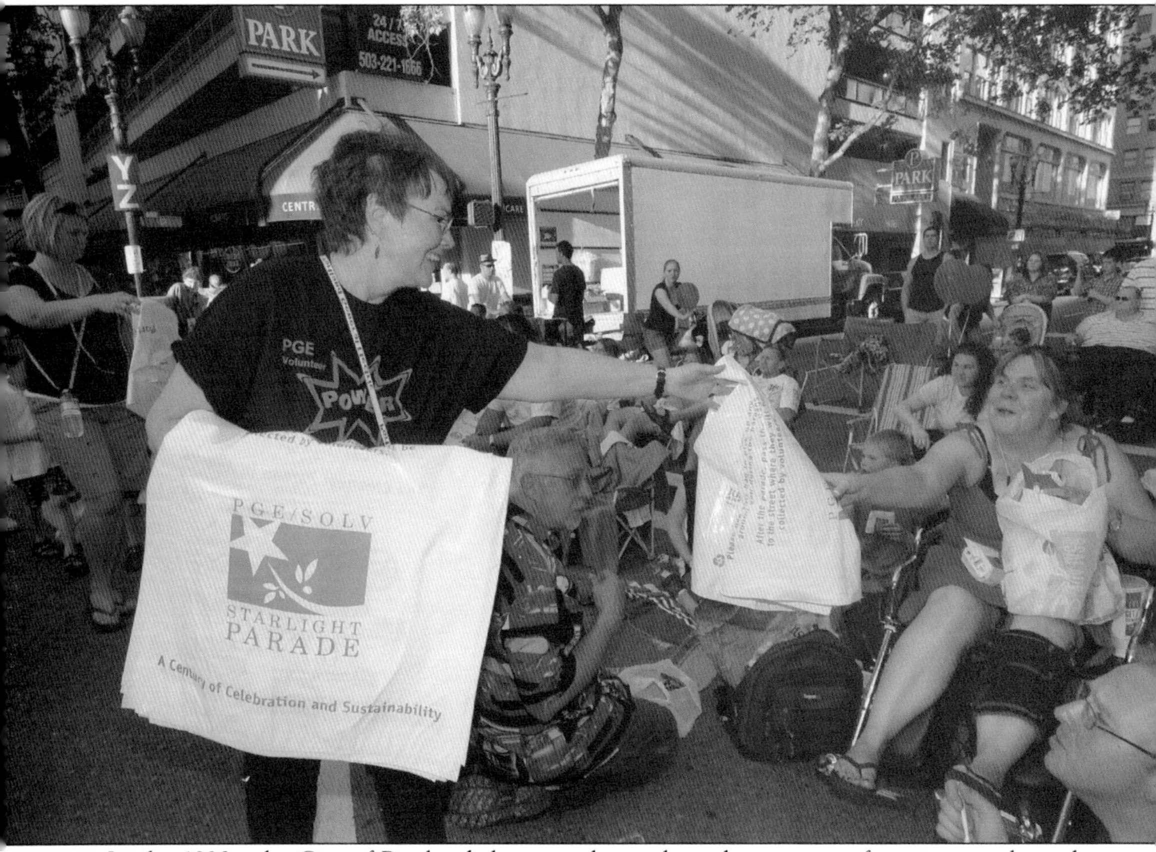

In the 1990s, the City of Portland threatened to reduce the amount of services to clean the parade routes, stating concerns about the cost. Leaders from the Rose Festival, the Portland Maintenance Bureau, Starlight Parade sponsor Portland General Electric, and the volunteer nonprofit SOLV, met to determine a solution for reducing costs. They instituted a volunteer parade cleanup that ended up saving the city tens of thousands of dollars annually. Paradegoers were urged to bag all their trash, and the volunteers pitched in to pick up the bags. Even local trash companies sent volunteer crews and equipment. The cleanup became the cornerstone of the Rose Festival's "Cleanest and Greenest Festival in the World" program, which to date has garnered 14 years of Pinnacle Awards from the International Festivals and Events Association for Best Environmental Program for festivals worldwide. In 2011, nearly half of the 4.1 tons of trash collected at the parades was diverted from landfills through recycling efforts. (Courtesy Portland Rose Festival Foundation.)

Ten

2001–2012
Rose Festival Renaissance

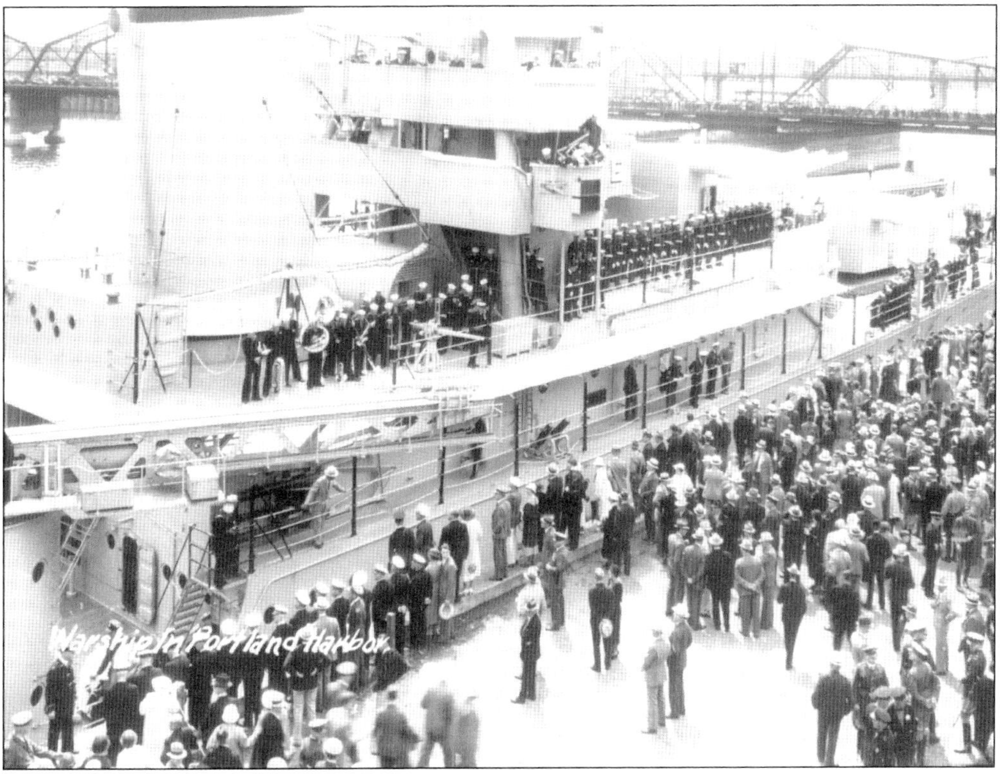

Prior to the tragic events on September 11, 2001, the Rose Festival fleet of naval vessels from the US Navy, the Canadian Royal Navy, and the US Coast Guard were annually docked along the Westside seawall at Waterfront Park, allowing easy access for the general public. After 9/11, the safety regulations of the fleet changed significantly, and the US Navy ships were placed in their own secured area and cordoned off. Limited ship tours were offered. The 2002 Rose Festival featured Oregon's Katie Harmon, who was the reigning Miss America, in the Grand Floral Parade. She sang the National Anthem inside Veterans Memorial Coliseum prior to the parade, and a ceremony was held to honor those who had and were serving the United States with a moment of silence to remember the fallen. (Courtesy Portland Rose Festival Foundation.)

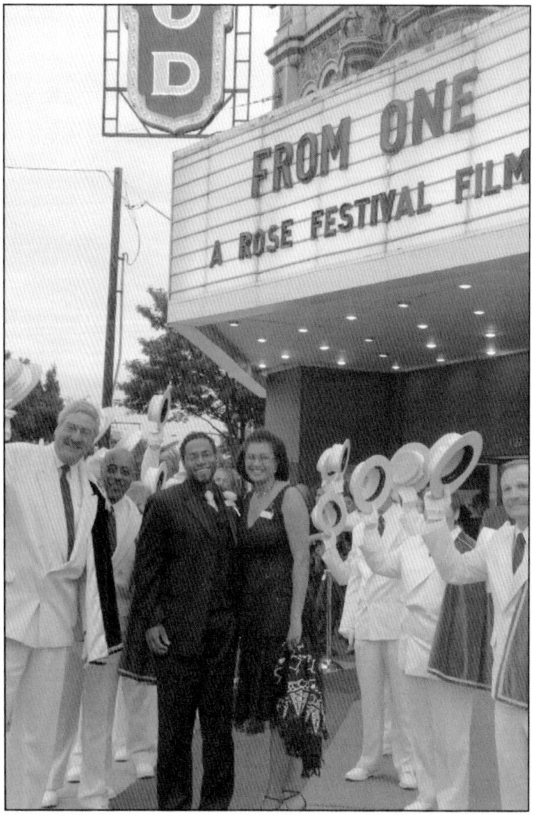

In 2007, the Rose Festival marked its Centennial Celebration. The scale of events was significantly increased, with the addition of several new activities and programs. The Rose Festival produced its own motion picture, *From One Rose*. In 2007, Leslie Goodlow-Baldwin was Portland Rose Festival Foundation president, the first African American to serve in that role, and attended the red carpet premiere of the movie accompanied by her husband, Richard Baldwin. (Courtesy Portland Rose Festival Foundation.)

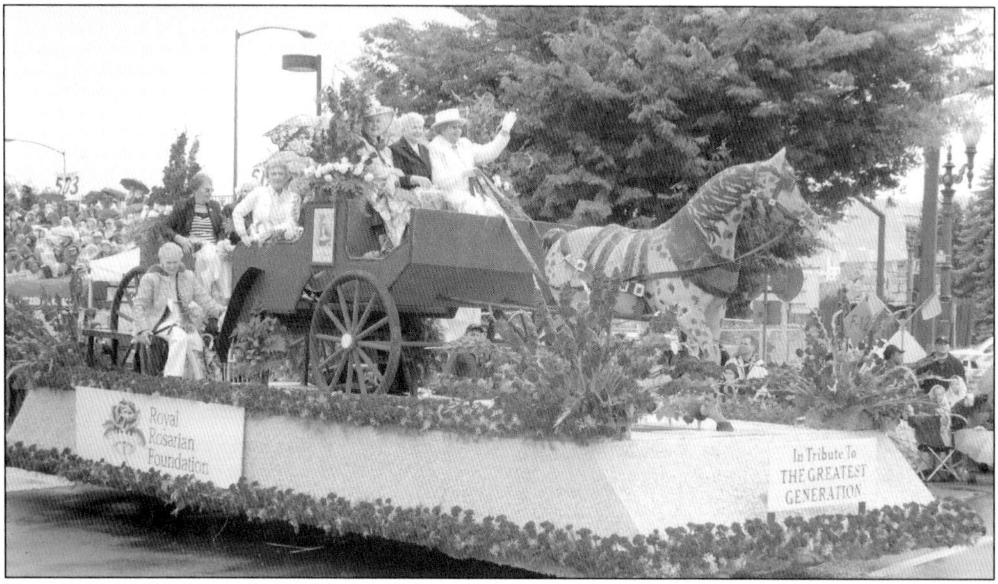

The Grand Floral Parade highlighted the past century. The Royal Rosarian Foundation float carried 12 wartime Rose Festival princesses from the 1940s, who had never had a chance to ride in the parade. The Rose Festival had purchased rain insurance for this important day, and by 1:00 p.m. that afternoon, the $100,000 policy had paid off as more than a tenth of an inch of water had collected in the official rain gage. (Courtesy Portland Rose Festival Foundation.)

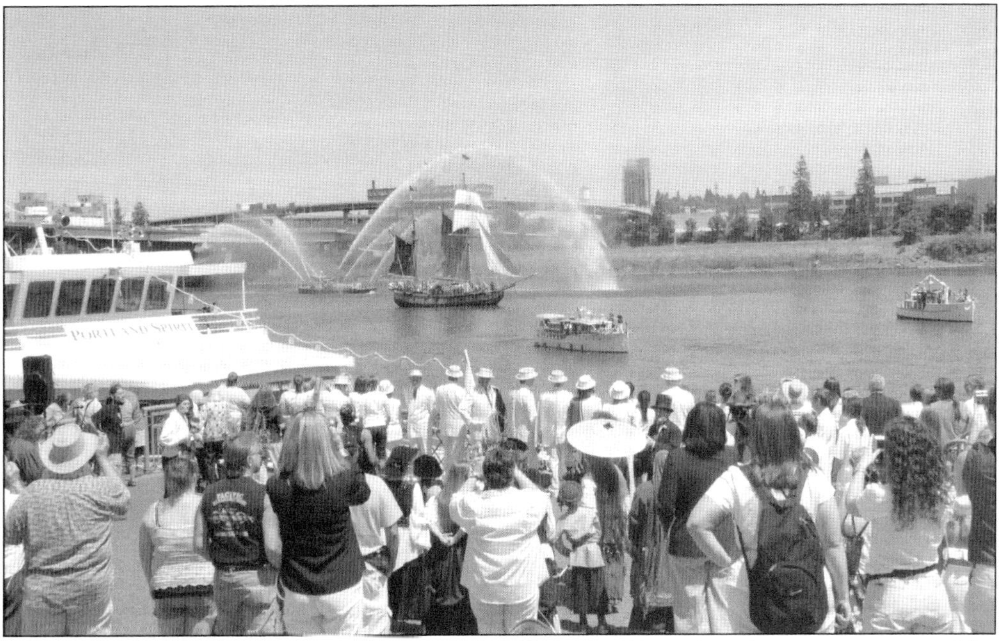

After years of not participating in the Rose Festival, carnival king Rex Oregonus reappeared for the festival's centennial celebration in 2007. As in years gone by, he arrived by "Royal Yacht" with his flotilla of boats. A special committee chose former Portland mayor Bud Clark to serve as Rex Oregonus. According to tradition, Rex's identity was kept secret until it was revealed at a special event, in this case the festival's opening celebration at Waterfront Park. Ironically, the well-known Clark had decided to shave his trademark beard while on vacation in Europe, so when he was unmasked, many people did not recognize him. One of Portland's most colorful mayors, Clark is shown participating in the Junior Parade in the 1980s. (Above, courtesy Portland Rose Festival Foundation; below, courtesy Oregon Historical Society, OrgLot850,B11,F1.)

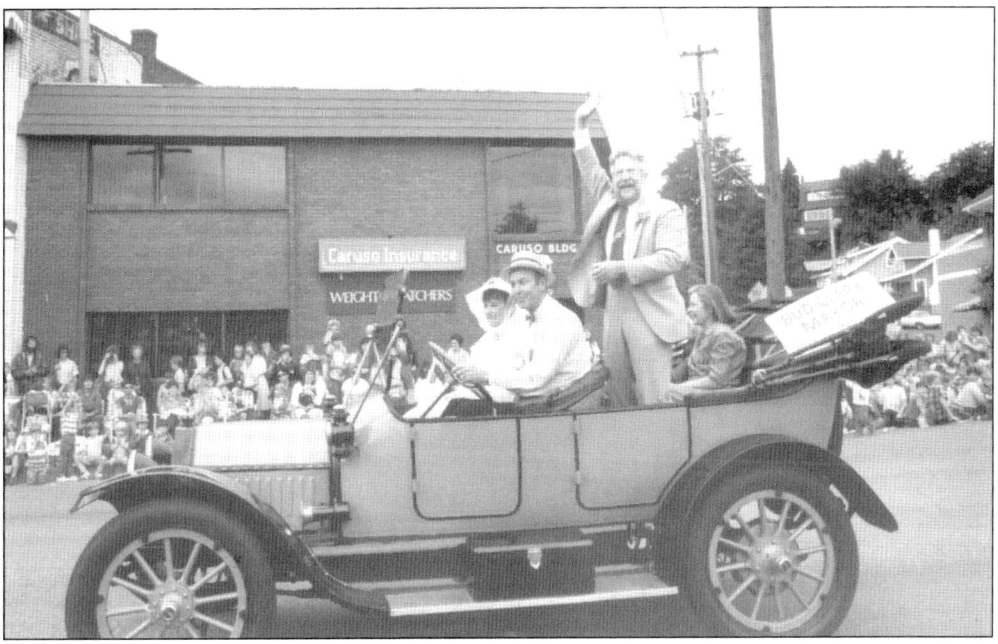

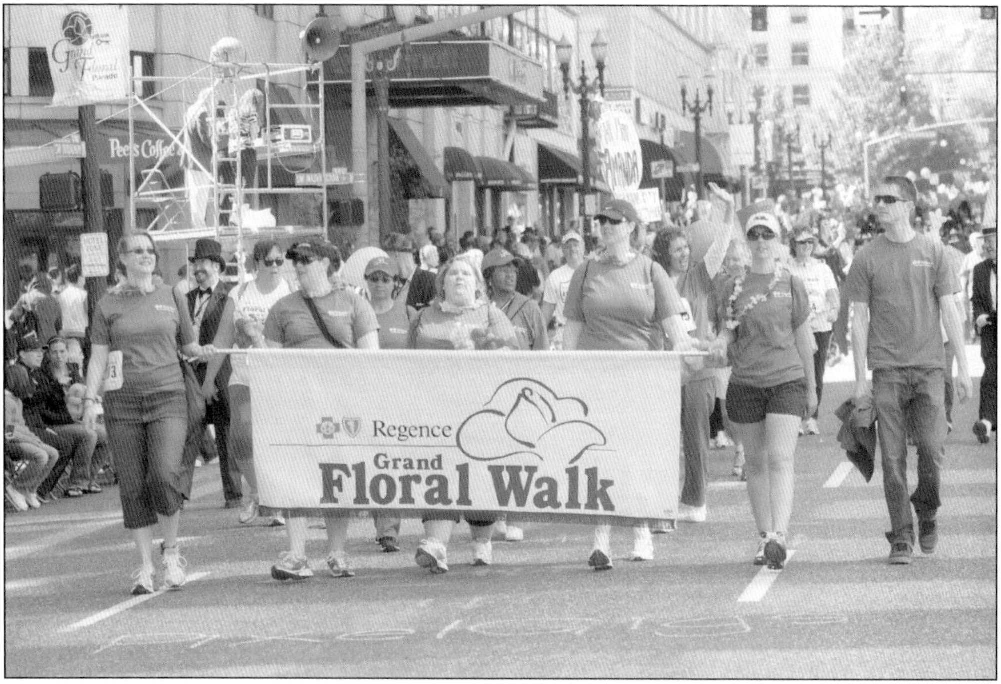

The Rose Festival was named the "Best Festival in the World" by the International Festivals and Events Association for its 2007 celebration, winning an award known as the "Grand Pinnacle." In 2008, the Rose Festival had to regroup, finding new sponsors and creating new events and programs. One of those programs was the Regence Grand Floral Walk, an event held prior to the parade, featuring around 2,000 recreational and fitness walkers. (Both, courtesy Portland Rose Festival Foundation.)

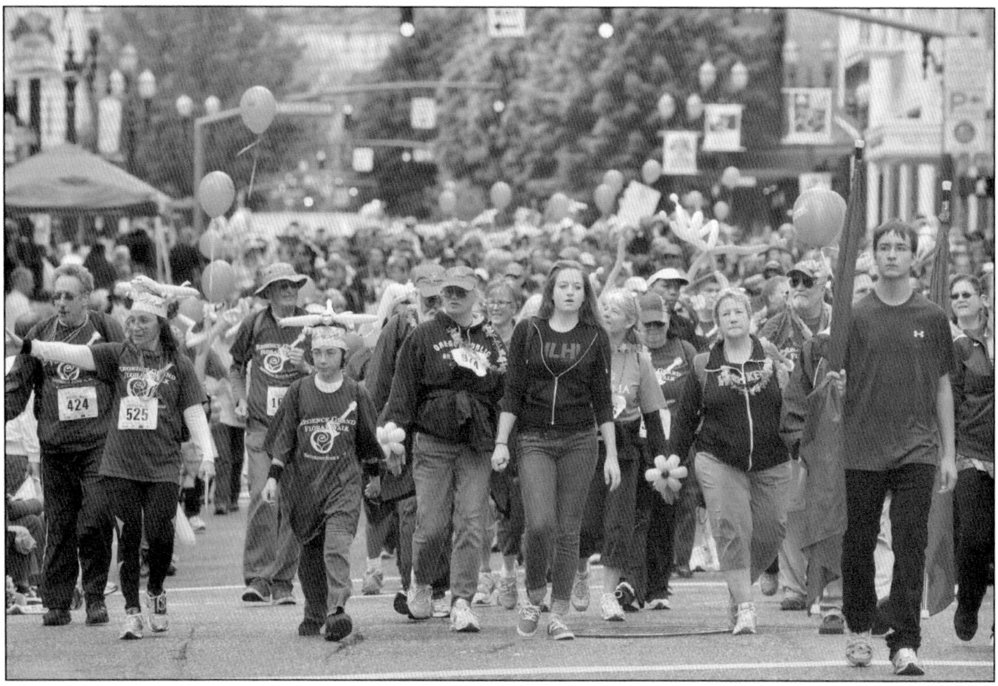

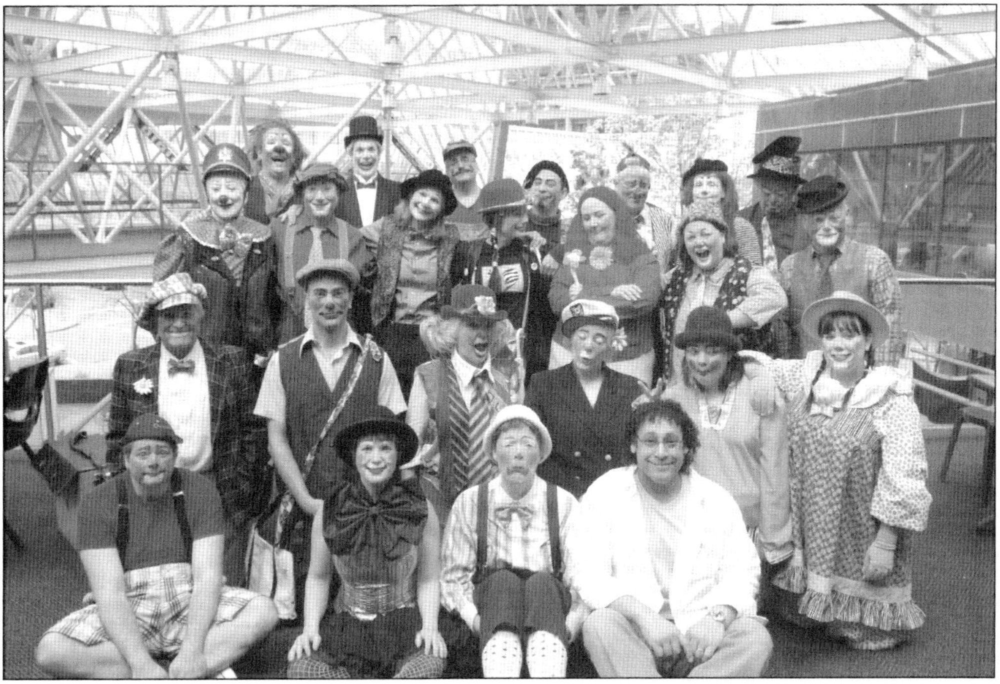

Another new program in 2008 was the Character Clown Corps, an opportunity for ordinary folks to become extraordinary entertainers. Originally conceived as an element for the Grand Floral Parade, the Clown Corps schedule was soon expanded to include many Rose Festival events. Fashioned after the European style of clowning, an annual class of around 20 volunteer clowns are put through a rigorous weekend of training and are transformed into their costumed counterparts. In 2012, the Clown Corps reached its fifth year, with no signs of slowing down. A new Rose Festival mascot, the "Clown Prince," was added in 2011. Here, Clown Prince Angel Ocasio is pictured being knighted by the 2010 Rose Festival queen, Victoria Dinu. (Courtesy Portland Rose Festival Foundation.)

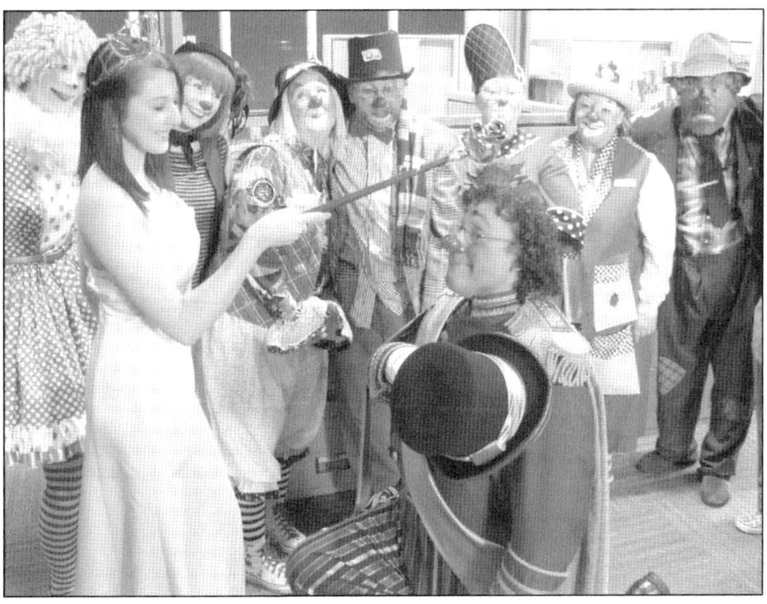

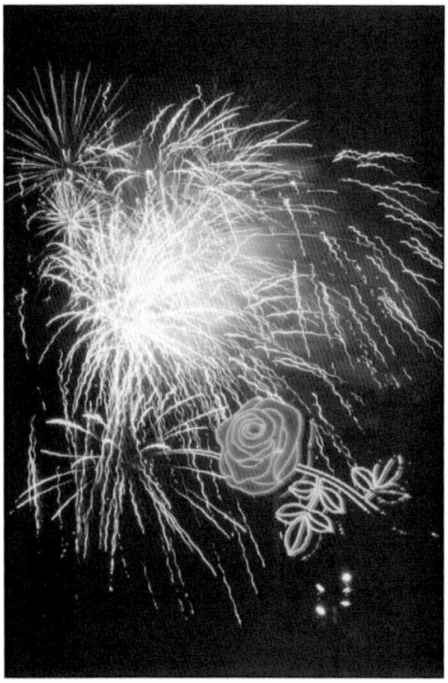

In 2009, the opening night of the Rose Festival enjoyed picture-perfect weather when a neon-rose sign was lit over the building that had served as Portland's Visitor Information Center in the late 1940s and was soon to become the home of the Portland Rose Festival Foundation office. The rose was designed and donated by Ramsey Signs in Portland. It now shines day and night at Waterfront Park. In 2009, it seemed to blend into the background of the festival's annual fireworks spectacular, a popular feature of opening night. (Courtesy Portland Rose Festival Foundation.)

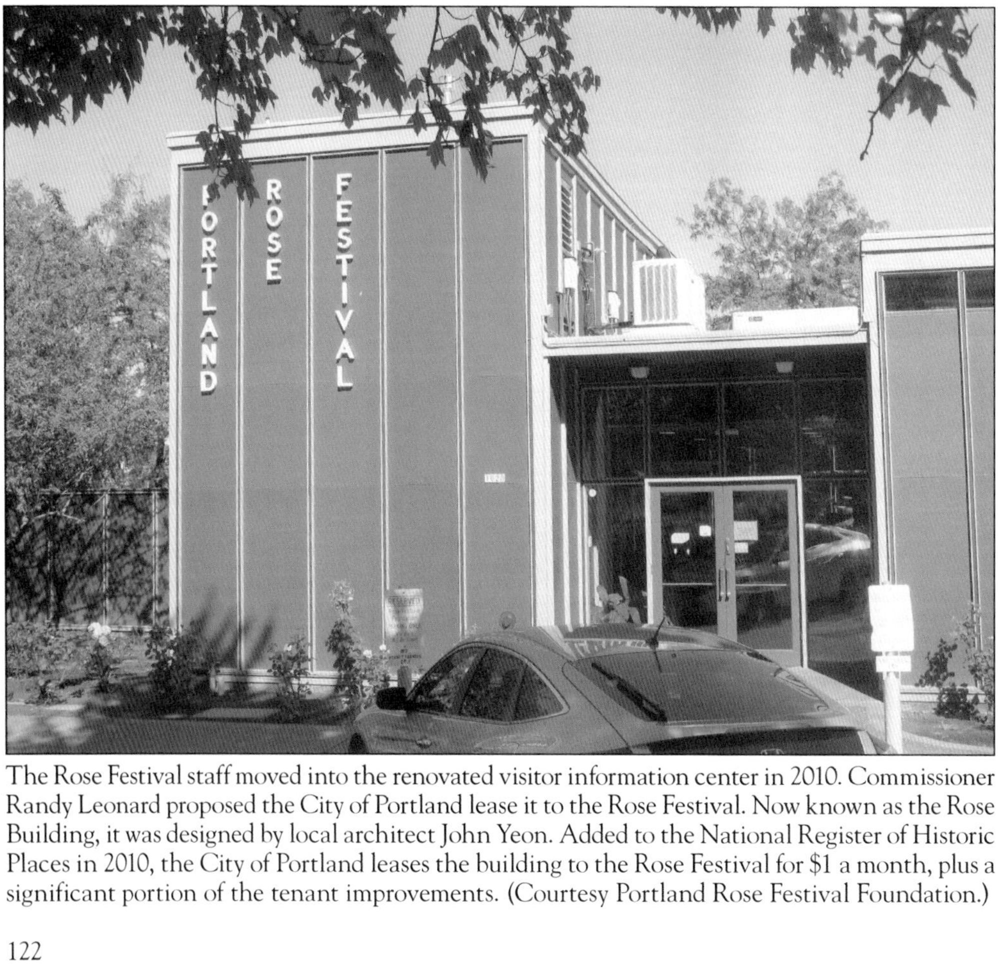

The Rose Festival staff moved into the renovated visitor information center in 2010. Commissioner Randy Leonard proposed the City of Portland lease it to the Rose Festival. Now known as the Rose Building, it was designed by local architect John Yeon. Added to the National Register of Historic Places in 2010, the City of Portland leases the building to the Rose Festival for $1 a month, plus a significant portion of the tenant improvements. (Courtesy Portland Rose Festival Foundation.)

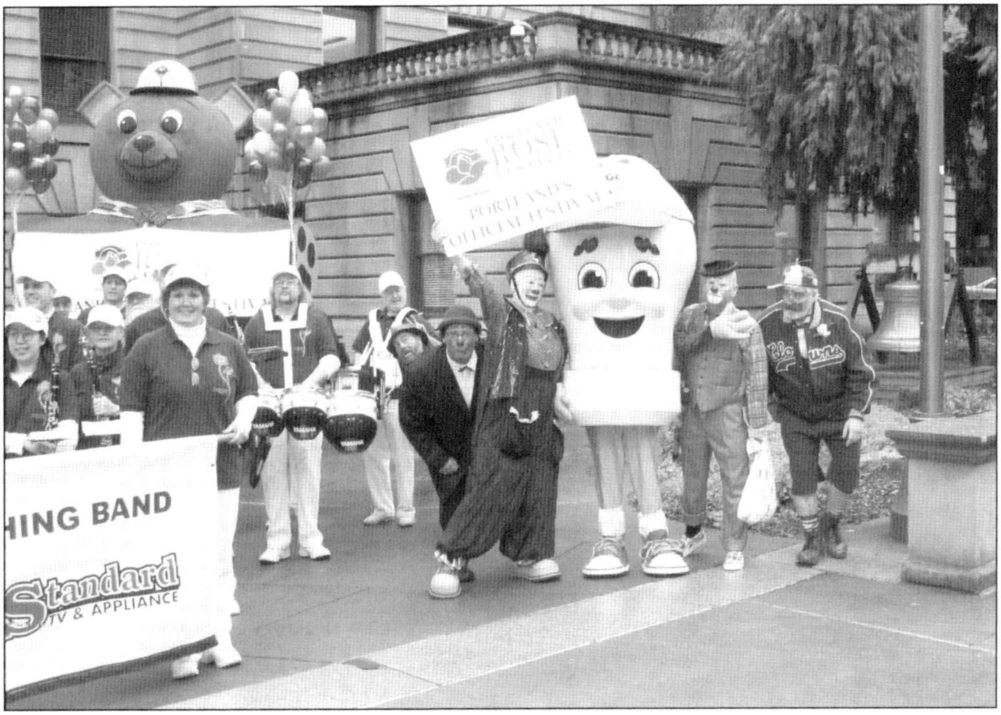

The One More Time Around Again Marching Band has been a festival favorite since the 1980s. The idea for the band was borrowed from the St. Petersburg Festival of States and its Second Time Around Again Band. The band marches in both the Starlight and Grand Floral parades and is famous for its rendition of The Kingsmen standard, "Louie Louie." In 2010, a portion of the 300-plus-person band appeared at city hall when the Rose Festival was finally declared Portland's "Official Festival" by the city council. (Both, courtesy Portland Rose Festival Foundation.)

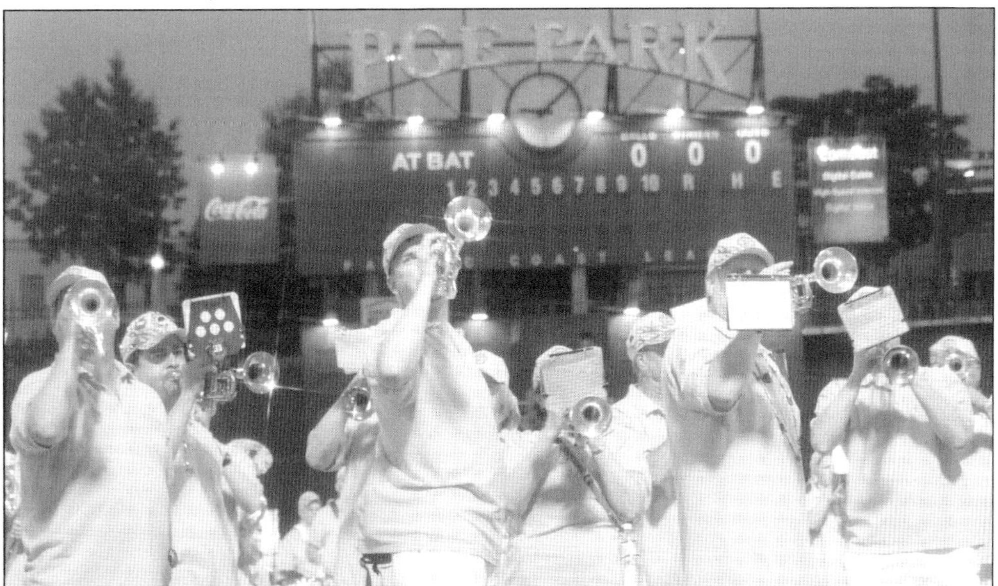

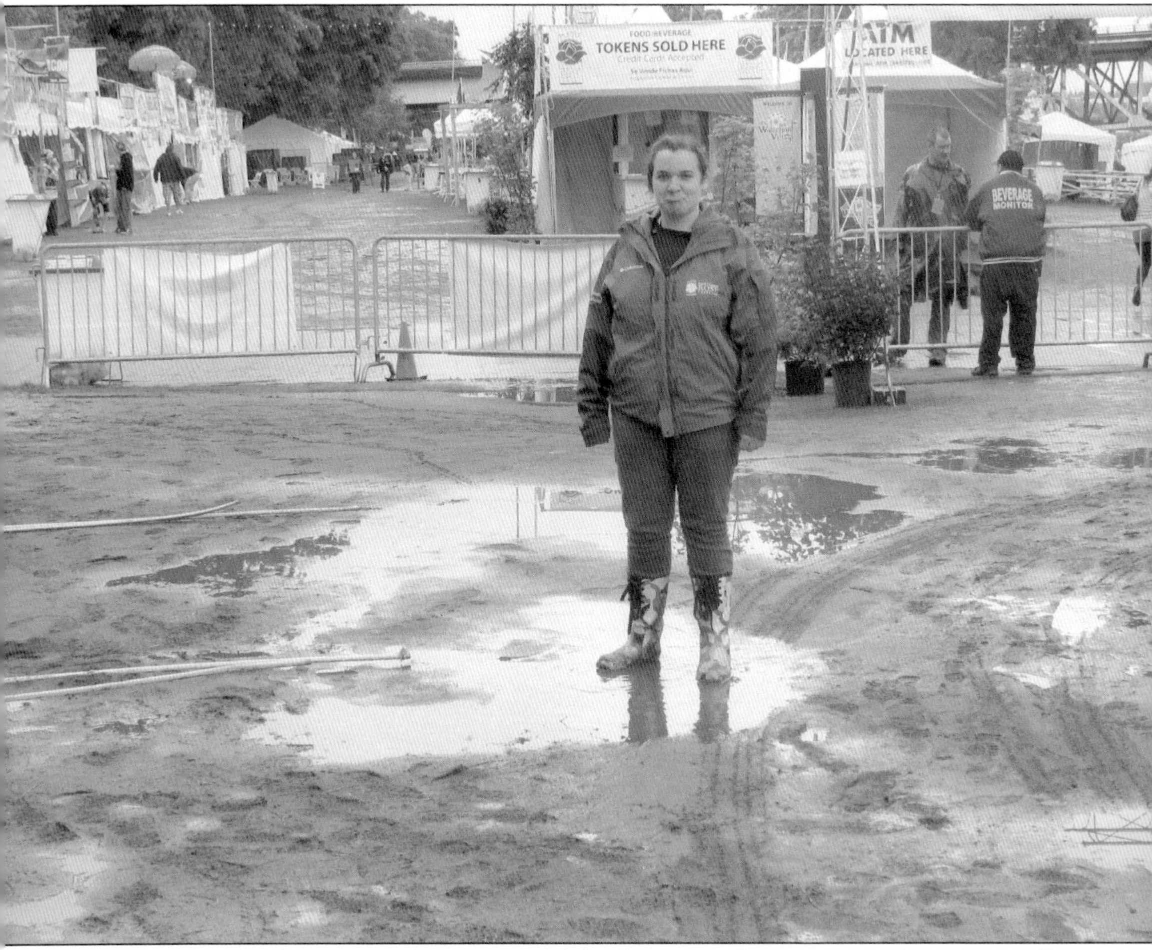

In 2010, Portland experienced record rainfall leading up to the opening of Waterfront Village, the event formerly known as the Fun Center. Rainfall for the month of June was 4.28 inches. However, nearly four inches of that fell during the first nine days. By Wednesday, June 2, the park was closed to the public to allow workers time to take steps to alleviate the muddy conditions. Festivalgoers were offered a free reentry if they wore their rain boots to the event. Rose Festival intern Caroll Casbeer is pictured standing in the puddles at Waterfront Park. Luckily, sunny weather greeted the Grand Floral Parade and a high temperature of 81 degrees on June 12. Some sunshine also blessed the Junior Parade, and for the Starlight Parade, it was mostly cloudy with no rain. That simple break in the weather ensured the Rose Festival was not a total washout. (Courtesy Portland Rose Festival Foundation.)

In 2011, the Rose Festival again revamped its festival center event, once known as the Fun Center, and newly christened Rose Festival CityFair. The urban entertainment fair was launched on opening day under the awning of a new illuminated sign designed and donated by Ramsey Signs. (Courtesy Portland Rose Festival Foundation.)

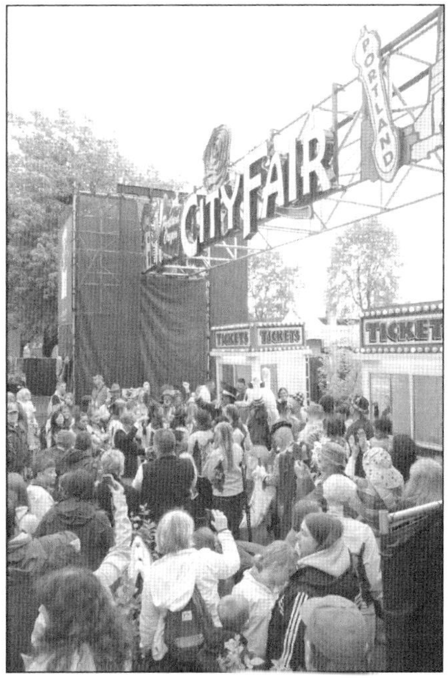

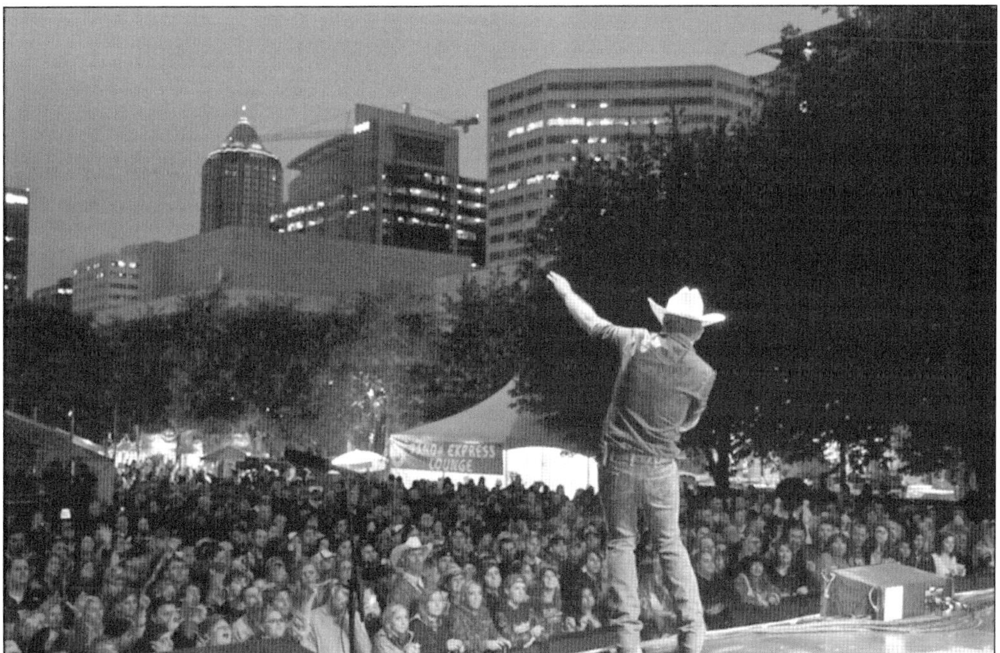

Live entertainment was an important part of the new format, attracting thousands of new customers to Waterfront Park. CityFair enjoyed unprecedented success, along with the rest of the Rose Festival events, heralding what was called a "Rose Festival Renaissance" by the media. After the 2011 season, the Rose Festival was named the "Best Festival in the World" by the International Festivals and Events Association for the second time in four years. Country singer Justin Moore is pictured performing in the RoZone at CityFair on the first weekend of the event. (Courtesy Portland Rose Festival Foundation.)

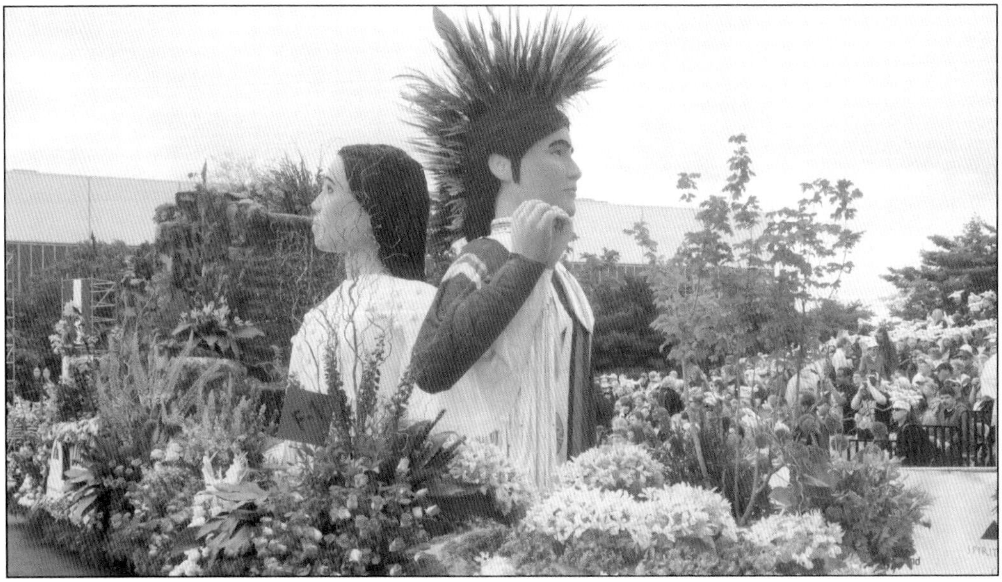

In 2011, longtime float sponsor Spirit Mountain Casino became the Grand Floral Parade's fourth title sponsor. Known for its beautiful floats featuring nature and native culture, the 2012 Spirit Mountain entry included a waterfall feature with running water. (Courtesy Portland Rose Festival Foundation.)

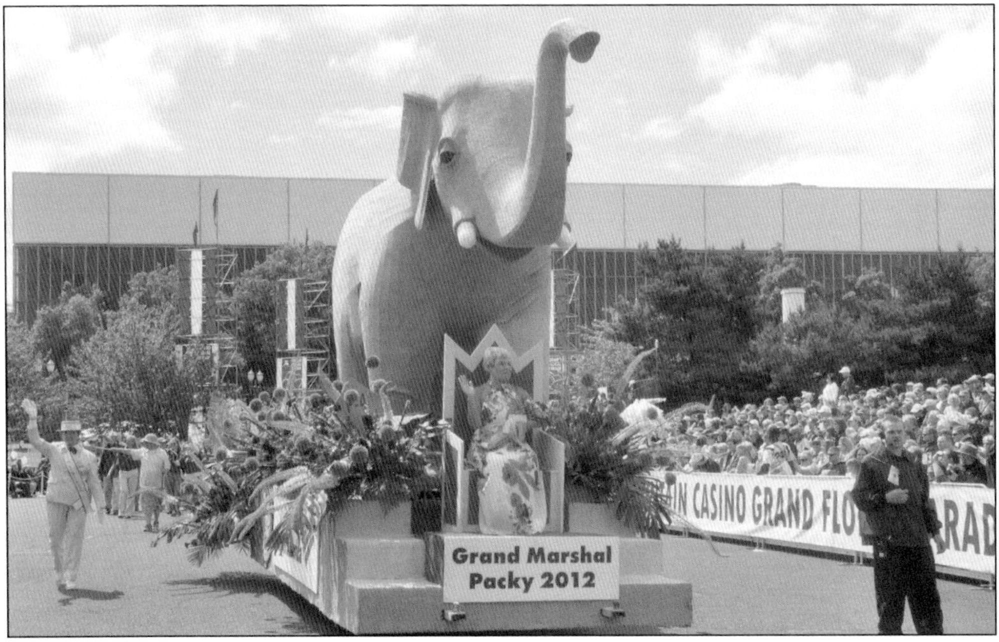

The 2012 Grand Floral Parade grand marshal, Packy the Elephant, was represented by a float, as the 50-year-old bull elephant could not safely appear in the parade in person. Newborn Packy had also been featured in the 1962 parade as a float element. The 1962 Rose Festival queen, Cherie Viggers Sanville, rode on the grand marshal float with Packy in 2012. During her original reign, festival officials had refused to allow her to ride the popular Packy float that the festival sent to Pasadena for the 1963 Tournament of Roses Parade, so the Rose Festival decided to finally give her the chance to appear with the popular pachyderm. (Courtesy Portland Rose Festival Foundation.)

EPILOGUE

As the pessimists have repeatedly said, "It always rains during the Rose Festival." When considering that the Rose Festival, from an initial three-day affair, has expanded to more than a five-week affair, that statement is generally correct. But June weather in the Pacific Northwest is fickle, and to go three weeks in late May, June, and July without rain is extremely unusual.

In many cases, dating back to the first Rose Festival, low clouds in the morning give way to sunshine in the afternoon at the Grand Floral Parade. This has been the case at least 20 times. Again, sometimes the low clouds do not fully dissipate, and the afternoon is left with partly sunny skies. This has happened at least 16 times. At least on 30 occasions, the weather has been sunny or mostly sunny during the Grand Floral Parade. There have been at least 10 occasions where rain has fallen just before the parade, but no rain fell during the parade. On only 11 occasions, however, has rain fallen throughout most of the parade. And on only five occasions did that moisture equal or exceed one-quarter of an inch. On at least six occasions, rain began falling after the parade was over. Remember, in several years there was no Grand Floral Parade, and in early years, there may have been three or four parades.

Then, there are always those who say, "Oh, it always gets sunny after the Rose Festival." During more than 40 years, rain followed the Rose Festival. For at least 15 Rose Festivals, the high temperature recorded was 90 degrees or higher, and it reached 98 degrees during the festival in 1941 as it did in 2003.

Yes, there have been some cool, cloudy parades when the thermometer barely reached into the mid-60s. On five occasions, the high temperature for the day of the parade did not reach into the 60s. But in 1909, the high temperature was 90 degrees for that afternoon as it was in 1963. In 2003, it was a sizzling 91 degrees in the afternoon of the Grand Floral Parade.

In 1912, the Electric Parade was canceled twice. The Children's Parade was canceled in 1923 and there have been several occasions when Coronation events held outside were canceled due to rain as well as balloon races and a few other activities. Taking a 10-day period from the opening of the Festival Fun Center on Friday to the following Sunday, on more than 40 occasions did less than one-tenth of an inch of rain fall during that period. There have been, however, many years when over one inch of rain fell during early June.

Photographs show in the book that paradegoers in Portland do not mind the rain. They cover themselves with plastic and umbrellas. As was mentioned, perhaps the Rose Festival officials worry more about the weather than the viewers. It definitely does not always rain on Portland's Rose Festival.